Skin Deep

SUNDAY *TIMES* BESTSELLING AUTHOR

CASEY WATSON

Skin Deep

**All she wanted was a mummy,
but was she too ugly to be loved?**

This book is a work of non-fiction based on the author's experiences. In order to protect privacy, names, identifying characteristics, dialogue and details have been changed or reconstructed.

HarperElement
An imprint of HarperCollins*Publishers*
1 London Bridge Street
London SE1 9GF

www.harpercollins.co.uk

First published by HarperElement 2015

1 3 5 7 9 10 8 6 4 2

A catalogue record of this book is
available from the British Library

PB ISBN 978-0-00-759509-9
EB ISBN 978-0-00-759510-5

Printed and bound in Great Britain by
Clays Ltd, St Ives plc

MIX
Paper from
responsible sources
FSC **FSC™ C007454**
www.fsc.org

To me, all children are beautiful. I often liken us parents and carers to gardeners. We work with what we are blessed with, and so long as we nurture and tend to our seedlings, and as long as we sort out what lies beneath – the tangled roots and weeds that threaten to prevent growth – then we can produce strong, healthy plants; some beautiful flowers, others not so aesthetic, but each with a purpose, and set to flourish and go on to create other life. This is all we can do, and all we need to do.

Acknowledgements

As ever, I'd like to thank the team I'm so privileged to work with. Huge thanks to everyone at HarperCollins, my agent Andrew Lownie and, of course, my lovely friend Lynne.

Chapter 1

The long school summer holidays. Who'd have them? We were only three weeks into them, so not even quite at the halfway point, but already that thought was uppermost on my mind several times a day. It was certainly the number one thing on my mind as I attacked the washing up and surveyed the scene of devastation that was supposed to be my garden.

More to the point, why had *I* always been such a staunch advocate for them? Silly me, I thought ruefully – that one was pretty obvious. It was because I used to work in a school, and those six precious weeks were like a gift from the gods. A vital pause between stints under the tyranny of the school bell. Fickle, fickle, fickle, that was me.

I raised a soapy Marigold and rapped hard on the open kitchen window. 'Tyler!' I barked. 'Denver! *Please*! Not so *rough*! And watch my flowers!' I added hopefully, though without much optimism that either boy would. Though they smiled and waved back at me, they also completely ignored me, chasing each other round the garden with

1

their water blasters just as manically as they had been for the past half hour. My poor windows were going to get it next. I just knew it.

Not that in normal circumstances I'd have much minded the devastation. Tyler had only been with us for a little over a year, but since we'd asked if we could keep him permanently – well, till he was ready to fly the nest – it almost felt like he'd been with us for half his life. And, in truth, I could never be cross with him for long. Well, except when I had to be, obviously. It had been a huge decision and we'd not yet had cause to regret it; now he was in a loving, happy home, he was blossoming.

Which was more than my flowers were being allowed to, however. This was probably par for the course when they were constantly being attacked by an almost 13-year-old boy and his boisterous sidekick. That's not to say that my flesh and blood family weren't partly to blame. Riley and Kieron, my own two, had both passed their quarter centuries, but Levi and Jackson – Riley's boys – were already following enthusiastically in the footsteps of their uncle Kieron, in that, if they saw grass, they immediately thought 'football'.

Now eight and six, perhaps it was a blessing that they weren't around to play today, as they were equally skilled at kicking a ball into a rose bush and creating a mud slick out of a previously lush patch of grass. Still, at least Riley and David's third child had been a daughter, and though my little grand-daughter Marley-Mae was only 16 months old I could already tell she was going to be a proper little lady.

But it was another little lady that was causing me to fuss and flap this morning. I'd had a phone call first thing from my fostering link worker, John Fulshaw, to inform me that he had something of an emergency on his hands – so could I possibly take on a young girl? In typical John style, he was fairly light on facts, operating according to his usual 'I'll tell you more when I get there' routine. So all I knew currently was that she'd been taken into care following a house fire, and that her mother was still in hospital being treated. Oh, and that, like Riley's Levi, she was just eight years old, and that though her name was Philippa she apparently only answered to 'Flip'. Oh, and one more thing. That they (as in John, the little girl and the social worker allocated to her) would be arriving at my house in – hell's *bells* – less than an hour.

As timings went, it couldn't have been much worse. I'd already agreed that Tyler's friend Denver could spend the day with us, which meant I'd had two boisterous almost-teens running wild both in and out of the house all morning, wearing nothing but swimming shorts, splashing around in Marley-Mae's little paddling pool and generally running amok in that way adolescent boys do, while my house, already messy after a Sunday spent with the very same grandkids, looked like a bomb had hit it.

For a clean-freak like me, this was naturally torture. Or would be, if I'd allowed it to remain in that state, but such was my horror of admitting visitors if it was anything other than pristine, it would be a cold day in hell before I allowed *that* to happen.

Which meant I needed to crack on fast. I popped the last plate into the drainer and peeled off my washing-up gloves. I'd need my heavy guns to come out for the rest of the chores that I'd be doing, so I went across to my cleaning cupboard to get tooled up: vacuum, duster, disinfectant and mop were my weapons of choice, and every speck of dust, or splash of dirty water, my enemy. The Blitz had nothing on me when I declared war on dirt and mess, and I was just preparing for battle when Tyler splattered into the kitchen, barefoot and grinning, not to mention dripping twin streams of water from the legs of his board shorts to the floor.

'Any chance of an ice lolly, Casey?' he wanted to know, accessorising his request with a smile that I knew one day was going to break some hearts in the same way he'd comprehensively stolen mine. 'Only with all that running about, we're Hank Marvin!'

I had to smile at that. It had been a term coined by a previous boy we'd fostered, Jenson, who'd learned it, if memory served, from his mother's latest boyfriend. It had since wormed its way into the family lexicon. It had probably been Kieron who'd passed it on to Tyler, who'd picked it up and run with it ever since.

He shook his dark hair like a shaggy dog would in order to shake off the water, further messing up my already messy floor. 'For goodness' sake, Tyler. Stop that!' I ordered. 'And an ice lolly is going to stop you feeling hungry, is it? No way, mister. It's almost lunchtime and I'm going to make a picnic for the pair of you. I'm sure you won't pass out from malnutrition before then. Now, hop it,' I added, swivelling him by the shoulders and frog-marching him back outside again. 'John and the others will be here soon, and I still have lots to do, so how about you and Denver start clearing a space to sit and eat your picnic on, while I do so.'

'Not even an ice-pop?' he tried hopefully.

I shook my head. 'No. Oh, hang on, though,' I added, reaching across and grabbing the sun spray from the kitchen windowsill. 'Give each other another good going over with this before you do. You've probably washed off half the last lot with those flipping blasters of yours, and I don't want the pair of you burning. Go on,' I said, giving it to him. 'Ice lollies after lunch, promise.'

'Oh, Casey!' Tyler grumbled as he took the bottle spray from me. 'You're such a fusspot. Look at the label. Look, *here* – where it says "once", see? That means we only *need* it once. That's why it *says* it! You've already covered us in it about a hundred times!'

'Covered you with it *twice*, actually,' I corrected. 'And twice never hurt anyone. It says "once" on the paint tins as well, and we all know how well they work, don't we? Go on, out with you! And put some more on!' I added, to his departing back.

I was mad, I decided as I surveyed my sopping floor. I was actually mad. Tyler was such a live wire, and had a best friend who was also a live wire, and yet not two hours back I'd gone and agreed to another temporary placement not with trepidation, but with an enthusiastic grin on my face, despite knowing almost nothing about the girl. But then if I was mad, then so was my husband, Mike, because when I'd phoned him at work to double check he was fine about us doing it, he'd agreed to it as well – and in an instant.

'Well, we said we would, didn't we?' he'd pointed out when I asked him if he meant it. These weren't light decisions to make, after all. But he was right; that had always been the deal. When we'd asked if we could be allowed to keep Tyler, we'd assured John that we'd still be more than happy to foster other kids who might need us – kids who could benefit from going on the specialist behaviour-modification programme we'd been trained to deliver. And this was apparently once such – though for what reason I knew not. But it was a little girl, and she was only eight, so there'd be no extra testosterone wafting around. No, it would be fine. It would work okay with Tyler.

'So I'll tell him yes, then,' I'd said. 'You know, assuming all seems well once they get here?'

'Course!' Mike assured me. 'You've had it easy for long enough, love. Time to get stuck back in.'

Cheeky sod, I thought now. I'd get him back for that later. Perhaps with a well-aimed water blast or two. Right now I had less than an hour – no, nearer 45 minutes – and, if not a mad woman, I was definitely a woman possessed. First impressions worked both ways, after all.

Chapter 2

Like mums everywhere, I always seemed to have several balls in the air at once, so even without the added health and safety risk of my sopping kitchen floor, it was odds on that I'd trip up and lose sight of one. And it seemed I had today. It was only because I was dusting the elderly house phone in the hall that I realised that, in my haste to get things ready for my unexpected visitors, I'd almost forgotten my poor son's daily 'un-alarm' call.

I checked the time, took an executive decision and went to find my mobile. If I didn't do it now, who knew when I'd next have the chance? And then there might be hell to pay. Keiron had – has – a mild form of what used to be known as Asperger's syndrome and which is now more commonly referred to as an ASD, or autism spectrum disorder. In an ideal world, I hoped that word 'disorder' might soon be changed to 'difference', but in the meantime it did mean certain challenges for him, so I supposed it was partly correct. It was something we were all used to, however, and if you met him you'd probably barely even notice it, but the management of it had been a big part of his childhood and even now, though he lived a full and fulfilling life, it still impacted on him in myriad little ways.

He and his long-term girlfriend Lauren were on holiday in Cyprus, which was something of a milestone for them both. As anyone familiar with autism knows, even in its mildest forms it can cause major anxieties, and often these are centred around routine and change. That was Kieron to a T – loved routine, hated change. And with a passion. So going on a holiday, when he'd been growing up, was a very big deal, and something we only attempted rarely.

It wasn't surprising, then, that when he'd popped round after work one day and announced they were going to Cyprus, just the two of them, I was shocked, as was Mike. This was a big step. It was the first time they'd been away on their own and they weren't just going away – they were going abroad!

The holiday had obviously taken a fair bit of arranging, and the strain of it soon began to tell. Though he was a grown man of 26, and was understandably keen to meet the challenge, he was terrifically anxious about how he might cope – or, rather, fail to cope – once he got there. Lauren, bless her, had taken on the mantle of chief organiser, planning it, organising their savings and making all the arrangements. But as the date had loomed we could all tell he was struggling with the thought of it, as he reacted just as he'd done since he was a little boy, by chewing off all the skin around his fingernails. That was always a bad sign. So much so that I'd begun to question the wisdom of going at all.

'Look, Kieron,' I said one afternoon, when he'd popped round for tea. 'If you really don't want to go to Cyprus, then you don't have to, you know. A holiday is supposed to be something you do for pleasure, after all. Have you spoken to Lauren about how stressed you are? I know she'll understand if you don't feel you can face it.'

But he was having none of it, and my heart really went out to him. 'I have, and that's exactly what she says as well. But no, Mum,' he said, 'I really, *really* want to go. If I can crack this once, I'll have it cracked for ever, then, won't I? Well, sort of. I'm just – oh, you know what I'm like. I can't stop thinking about all the things that might go wrong on the journey. What if I get stressed and need to talk to you?'

'Then *call* me. Get that Euro-travelling package-thingy they do.'

'And what if I don't know where to go at the airport, or what queue to join, and Lauren doesn't either? What if we accidentally get on the wrong plane?'

I was pretty sure Lauren would have had all of that under control, because she was a brilliant, capable girl, not to mention the fact that air travel was almost like bus travel these days. But I also knew my son and how his anxieties could overtake him; so much so that he'd stopped coming on family holidays at the age of 16, preferring to stay instead with my sister Donna.

No, Kieron just needed to know there was a safety net, that was all. 'So, like I said,' I repeated, 'if Lauren can't sort it, get your phone out and *call* me. And, I tell you what. How about I call *you* from time to time in any case. You know, just to see how you're doing?'

'Would you, Mum?' he asked, and I knew right away that this was what he needed. Better for me to keep in touch with him than for him to de-stress himself by reaching for his mobile to call me every five minutes. Just knowing I'd be popping up on his screen at every stage would probably be enough to keep him on top of his anxiety, but without the added anxiety of feeling Lauren would think he was being silly, even though *I* knew she wouldn't. Oh, it was a game, it really was, fathoming it all out.

'Course I will,' I said. 'I'll be like the BT woman, ringing up with alarm calls. Except they'll be "un-alarm" calls, because there *won't* be any alarms, I'm sure of it, as Lauren will have everything under control. And if anything unexpected *does* happen, you can call me, like I say. Except nothing will, I promise.'

He looked 100 per cent happier. 'Thanks, Mum. Just till we're there and settled and that, anyway.'

'Exactly,' I said. 'You're just anxious about the travelling, love, which, trust me, is perfectly normal.'

And my 'un-alarm' calls had clearly done the trick. We'd spoken four times on the Saturday, three on the Sunday, and now, when I told him I'd got to go as John was due at any moment, he'd hung up before I'd barely taken the phone from my ear, leaving me secure in the knowledge that they were having a good time, and free to concentrate on my young visitor.

Who seemed to be arriving even as I put my mobile back on its charger. With all the windows open, in order to counteract the sweltering heat, I could hear a car pulling up outside the house even before I saw it. I felt the usual stirring of intrigue. It wasn't quite excitement; that was the wrong word to use in such a circumstance – this was a child who'd been taken into care as an emergency, after all. But there was still a certain frisson; I'd opened several front doors by now, to several different children, and perhaps because ours was a kind of fostering that often took place at short notice I really had to be unshockable when I pulled it back to greet whoever was standing nervously on our front doorstep.

In this case, however, it was only John. And he didn't look nervous in the least. Just very hot.

'Oh,' I said, looking beyond him towards the car. 'Are you on your own, then?'

'Only for a little bit,' he said. 'They've had to go back. For a forgotten Barbie doll. Shouldn't be long.'

I ushered him inside. 'Come on in, then. Do you want a cold glass of something? Or an ice pop?' I said, grinning. 'We're very well stocked with those currently, as you can imagine.'

'Just a large glass of water,' he said, loosening his tie, and following me into the kitchen. 'I'm parched. Like a flipping furnace, my car is, in weather like this.' He grinned ruefully as he placed a manila folder on my kitchen table. 'Actually – hmm – under the circumstances, perhaps I'd better rephrase that.'

It took me half a second to work out what he was on about. Of course. The *fire*. 'Sorry,' I said, placing a pint glass of water down beside the files. 'Bit slow on the uptake there, wasn't I? Sit down, I'll' – I stopped and went over to the window, which was being liberally sprayed with a blast from one of the water guns. 'Oh, for goodness' sake, Tyler! Will you STOP that!' I called out of the window. 'Sorry, John. Think the heat's getting to the boys, too. They're both completely manic.'

John chuckled. 'Enjoying the holidays, then? Sounds like young Ty is, anyway. Actually I could use that kind of dousing right now.'

'Be my guest,' I said, waving an arm towards the door out to the conservatory and garden, before pulling out a chair to sit on myself. 'Though not till you've given me some detail on our new arrival. What's the lowdown? How's the mum? Badly burnt?'

John shook his head. 'Apparently not. She's still in hospital, but it's mostly smoke inhalation they're treating her for. A lucky escape.'

'And the little girl's okay?'

'Yes, absolutely fine. Completely unharmed, which is something of a miracle, by all accounts. The blaze all but gutted the entire house, and the mother was lucky to get out alive. Philippa – Flip – was found quite a bit later, by all accounts, hiding in a wardrobe upstairs. Rescued by the lady next door, it seems, while the fire crew were attending to the mother. I just met her, as it happens – she's become something of a local hero.'

'I'm not surprised. How did it start? Do they know?'

'I'm not sure they know for definite, but the assumption is that the mother fell asleep with a cigarette in her hand. Alcoholic,' he added, opening his files.

I smiled. John had dropped the word into the conversation as if it was something bland and innocuous, like her hair colour or job description or star sign. As he would, because these were the conversations we tended to have. Ah, I thought. So we were getting to the nub of it now. There had to be *something*, after all. A child could and often would go into care as the result of a major house fire. If their home was gutted, the parent or parents hospitalised, and with no family or friends to take them, a child would invariably end up in temporary foster care. I imagined the little girl on her way to us was coming from temporary foster care herself; an emergency placement, while social services sorted out what needed to be done in the longer term, be it to keep the child there till the responsible adult was in a position to have them back again or, if they'd been orphaned, to find them adoptive parents.

But in this case they were moving her on to us, which meant it was slightly more complex than that. Mike and I, however, weren't those regular kinds of foster parents. We were trained to foster children who were tending towards being 'unfosterable'; our specialist programme was designed to modify the behaviour of the most challenging children in the care system, in order that they could be socialised sufficiently to have a hope of going into mainstream foster care and/or being put up for adoption.

Yes, from time to time we did respite care, to help the fostering agency out, just as Riley and David were doing at the moment, but, generally speaking, if a child needed to come to us there was usually an extra problem, and I already knew, from John's initial call, that there was a reason why he wanted us to have Flip. And this was apparently it.

Well, half of it. The mother being an alcoholic wasn't the whole story, I was sure. No, there would have to be some sort of challenge to address with the little girl as well.

'Ah,' I said. 'And?'

'And she's a long-standing alcoholic. Well known to social services. As is the daughter, because she has foetal alcohol syndrome. Something you've probably –'

At which point he stopped, because there was a rap on the front door.

If I'd finished his sentence correctly, John was right. I had heard of foetal alcohol syndrome (commonly known as FAS), because we'd touched on it in training. 'Touched' being the operative word; we'd touched on lots of things in training, but with so many ways in which a child could be damaged by the things life had thrown at them, if we'd done more than touch on most of them we'd still be in training all these years later. So, as I walked to the front door, it was with the usual thing in mind – that what I didn't know I would now simply learn, on the job, so to speak.

I opened the door, the sun streaming in almost bodily; certainly casting my guests into deep shadow, almost silhouetting them on the step. But not for long, because the little girl stepped straight over the threshold. 'Hello,' she said brightly. 'Do you think I'm ugly, Mummy?'

As first lines went, it was an unusual one, to say the least, but as I smiled down at the dot of a girl who now stood before me, I was more struck by what I saw than what she'd said. She was dressed for the weather, in a flower-sprigged cotton sundress with a shirred bodice, the straps tied in neat bows on her skinny shoulders, but my eyes were immediately drawn upwards, to her face.

I'd clearly absorbed more about her syndrome in training than I'd realised. I took in the small head – which seemed too small, even on her tiny little body, even with her fullish head of wavy dark-blonde hair. I took in the far-apart eyes, the upturned nose and the thin upper lip. It was almost like ticking off boxes on a checklist, and I was surprised how immediately the details of FAS came back to me.

But ugly? No, call me soft, but she definitely wasn't that. Arresting, unusual, but definitely not ugly. Bless her little heart.

'No, of course you're not, sweetheart!' the young woman with her supplied before I could, as she steered Flip around me so she could step inside herself.

'There,' I added, smiling at her. 'Took the words right out of my mouth. Come on in – Flip, isn't it?'

The girl nodded. 'And this is Ellie. She's my social worker. She's pretty, isn't she, Mummy?'

'She is indeed,' I said, smiling at the social worker, then gesturing towards the doll in Flip's hand. 'And who's this?'

'It's Pink Barbie. We nearly forgetted her.' She raised her other hand, which was clutched around the handle of a small pink vanity case. Both looked new. And apparently were. 'She goes with this,' Flip explained. 'It's to keep all her clothes in. I gotted them from Mrs Hardy. As a present.'

'And we nearly came without her, didn't we?' the social worker added. 'As John no doubt told you. Still, we're here now. All present and correct. Well, such as we can be.' She too raised a hand holding a bag; in this case a 'for life' one, supplied by a well-known supermarket. 'This is pretty much it.'

'And I'm pretty, too,' Flip reminded her. 'Mummy said so.'

We went back in the kitchen to find that John had filled the kettle and put it on, and was busy pulling mugs from one of the cupboards.

'You must have read my mind,' I said, pulling out a third chair. 'How about you, Ellie – coffee? And what about you, Flip?' I added, as the social worker nodded an affirmative. 'Would you like some juice?'

Flip turned to her Barbie – clearly now a very precious possession, even though she had managed to forget her temporarily along the way. 'Yes, please,' she said, having put the doll to her ear. 'And Pink Barbie says do you have any teeny-weeny cups, Mummy?'

'I'm sure we can find something just right for her,' I assured her. *Mummy*. *And three or four times now*, I mused, as I rummaged in my 'teeny-weeny cups' drawer for something Barbie-sized the doll could sip from. What an unusual prospect this sweet little girl looked like being.

Unusual, interesting and definitely bordering on the profoundly challenging. Or so I was about to find out. First, though, there was the usual raft of paperwork, and, of course, the formal introductions. Ellie turned out to be called Ellie Markham, and had only just been assigned to Flip, as a consequence of her having been transferred from out of our local authority area. Though, thankfully, they'd been prompt in transferring all her notes, I felt for Ellie;

guessing at her age, my hunch was that she'd not long been qualified, so she was probably diving straight into the deep end while still a little wet behind the ears.

As she wasn't in a position to give us much in the way of background, I suggested she and I take Flip outside to meet Tyler and Denver, and that perhaps Tyler could take them on a little tour of the house and garden. It was a job that usually fell to Mike while John and I and the attending social worker dealt with all the forms, but with it having been too short notice for Mike to get away from work, we were having to improvise on that front anyway.

Which was fine; I also thought it would be nice for Tyler to meet Flip with his role in the family clearly evident, i.e. that she could see he was very much *one* of the family, and would naturally assume a big-brother role while she was with us, for however long that looked like being. We'd already primed him a while back, and with the respite work we'd done since we'd had him I was confident he'd adjust to a new child pretty quickly, just as long as he didn't feel insecure.

Indeed, he seemed puffed up with pride at being given the responsibility, and it was only Ellie's insistence that she stay by Flip's side that meant she wasn't back with John and me herself. 'Crossing the Ts and dotting the Is,' John explained when I returned to the kitchen so we could make as short work as possible of the formalities. 'She has a tendency to wander, I'm told. No sense of stranger danger either – one of the features of her FAS.' He patted a pile of papers in a slip case. 'There's plenty for you to get your teeth into here.'

'And this is it, is it?' I asked him as I retook my place at the table. 'She's in the care system now? No likelihood of her being reunited with her mum?'

John shook his head. 'That's not the plan. She's been on the "at risk" register for quite a while now, apparently; there have been repeated attempts to get Mum into alcohol abuse programmes, parenting classes and so on, so this fire's really just been a line drawn in the sand. It was probably only a matter of time in any case. There's no home for either of them to go back to now, anyway. They've apparently lost everything.' He pointed to the bag Ellie had parked by the table. 'That's all she has; the bits and pieces the respite carers pulled together for her. So she'll need kitting out ...'

'That's no problem,' I said. 'Well, in terms of stuff to run around in, anyway. I have a boxful. Not that any of it's pink. Poor mite. She must be reeling inside, even if she's not showing it. Probably too dazed by it all ... When did it happen?'

'Friday evening,' John said. And we were now into Wednesday.

'She must be in shock still,' I said, as I took the forms he was handing me. Copies of the care plan, the risk assessment, the moving forms and so on, all to be signed three times. Nothing in social services ever happened except in triplicate.

John shook his head. 'Apparently not,' he said. 'Ellie tells me what you see is what you get. One of the main problems Flip has is a lack of empathy, which I'm told is quite common. I'm sure you'll be Googling it all later, and, as I say, there's more about her background in the file here, but she's a tricky one; she's already been dealing with the legacy of being born the way she is, and it's been compounded by the rackety way she and her mother have been living. Oh, and she's on Ritalin for her ADHD, so *that* needs managing too. And probably hasn't been, not properly ...' He grimaced as he tailed off. 'You know how it goes.'

'Indeed I do,' I said, mentally ticking off another check-list. Of all the things we'd need to get put in place as a priority; of all the things we'd need to establish in terms of ground rules and routines and behaviours. Of how many ways in which my first impression had already begun changing about this outwardly sweet, biddable, idiosyn-cratic little girl.

'Oh and one other thing –' John began, but once again we were interrupted. By Tyler, who blew into the kitchen like an EF5 tornado, with Denver close behind.

'OMG, Casey!' he panted. 'OMG! Yeuch! You gotta come!'

'Come where?' I wanted to know. 'And what are those faces for, the pair of you?'

'Casey, it's like, *soooo* gross,' Denver supplied. 'You won't believe it, honest.'

'Like, *so* gross,' Tyler added, grabbing my hand and tugging on it. 'And that social worker lady, she says can you bring, like, a plastic bag and stuff? That girl –' he gestured behind him. 'She's only gone and done a poo on the grass!'

I looked at John. 'That the one other thing, by any chance?'

He nodded. 'Yup.'

Chapter 3

Mike and I have dealt with our fair share of 'accidents' with children over the years, so while Tyler and Denver continued to express their horror via the medium of extreme face-pulling, I simply reached for a pack of baby wipes, my disinfectant and my heavy-gauge rubber gloves, while John, following my instructions, pulled a plastic bag from the roll in the utensil drawer.

'Boys, *hush*,' I told them as we all trooped in a crocodile out to the garden. 'It's just a poo, not the Four Horsemen of the Apocalypse!'

Ellie and Flip were in the far corner by our trio of plucky rose bushes – which seemed appropriate; roses loved a mulch of manure, didn't they? Ellie was squatting on her haunches, talking quietly to Flip, as she carefully helped her step out of the pants she'd had on and had presumably pulled down before squatting on the grass herself.

I strode across to them, aware of the boys keeping a wary distance, and of John sensibly electing to stay with them and chat.

'Here we are, sweetie,' Ellie said brightly as she took the baby wipes from me and proceeded to pluck one from the packet to clean Flip up. 'Let's get you sorted now, shall we? And what do we say to Casey?'

Flip was now standing wide-legged, as if recently alighted from a long journey on horseback, which point I noted, wondering as I did so what life with her alcoholic mother had been like. She was eight. Not 18 months. Yet she was obviously used to being cleaned up in such a fashion. So this – this tendency to go *where* she needed to as well as *when* she needed to – was probably a long-entrenched behaviour.

'Sorry, Mummy,' Flip said, looking genuinely, if only very slightly, contrite. 'I didn't know it wasn't allowed.'

'Now that's not *strictly* true, lovely, is it?' Ellie corrected gently. 'We go to the toilet *in* the toilet. *Nowhere* else. Remember?'

'But I was despret,' Flip countered. 'I couldn't help it. It just comed out.'

Since I could see for myself that this clearly wasn't a case of a tummy upset, I doubted that very much. But perhaps she had never learned to 'feel' the usual signals; or, perhaps more likely, not to worry about the necessity to act on them as a priority. I sensed John was right. This wasn't a signifier of emotional stress. It was a lack of house-training.

'Let's not worry for now,' I said, as I pulled the gloves on and dealt with the other half of the equation. 'We can have a chat about all that later, can't we? In the meantime, let me deal with this' – I tied up my bag – 'and then we'll see about finding you a swimming costume so you can have a play in the paddling pool with the boys. How about that?'

'And Pink Barbie?' Flip asked, beaming now, while Ellie used another baby wipe on her hands. 'She's got a cossie, she has. A sparkly one. She's a beach Barbie, too.'

'Excellent,' I said, as Ellie rose to her feet and we followed a now skipping Flip back across the grass. 'How about you get Barbie changed, then, while I see what I can find for you?'

She was back through the conservatory doors and off into the kitchen like a rocket, and I realised what we were dealing with felt more like a four-year-old than an eight-year-old. And then realised something else. The effect the something I was carrying was now having.

'Oh my *God*!' Tyler shrieked theatrically, seeing the plastic bag swinging from my hand and immediately shrinking away from me. 'That's just *too* gross. You're not going to let her live with us, are you?'

I surveyed the offending bag, recalled the lack of mortification in our young visitor, and wondered if I should start the toilet training sooner rather than later, by having Flip accompany me to the downstairs loo for a ceremonial flushing away before we did anything else.

There were a multitude of challenges that we'd be facing with this slip of a child. I knew that, because John had already told me. Issues of her ADHD (attention deficit hyperactive disorder), of her lack of empathy, of her apparent tendency to wander, of how the huge change in her life might impact on her emotional health. All of this fazed me not a jot, and I knew it wouldn't faze Mike either. Our programme was designed to take a pragmatic, systematic approach to those challenges and we'd done it enough now to feel confident we would deliver it well.

But I also thought back to previous placements, and one in particular; a pair of almost feral young siblings. And, by extension, to the uniquely soul-sapping business of having a child or children regularly soiling around the house. No, it wasn't a deal-breaker – well, hopefully – but as Tyler stood waiting for my answer I wondered if his question might be echoed by Mike, just as soon as he got home.

The soiling, however, wasn't Mike's main concern that evening. Nor was it mine, because, though my hunch was that she wouldn't need to go again (not in that way), I watched Flip like a hawk. As did Tyler and Denver, with a kind of appalled fascination, as, once John and Ellie had been dispatched (the latter promising to return on the Friday to catch up and see how things were going), she darted from kitchen to conservatory to garden to living room, all the time chatting thirteen to the dozen to Pink Barbie, and seemingly physically unable to stay in one place, or engaged in one activity for more than five minutes at a time.

I'd had several children in my care who suffered the symptoms of ADHD, so the mile-a-minute behaviour and tendency to be easily distracted weren't unfamiliar territory. What did strike me, and struck Mike as soon as he'd spent half an hour in her company, was that, very much unlike the majority of children we'd fostered, little Flip seemed not the least concerned to find herself in the company of complete strangers.

'It seems like almost the opposite,' he remarked, once we were flaked out on the sofa, half-watching Tyler's favourite soap. 'I've never seen a new kid so pumped up with excitement about being here. Weird.'

It was probably adrenaline, I'd decided. And it had clearly worn her out. When Flip had crashed, she had crashed good and proper. Having wolfed down her plate of bangers and mash – of necessity, it had been a cobbled-together kind of tea – she announced that Pink Barbie was tired and needed to go to bed and she thought it would be a good idea if she went with her.

We'd tried not to smile at Tyler's fist pump (we knew how he felt) and, as Mike and he dealt with the dishes, I took her upstairs and found her some pyjamas from my stash, upon which she was in bed and fast asleep within a matter of minutes, Pink Barbie in her own pink pyjamas tucked in the crook of her arm.

'She's *weird*,' Tyler observed now. 'She's like a loony, isn't she, Casey?' He glanced at Mike, then, presumably to check that the use of the word 'loony' was acceptable. Which it wasn't, of course, but, as he already knew that, Mike didn't press it. This was an adventure, and a challenge, that was going to involve him as well, after all.

'She's certainly one of a kind,' Mike agreed, diplomatically. 'And I'm sure she's going to keep us all on our toes.' He turned his gaze away from the television and leaned forward so he could look at Tyler properly. 'But you and me are well up to that job, aren't we, kiddo? Because I think Casey here's going to have a lot on her hands, don't you?'

He accompanied his words with a wink and raised a hand, with the palm towards Tyler. 'Deal, kiddo?'

Tyler slapped the palm with his own and grinned. '*Deal!*'

I could have kissed Mike for that. There I'd been, getting increasingly stressed about whether Tyler potentially might find it all much too difficult to handle, and with a scant half dozen words Mike had him completely on side: we were Team Watson and we were in this together. I knew there would be flashpoints and disaffections – I'd be mad not to expect that – but I also felt confident we could rise to them; especially if Flip went to bed at a reasonable time every night, giving us all that precious space to recharge.

And we would need to recharge, if today had been indicative. Ellie had assured me Flip had been given her morning Ritalin by the respite carer, and I'd given her a dose at teatime, but if that was her dosed, I could only wonder incredulously what she might be like unmedicated. She was like a Duracell bunny as it was.

'You're telling me I'll need back-up,' I confirmed, nudging Tyler and grinning. 'She's only got one speed setting, hasn't she, Ty? Billy Whizz.'

He looked confused. 'Who's Billy Whizz?'

'He's out of a comic,' I explained. 'One I used to read when I was Flip's age. It's called *The Beano* and Billy Whizz was a boy who went everywhere super-fast. You've heard of Dennis the Menace?' Tyler nodded at this one. 'Well, he's a character from the same comic. I'll have to pick you up a copy some time.'

Mike chuckled. 'And with a bit of Minnie the Minx thrown in for good measure, by the sound of it.'

'Or Flip the Fast and Furious,' Tyler suggested, pretty sagely.

Later, once we were all in bed and Mike was snoring under the duvet beside me, I sat up and properly read the notes John had left for me, which fleshed out the picture he'd already sketched. It was the same depressing scenario as I'd come across many times before, both as a foster carer and, prior to that, running a behaviour unit in the local comprehensive school. Little Flip (little *Philippa*; how had the name Philippa come about, I wondered) had her potential in life stunted before she'd even been born, due to being born brain damaged as a result of her mother's addiction.

I thought back to Tyler, whose early life had been so tragically blighted by his own mother's addiction to heroin, and sent up a silent curse to the forces, and in Tyler's case more specifically to the dealers, that saw young women trapped in that same desperate downward spiral that not only meant their own lives were blighted, often permanently, but that also led them to the reckless sexual behaviours that saw them bring children into the world.

It also struck me that, in one sense, Flip had had it tougher. Though Tyler's mum's poison had killed her when he was a toddler, it had left no long-standing physical mark on him. Yes, he'd suffered horribly, psychologically, in a zillion other ways, but he was young, fit and strong now. He could grow up and be and do anything he wanted.

There would be no heady potential for Flip, as far as I could tell, because – damningly and cruelly – alcohol had poisoned her too. And once I'd refreshed my knowledge of the damage FAS could wreak, I was reminded that there were things that could not be reversed; that the damage to her brain was going to be permanent.

I tried not to judge. To be a foster carer and be judgemental is a fool's game, and often inappropriate, as well. Though revulsion at abusers is a normal human reaction, there are many cases where the parents who've had their children removed from them are very much victims themselves. But as I read, I still felt a stirring of something like anger. There were apparently grandparents. There was a brother. This was a child who *did* have family. Just a mother unwilling or unable to conquer her addiction and an extended family that didn't seem to want to know her.

I read the previous social worker's lengthy set of notes with care. John had been right when he said mother and daughter had been known to the authorities for some time; the notes went back to when Flip had been little more than a baby, one who hadn't been reaching her developmental milestones.

There was no father's name recorded on Flip's birth certificate, but it seemed social services had had some contact a long time back with the maternal grandparents, who were both in their seventies, and apparently not in the best of health. Their daughter Megan was the younger of two children – there was also a brother, but he was a soldier who lived in Germany and was recently divorced. Hardly knowing his niece in any case, he apparently wanted no involvement.

Neither, it seemed, did those very same grandparents – well, at least according to the most recent note about it, which was a few years old now. This was another sad state of affairs. They had apparently tried hard to help out their daughter when Flip had been a baby, but when they practised tough love and stopped helping Megan financially her retaliation was swift and decisive. She refused to have anything more to do with them, in protest.

And it seemed that they'd long since given up on both daughter and grand-daughter – washed their hands of the pair of them, despite entreaties by Megan's then social worker to try to build bridges. '*It's difficult,*' she'd noted in an email to her manager, '*because Flip has so little in the way of attachments; with the best will in the world, it's hard to appeal to their better natures when Flip herself seems to have not the slightest affection for them, while professing to love people she has only just met. One of the many frustrations of dealing with FAS! Will just have to keep trying …*'

I recalled Flip's last words to me when I'd kissed her goodnight; a hug and then a completely guileless and affectionate 'I love you, Mummy.' What a complicated business her disability was, I decided, making a mental note to find time for a session at the computer the following morning, just to gen up on things more comprehensively.

I closed the file, dropped it on the rug and switched the bedside light off. Still, I thought, as I wriggled down and put my head gratefully on the pillow, at least she was whacked out and sleeping soundly, and tomorrow was another day – one which I was actually rather looking forward to. Get a plan going, get a chart going, start getting to know our new charge a little better. First, however, sleep. A good solid eight hours till the alarm.

Though it turned out to be only two till her ear-splitting scream.

Chapter 4

'What the *hell*?' Mike said, shooting bolt upright in the bed just as I was leaping out of it.

I switched on the bedside light and checked the time. It was just after half past one in the morning. 'I've no idea, love,' I said. 'But you try and get back to sleep. I think Flip must be having a nightmare or something.'

Mike sighed and snuggled back down under the duvet as I grabbed my dressing gown and left the room to investigate. The door to Flip's bedroom was ajar and as I approached I could already see her, sitting crouched at the top of her bed with her back to me, holding on to the headboard, still screaming.

'Shhhh,' I soothed as I rushed to sit with her and stroked her back. 'What is it, sweetie? You had a bad dream?'

Flip recoiled from my touch and shrieked even louder as she squashed herself further against the headboard. It seemed clear she didn't know where she was or who I was.

'It's just me,' I said softly. 'Casey, you remember? Mummy.' She twisted her head; her eyes were like saucers.

I didn't touch her this time. I just smiled and hoped that she'd recognise me enough to calm down. She really did look terrified and I imagined she'd had a nightmare. Perhaps reliving the terrifying events of the last few days. I'd also heard about night terrors in toddlers and very young children, and as she seemed unable to regain full consciousness and shake off whatever had terrified her, I decided to add some research on that to my 'to do' list.

In the meantime, however, she needed to wake up. It seemed nothing else was going to stop her screaming. I cast around, my eye fixing on Pink Barbie, still on her pillow. 'Flip,' I said in a voice that I hoped was akin to that of a diva like the eponymous Barbie, as I held the doll close to her face. 'Flip,' I said again, moving Barbie's head to suggest she was the one talking. 'New mummy is sad because you're screaming, and you're making *me* scared now as well.'

The effect was almost instantaneous. The screaming stopped as abruptly as it had apparently begun. And much as I was concerned about this vulnerable little thing apparently deciding I *was* her new mummy, my hunch at that moment was that it was the right word to choose. I continued in my Barbie voice. 'Oh that's *much* better, Flip,' I trilled. 'Now, why don't we tell this new mummy what's wrong?'

To my surprise, Flip immediately launched herself straight into my arms, and with such force that I nearly fell backwards on the bed. More bizarre was that she giggled then, all fear forgotten. 'It's *you*, Mummy!' she said. 'I forgotted what you looked like an' I was frightened.' She raised her eyes towards mine. 'I *am* a silly sausage, aren't I?'

I laughed, more out of sheer surprise than seeing any humour in the situation. 'Yes, you *are* a bit of a silly sausage, sweetie,' I agreed, stroking her hair. 'Did you have a nasty dream?'

Flip lifted her head again, and shook it. 'I don't think so,' she said, seeming to be struggling to remember. 'I know,' she said brightly. 'I need a picture by my bed, don't I? Could I have a photo picture of you? In a frame? So I can put it by my bed? Then I'll remember.' She paused. 'And a mirror? Can I have a mirror as well?'

'What, *now*?' I asked, bemused by this unexpected shopping list. 'Tell you what,' I said, gently disentangling her from me and passing her the doll. 'If you and Pink Barbie get back into bed and go back to sleep, I promise I'll get you those things tomorrow for you, okay?'

But she clearly wasn't ready to hop back into bed yet. 'Could you just take me to the toilet then?' she asked. 'Just to look in the mirror?'

What, now? I thought. This was something I'd never come across before, and I was intrigued. What on earth was wrong? I stood up, holding my arms out to her. 'Come on then, miss,' I said, 'But *quietly*. And then straight back to bed, before Tyler wakes up.'

Indeed, it was a miracle he hadn't already, I mused, as Flip threw herself at me, this time straight onto my hip, curling her legs around my waist like a little koala bear. She planted a kiss on my cheek. 'Thanks, Mummy,' she said.

Once in the bathroom, and with the door closed so the light wouldn't spill out into Tyler's adjacent room, I held

Flip in front of the mirror above the sink. What struck me most forcibly was the intentness of her expression as she traced a finger around both her eyes, then down her nose and then around the curve of her narrow chin. I then had to struggle with my own troubled expression as a single tear fell from her left eye and slid noiselessly down her cheek. She turned away from the mirror then and buried her face into my neck. 'I'm still ugly, Mummy, aren't I?' she said.

I continued to hold her where she was. 'Flip, you're *not* ugly, not at *all*, sweetie. You're very, very pretty. Look. Look at your beautiful wavy hair. It's just like Pink Barbie's, isn't it? And those lovely lips – just like a rosebud – they look just like Barbie's too.' I kissed her forehead, thinking wryly how this was so entirely off message. Girls, in the main, needed to know that beauty was only skin deep; that being beautiful on the inside was the only thing that *really* mattered. But not in this case. This was something different. This was a deep-rooted canker. I wondered where – or whom – she'd absorbed it from. 'Now,' I whispered, 'one thing I *do* know for sure is that pretty girls need their beauty sleep. Have you heard about beauty sleep?'

Flip shook her head. 'Is it a special sleep that makes you pretty?'

I nodded. 'Even prettier. You are already very pretty. But a good night's sleep makes you bright-eyed and bushy-tailed, and that is *especially* beautiful. Now, then. Are we ready to go back to bed?'

Flip's mouth bloomed into a smile. 'You mean like a squirrel? Now *you're* the one being a silly sausage, Mummy, aren't you?'

Quite possibly, I thought ruefully, as I slipped back under my own duvet some ten minutes later. Mike was fast asleep, and, having looked in on him en route, I could see why Tyler hadn't woken up; he'd fallen asleep with his earphones in, listening to music, as per.

It took me a good while to get back to sleep myself, my head full, as it invariably was when we took on a new foster child; of all the questions that popped up about the multitude of whys and wherefores and how we'd go about unlocking the mystery behind whatever psychological muddles lay behind her challenge in living an easy life. And, in this case, physiological muddles also. That much about FAS I already knew. But what, if anything, could be done about it?

Over the next few days I began to at least gain more understanding about the problems our latest foster child was facing. Night terrors and what seemed to be unfathomable bouts of screaming seemed to be as much a part of Flip as was her ADHD; another common manifestation of her FAS.

All these letters, I thought, lined up like ducks in a row, but where the numbers were concerned things were rather less tidy; there seemed no clear consensus on either the quantity or timing of the medication she'd arrived with, and it seemed to me that nailing that was a priority.

'Definitely,' Ellie agreed when she made her visit the following Friday, by which time Flip had been with us for ten days. 'You're currently giving her two a day, right? First thing and teatime?'

I agreed that I was. 'Not that it seems to have much of an observable impact on her mood or behaviour, I have to say,' I added. 'Or maybe the impact of her FAS overrides all that?'

Ellie frowned apologetically. She clearly knew as well as I did – or at least thought I did – that the pills should have *some* effect, and fairly quickly, too. Most people who spent time around kids with ADHD knew that. When they didn't have their meds the term 'all hell broke loose' had serious resonance. 'It's still early days with the meds,' she said. 'Or so I'm told. And I'm really sorry it falls on you and Mike, Casey. But it's really a case of trial and error till a routine is re-established. School will help with that, won't it? And everything, you know, settles down after a bit ...'

'Settle' and 'down' being the operative words. Because it seemed the night terrors weren't confined to the night-time. Flip could 'lose it' – and properly lose it – seemingly without warning in the daytime too. Only the previous day she'd gone into some sort of major meltdown in the living room, leaving both Tyler and me dumbfounded.

'They'd been sitting there watching TV, not six feet from me,' I explained to Ellie. 'Weren't even talking to each other; just sitting there, opposite ends of the sofa – watching a nature programme, I think it was – when suddenly she was screaming at the top of her lungs.'

'Something she saw on the screen?' Ellie suggested. 'A big spider, perhaps? Something like that?'

I shook my head. 'Not a spider. It was a lion that set her off, apparently. A lioness, actually, carrying a cub in her mouth. Which completely freaked her out. And I *mean*

35

freaked her out; it was almost as if she was having some sort of fit; she'd thrown herself on the floor, still clutching her doll, thrashing about, limbs flailing, the lot. And she was *really* thrashing about, too – took me a good while to get a proper hold of her, let alone calm her down. And even *she* couldn't articulate quite why it had set her off the way it had. So it's not like a phobia, nothing like that. It can come out of nowhere.'

And could do so at school, too, I reflected gloomily. Ellie shook her head and sighed sympathetically. 'Well, there's nothing in her notes, as you know,' she said. 'So perhaps this is a new thing. You know, with all the upheaval. And being separated from her mum, of course. Or perhaps it's just a new manifestation of the ADHD. I guess all you can do is keep on recording everything; see if there's any pattern to it, any obvious triggers.'

Along with the episodes of soiling, the night waking, the obsession with being so 'ugly', the myriad little ways the strangeness of our little house-guest was becoming ever more apparent. I was at least forming a picture of sorts, however dispiriting the colouring-in part. 'Will do,' I said. 'Early days. I'm sure there's a lot still to learn. We'll get there – try our best to, at any rate.'

'And you're doing a *great* job,' Ellie reassured me, smiling a bright, encouraging sort of smile, which couldn't help but remind me of just how young and inexperienced she was, even as she affected the role of sage supporter. 'Casey, I *know* you'll do your best,' she said. 'You and Mike both.' She grinned. 'Trust me, you came *highly* recommended. So we have no concerns. None. And Flip seems to love it here.

You all got a *very* big thumbs up, I can report. As did your cooking. *And* her room. So that's positive, isn't it?' she finished brightly.

I couldn't help but laugh. This, too, was a part of the process. The business of 'bedding in' – with both the child and the social worker that came with her. And one of the key things that happened during every home visit was that the social worker spent time alone with the child privately. This was a necessity, obviously, because it gave the child a voice; a chance to share their own thoughts about the place where they'd been billeted – to comment on how *they* felt about aspects of their care.

It was a dialogue that invariably had to be adapted to a child's age and stage. An older child might well be able to articulate their feelings easily, but a little one might need a simpler schema to work with; a question-and-answer format that could elicit, say, a thumbs-up or thumbs-down response. And it wasn't just valuable for the child. As a foster carer myself I knew what many of us were like. If given a thumbs-up, thumbs-down or halfway-between selection, we'd err towards the 'up' almost every time. That was the nature of the job – and perhaps the psychological make-up of the majority. You didn't go into fostering if you were generally beset by negativity; that a person tended towards the positive was probably an essential to do the job. You definitely had to see hope where others didn't.

Which made us unreliable witnesses. Given the opportunity to tell it like it was, I knew for a fact that the majority of us didn't. We'd make light of problems if we could, wanting to try to deal with them ourselves, and only when things got really bad did we want to ask for help. Silly, really, and definitely not in anyone's best interests, but definitely also par for the course.

Which meant that social workers, who didn't always get a chance to see the extent of a child's idiosyncrasies for themselves, sometimes failed to hear the full extent of them either. Today, however, Ellie was in luck because just as she was preparing to leave, having given me my pep talk, Tyler blew into the kitchen like the proverbial East Wind.

'Casey, you best go outside,' he said. 'Go and see to her. I think she's going Loony Tunes again.'

'Tyler!' I admonished, while Ellie slipped her files into her bag. 'What have I told you about using expressions like that in this house? What do you mean, exactly? What's Flip actually *doing*?'

'Three guesses,' he suggested as we both followed him out into the back garden. 'Only *much* worse,' he threw over his shoulder.

He wasn't wrong. Flip, who as far as we'd known had been playing in the garden with Pink Barbie while we'd chatted, was squatting on the grass, holding the doll above her, swooping it back and forth like a boy would do with an aeroplane. She was also singing. Singing lustily, at the top of her voice. But it wasn't the song – 'Under the Sea', from *The Little Mermaid* – that stopped me in my tracks. It was the fact that her hair and face, and that of the doll, were covered in what looked like something I hoped that it wasn't but which I feared, from Tyler's tip-off, that it more than likely was. 'Flip!' I shouted. 'Is that poo that you're covered in?'

Flip looked up as if surprised and then smiled and waved at me. She then put the Barbie – and I cringed – close to her ear. Then she spoke. 'Yes, it's Mummy, Barbie! Look! Wave to Mummy.'

Barbie waved. Tyler wrinkled his nose. Ellie tapped me on the shoulder. 'Erm, Casey,' she said, 'I've got a meeting I really shouldn't be late for. So unless you need me – and just say, because it's *absolutely* no problem – I think I'd better get going and leave this to you.'

Would I do any different in her shoes? Probably not, I conceded. 'No, no,' I said, 'you get off. We've got this one covered. No problem.'

'No problem?' squeaked Tyler, sharp enough not to have missed my royal 'we'.

I turned back to Flip. 'Come on, miss. Indoors, please. Time for a bath. Honestly, Flip, *how* many times?' I added, as she ambled across the grass. 'Why would you poo in the garden *again*? You *know* you must use the toilet. Come on. Inside.'

Tyler stood back, making a big show of retching as he did so. 'Urgh! You're disgusting, Flip! Urrrrgh!'

I shared his sentiments. Up close and personal the smell was indeed disgusting, encouraging Ellie all the quicker to say goodbye and head for the front door. I changed my mind then. Perhaps the bath indoors needed to be preceded by an al fresco soaking. It was another scorcher and we had the hose and paddling pool out, after all.

'It wasn't Flip, it was *me*, Mummy!' she said in a squeaky voice, brandishing the doll. 'It wasn't Flip. Flip's a good girl an' she *knows* to go to the toilet. I'm sowwy, Mummy.'

Great, I thought, ruing the fact that the other night I'd unwittingly given this diminutive plastic goddess a voice. I could see Tyler opening his mouth to offer his own take on the subject too.

'We can talk about all that in a bit,' I said to both of them. 'Now come on over here, miss,' I said, directing Flip towards the coiled hose with a carefully placed finger. 'I think you and Pink Barbie need a bit of jet wash.'

Tyler cottoned on then. 'She's not getting in the paddling pool!' he shouted after us, his voice indignant. 'I'm not fishing that stuff out as well as all the flies!'

I had a re-think. 'No, of *course* I wasn't going to put her in the paddling pool,' I lied, the words 'creek' and 'paddle' springing instantly to mind as I herded her across the lawn and told her to stay put.

Tyler handed me the hose with an air of resignation. 'I *knew* she'd be trouble,' he sighed.

Chapter 5

To say I was relieved when the start of September came around was a bit of an understatement. It wasn't the fact that I had two full-on children in the house particularly; I'd obviously dealt with that many times before. It was that having our very own Minnie the Minx around – as Tyler had taken to calling Flip – was physically and emotionally draining, and I was exhausted.

Flip simply didn't seem to have an off switch. She chattered on ceaselessly, about anything and everything, from the minute she woke up to the minute she went to sleep. And if she had no actual human available to chat to, she chattered on to Pink Barbie instead.

'Mummy, why is the sky blue? Mummy, what are leaves made of? Why do they taste nasty and peas don't? Where do clouds live when they go home at night? Why has the daddy got silver bits in his hair?' The stream of never-ending questions (not to mention the answering of them, which invariably threw up even more questions) was beginning to take its toll, even if it did at least point to a healthily enquiring mind, and even if the Mike-centred questions did make me giggle. Where we used to stay up until around 11 o'clock, we found ourselves clock watching from eight, when Flip went to bed, and would follow her and Tyler (who would be back to bed at nine on school days) as soon as we were confident they would be asleep – so keen were we to get our heads down ourselves. We knew we had to; the small-hours screaming sessions could start at any time, and seemed to be happening two nights out of three, and at least that way I was sure to get some sleep in before they started and I had to begin the laborious process of settling Flip back down again.

No, she needed to be back in school, badly. Though I'd had a fight on my hands to get her placed where I wanted her, because Ellie's manager felt it best that she return to her old school, thereby making the transition into care less traumatic. I disagreed. 'I just don't see that,' I'd argued, when Ellie had popped over at the end of August. 'She's already *made* that transition. And from what I can see in her notes, she was barely attending anyway; I certainly get no sense that she's pining for a gang of girlfriends. She's mentioned no one, and it seems clear to me that she's not really formed any real attachments. To my mind, it makes more sense for her to have a fresh start at the local school.'

It was also a lot closer, which was a big consideration too. It made no sense to cart her several miles there and back every day – no sense for either of us. Plus if she *did* make some friends, they'd be local as well, which meant she'd at least have the option of seeing them out of school too.

Thankfully, Ellie agreed with me. 'Leave it with me,' she'd said firmly. And within a matter of no more than 48 hours she'd not only got her hands on Flip's school files for me to look through, she'd also spoken to the school Special Educational Needs Co-ordinator (Senco) there, a lady called Sonia, who'd said she'd be more than happy to chat to me and answer any questions she could. For a relative rookie, Ellie was proving to be a pretty good ally, clearly unafraid to state her case.

And Sonia was extremely helpful too.

'Oh, I'm so pleased that someone has acted at last,' she said after I introduced myself. 'Well, perhaps not in the best of circumstances, but you know what I mean. That poor mite was such a worry for me. You know, it was almost as if she were bringing herself up,' she explained. 'Some days she'd turn up for school half starving. And I mean *really* hungry – give her a biscuit and she'd wolf it down like an animal; I often got the impression that she might not have had a single thing to eat since her school dinner the lunchtime before.'

'She certainly seems to love her food,' I said. 'Though I'm not sure where she puts it.' Despite her eating like the proverbial horse, Flip was no less scrawny than when she'd come to us – no doubt a result of using up so much nervous energy.

'Oh bless her. Such a terrible business. And there would always be some excuse; Mummy was asleep, Mummy was ill, Mummy was out ... And we reported everything, naturally, not least because she'd turn up at school at such odd times as well. Mid-morning, mid-afternoon – well, when she turned up at all, that was. You know, one day she fetched up at half past four in the afternoon, seemingly oblivious – and, of course, there were only a handful of us left. It was only luck that someone glanced out and saw her crossing the playground. By the time I got there, she'd hung up her bag and coat on her peg and was just sitting there in her seat, smiling. I honestly don't think she had the slightest idea what time of day it was.'

Which all seemed to fit. Sonia paused. 'Well, until I explained to her that school had finished and that everyone had gone home. Soon as I told her that she burst into tears and it took an age to calm her down. Said she'd come in specially because she wanted to do some drawing. I feel dreadful about sending her away that day, I really do.'

I didn't doubt it. For all that Flip had come into our lives like a small fizzing tornado, the thing that screamed most loudly at me – louder than she did – was her extreme vulnerability. No, it was absolutely right that she come to our local school, where I'd only ever be ten minutes away.

Not only that, our local primary was the school that Levi attended, and that little Jackson was starting at this term as well. It really made no sense to send her anywhere else, so I was glad when John confirmed, after stating my case to social services as well, that they'd agreed she could be educated in our area, even if it was slightly reluctantly.

A trip into town to get a new uniform was therefore a priority, as Flip would need the whole kit and caboodle, including a pair of shoes. It would also give me an opportunity, thankfully aided and abetted by Riley, to make my first foray out into the wider world with our new charge, who thus far had only ventured as far as Kieron and Lauren's, when I'd popped over with her to drop some milk and a loaf of bread round for the pair of them, as their flight back from holiday brought them back in the wee hours.

No, this trip would be something of a learning curve, I reckoned, giving me an opportunity to observe how she managed out in the wider world and whether the business of her wandering off was one I needed to be hyper-vigilant about. Not that we were short of pairs of watchful eyes. As well as Riley, who was driving (she being the one with the people-carrier), we also had Levi and Jackson with us, plus Tyler, who needed a new uniform as well. He was starting in year 8 – he'd be 13 in no time at all now – and, as boys often do, he seemed to have grown three or four inches in as many weeks. Well, if not quite that, certainly in less than as many months. Needless to say, with Marley-Mae in her buggy, we were all but mob-handed. And with the lads being lads, somewhat rowdy.

'Ha-ha! Girls have to wear PE knickers,' Levi pointed out to Flip as we browsed through the list in the school uniform section of the department store. 'Big black ones. HUGE black ones,' he added helpfully. 'Really baggy.'

Although Levi and Flip were almost exactly the same age, the huge social and intellectual gap between them was often apparent. Flip immediately began to fret about this nugget of information. 'But I don't wanna *do* PE. *Or* wear them knickers. What if I need a poo?'

Levi grinned widely. 'Ha-ha!' he said, laughing. 'Mum, she said poo! She said she might need a poo in PE!' Then something else seemed to occur to him. 'I hope you're joking,' he told her, 'because you can't say things like that at school. People will laugh at you,' he added, looking suddenly anxious. '*And* at me,' he said, as if becoming aware of a worrying possibility. 'Mum, she's not gonna be in my class, is she?'

Riley and I exchanged glances as Flip beamed at a now concerned-looking Levi, then threw her arms around his neck. 'I think I *will* be in your class,' she said, as he wriggled free from her clutches. 'It'll be good, won't it? We'll be just like a real brother and sister!'

She then turned and patted Jackson. 'An you can be my brother too,' she said, pinching his cheek, while Levi watched them, clearly appalled.

He wasn't the only one. 'God,' Tyler said, with some feeling, looking at me. 'I am *so* glad I don't have to be a part of this. You're all right, Flip,' he said, as her attention turned towards him. 'And if anyone asks, I'm the black sheep of the family, okay? No relation.'

Which set Marley-Mae off on an impromptu rendition of her current favourite song, so that anyone who hadn't heard our arrival in the school uniform department could be assured of at least noticing our exit.

Having lunch in town with five children and a buggy is never easy; not if you want it with a modicum of decorum and your coffee served in mugs rather than cardboard. Fortunately, there was a big friendly café just off the high street, which just so happened to be run by my younger sister, Donna, and was invariably the obvious choice. So, with the kit part done (and just the shoes, and the caboodle part, presumably, left to deal with) we headed there to get everyone fed.

Less fortunately, it was busy and there was no large table left, so the logical thing seemed to be to spread across two adjacent ones. 'There you are, boys,' Riley told them, as she unbuttoned Jackson's jacket. 'You boys can have a boys' table – you're officially in charge, Tyler – and we girls can have a nice quiet one next door.'

'Ye-ess!' Levi said, doing the little fist-pump he'd learned from Tyler.

'So, Flip,' he finished, 'would you like to help take off Marley-Mae's coat?'

But it seemed Flip didn't want to take off Marley-Mae's coat. It seemed Flip didn't want to do anything.

Except scream. Which she immediately did, at an ear-splitting volume. As ever, it seemed incredible that so many decibels could come out of such a tiny pair of lungs. I jumped from the seat I'd been just about to park my bottom on and knelt down in front of her in the aisle between the tables, conscious that every head in the place had turned towards us.

'Flip! Stop that!' I tried, speaking sternly in the hope that it might work. It didn't. In fact, her face started to go an alarming shade of purple. She threw back her head then and screamed even louder. I knew my own face was probably well on the way to matching hers for colour; even though my focus was on her, I could hear Tyler groaning, and also the low but rising hum of incredulity from our fellow diners – well, former diners; I doubted anyone was enjoying a quiet lunch any more.

Riley squatted down beside me and placed her mouth close to my ear. '*God*, mother,' she whispered. 'I mean, I know you told me, but, oh my *word* … Look, can I try?'

I leaned to the side, only too happy to accept a third-party intervention, it coming to me immediately that a less familiar figure might bring her 'back' more readily than I seemed to be able to.

Riley placed her hands on Flip's shoulders. 'Flip,' she said, giving her shoulders a gentle squeeze to get her attention. 'Something has upset you, clearly, but we don't know what, do we? And unless you stop this silly screaming, you won't be able to tell us what it is, will you? We'll just have to get the boys … are you listening to me, Flip? *Get the boys and leave here*. *Are* you listening? Are you hearing what I'm saying?'

Flip's mouth clamped shut. It was almost an instantaneous action. From one state to a different state in the blink of an eye. She then glared at Riley. 'Thems are *my* boys!' she shouted at Riley. 'Thems my brothers and I wanna *sit with them*!' Then – ping! Blink of an eye again – the screaming started up again.

My mind was whirling with thoughts as I took in the components of this short exchange. Was this simply a manipulation tool? Was this just a classic toddler tantrum? No, it wasn't that, clearly. No toddler could switch emotions on and off in that way. When a toddler had a tantrum there was a long tail at the end of it; the child in question was invariably an emotional wreck immediately afterwards – a limp rag, hot-cheeked, shuddering with the last remnants of tears. No, this was different. This was knowingly manipulative behaviour, and the name Violet Elizabeth popped unbidden into my brain. Violet Elizabeth from the *Just William* books I'd read to my own children. Violet Elizabeth, who when crossed always said 'I'll scream and I'll scream and I'll scream!'

Despite the spectacle we were making of ourselves, it even made me smile. Though somewhat grimly, and I could see Riley was thinking the same. This was no spoilt brat – not in a million years – but this *was* possibly a learned behaviour; a blunt instrument of a communication tool, in order to get her way. And it was one that we didn't do her any favours by giving in to for the sake of peace. To give in to it would simply be to reinforce it.

I could read Riley's thoughts as she took Flip's hand, and, smiling at the boys (the younger two of whom looked like they might start crying), stood up again. 'Right, boys, everything is fine,' she reassured them. 'Levi, could you help take off your sister's coat while your nan orders some drinks, sweetheart? Me and Flip here just need to go outside for a minute or two.' And with that she tugged on a now stunned Flip's arm, and pulled her, thankfully mute again, out of the café door.

The low hum around us mushroomed into a more familiar burble; cutlery clinked, chairs scraped and normal service seemed to be resumed. 'Help Levi with Marley-Mae, will you, Tyler?' I asked him, before heading up to the counter and prefixing my drinks order with a profuse apology to the new woman manning the till, Donna having nipped home for her break. I wasn't sure how much luck Riley would have with Flip out there, but if it looked like we'd have to cut and run rather than actually eating – or, indeed, without finishing our shopping – I at least wanted a decent slurp of coffee before we did so.

Riley and Flip still hadn't reappeared when I brought the tray back to the table but, as far as I could see (not to mention hear) through all the menus and various 'dish of the day' stickers, Flip had at least not resumed screaming. I duly sat down and sipped my scalding drink. Fingers crossed then.

'I don't like her when she does that, Nanny,' Jackson said quietly. 'What's *wrong* with her?'

Before I could think of an answer, Tyler provided one for him. 'She's not right in the head, kiddo,' he said conversationally. 'We get it all the time at home, don't we, Casey?'

I shook my head. 'Tyler!' I admonished, albeit equally quietly. 'How many times have I told you? "Not right in the head" is not a nice thing to say! She has some *problems*, sweetheart, that's all,' I corrected for the benefit of Levi and Jackson. 'But we're working to help her – *all* of us; Tyler's doing his bit, too – and hopefully you boys can just be a little bit patient while we try to work out how best we can do that right now. Is that okay?'

Jackson nodded and then pointed at the door. 'It's all right, Nan, she's all better now. Look, they're coming back in again.'

She did indeed seem largely 'all better'. Riley winked at me as she sat opposite and pulled Flip into the chair next to hers. 'All sorted, Mum,' she said, turning to smile at Flip, who seemed to be looking up at her adoringly. 'Flip just wanted to sit somewhere different, didn't you, sweetie? But she now sees why we *ladies* should all sit together, and I've explained that screaming is most definitely not a good way to get people to listen to her. In fact it's more likely to get people to close their ears and not listen. Isn't that right, Flip?'

Flip nodded and picked up the orange juice I placed in front of her. 'I was just scared, Mummy,' she told me.

'Scared?' I asked her. 'Scared of what?'

She glanced past me to where the boys were. 'Scared I wasn't allowed to sit with my brothers because they didn't like me –'

'I never said that!' Levi interrupted indignantly. 'I never!'

Oh, God, I thought. *Here we go again*. But Tyler was already shushing him.

'Because I'm so ugly,' Flip finished, with a new sob in her voice, and clearly so taken up with her own train of thought that she wasn't even listening to him.

'Well, what a silly sausage thing to think!' I said, reaching across to pat her hand reassuringly. 'As if those boys would even think that! *Nobody* could *possibly* think that, sweetie. I keep telling you how pretty you are.'

'I did too,' Riley said, looking at me. 'In fact, we've even had a chat, Flip and I. And the next time you bring her round to our house she's going to play Princess Dress Up with me and Marley-Mae, and we're doing hair, make-up, the whole girly lot, aren't we, love? I might even get Lauren over too, now she's back from holidays. Now, who's for food? Are you all Hank Marvin over there, Ty? I know I could eat a whole woolly mammoth.'

With woolly mammoth not on the menu, it was chicken nuggets and French fries for the kids, and while Riley and

I shared a plate of spaghetti and meatballs we tried to ignore the glances of the customers who had witnessed the performance and seemed so keen to express their feelings – via the medium of dark looks and meaningful stares as they exited.

Which was fine. I'd been in similar scenarios more times than I cared to remember, and it was odds on I'd be in similar scenarios many times again. Indeed, likely as not before the week was out, with our little pocket rocket. Which reminded me that I should perhaps be a little more proactive; rather than wait to be told, I should get down to the GP's and get Flip registered and re-assessed, because it seemed clear things were not working out with her medication.

Seemed *crystal* clear, in fact. Because lunch finished, and while Riley was off in the ladies with Flip and Marley-Mae, a kindly-looking older lady stopped on her way out of the café. 'Bless you, you have got your hands full,' she remarked.

'We have indeed,' I agreed ruefully, while I helped Jackson with his coat.

'Not meaning to interfere,' she added, obviously keen to tell me something. 'But she reminds me of my grand-daughter, that little 'un with the lungs on her. I was saying to my friend. She might have that ADH thingy.' She lowered her voice a touch. 'You can get pills for it. Like a miracle, they are. Like a different girl, she is now. Anyway, dear, just thought I'd mention.'

'Erm …' I began. But where to start? In fact, *why* start at all? After all, she'd just proved my point.

Chapter 6

The morning I waved Tyler off to school for the start of a new term didn't turn out to be the day that Flip joined her class. Despite getting the go-ahead from the local authority – and I had carefully guarded the confirmation letter as evidence, should it be needed – the school had already been informed about her history and her lack of attendance at her previous school, so, before deciding which class to put her into, they wanted to meet Flip and me for a chat.

Given the time we'd had with her so far, this did make sense, even if it meant that in the end they didn't take her. Should that be the case, then perhaps a more specialist school was going to be the way forward in any case, though the big stress was the time it would take to get her a place at such an institution – I knew things like that could take weeks, and Flip needed to be back in the routine of education, for everyone's sakes.

I'd also made an appointment with our GP's surgery, with a view to discussing where she was with her medication, and coming up with a slightly more scientific answer than 'Aargh!'

As for giving her a morning dose of Ritalin, I was very much in two minds, but reasoning that, for the most part, it was a drug that calmed children down rather than making them go off pop, I opted to give it to her and hope for the best; odds on, it would surely only help our case once we got to school.

'Here you go, sweetie,' I said, passing Flip a glass of water and her pill. 'Take this and then we'll have a nice walk down to see the doctor.'

Flip pulled a face at me, wrinkling her nose. 'Thems horrible, Casey. They make me feel funny.'

It was the first time she'd made reference to how the drugs made her feel so I pressed her for more, thinking it may help the doctor. 'How do they make you feel, love? Funny how?'

She swallowed the pill and put the glass down, then shrugged. 'Just funny. And I don't like it. Sort of wonky.'

I supressed a smile as I took the glass. It wasn't the first time I'd heard a child try to explain how Ritalin affected them, but it was the first time I'd heard the word 'wonky'. But perhaps she had hit the nail on the head. I couldn't imagine having to take a pill that made me feel out of control, and from what I knew of this particular medication, that's kind of what it did. Other children had described it as making them feel that they were stuck in a dream, and 'not quite there'. Wonky. I got that. And I mentally filed it. Whatever it did, I didn't suppose it was very nice.

In most cases there was no doubt Ritalin had the 'desired' effect – it subdued the need to be constantly on the go, increased the ability to concentrate for more than five minutes and, I guess more importantly, it allowed parents who were at their wits' end to cope and teachers to allocate their time to *all* of their class, rather than having to be constantly tied up with a child who had ADHD. Which was obviously important in a world full of 30-strong classes, a curriculum to be delivered to a timetable and, of course, those frazzled parents.

Which was why I was slightly open mouthed at Dr Shakelton's suggestion when we were sitting in his consulting room half an hour later.

'What I'd like to do, Casey, if you're okay with it,' he said, after we'd discussed what we both knew of Flip, and he'd chatted to her himself, 'is to have a bit of a trial run *without* the Ritalin.'

I looked at Flip, who was now disengaged from us, sliding her new school socks up and down her legs. Then I turned back to the doctor. '*Without* the Ritalin? I don't understand,' I said. 'She's been assessed as having ADHD – well, as far as I believe, and she's very hyper even though she's *taking* the tablets.' I frowned, choosing my words carefully as she was in the room with us. 'I don't know what it would be like without them.'

'And that's precisely my point,' the doctor said. 'Despite popular opinion, Ritalin can actually have an adverse effect on some children. From what you've told me – and her records seem to suggest the same – the medication isn't doing much to control the hyperactivity at all.' He smiled at Flip, who smiled back at him as if he was Santa in a suit. 'Young Philippa here says she doesn't like the tablets, so we ought really to have some time off from them, shouldn't we? Just to see what happens.'

Flip's smile became a pout. 'S'not Philippa!' she said crossly. 'It's *Flip*. With a "F"! Mummy, can we go now?' she whined, turning to me. 'I'm bored an' I wanna go to school.'

Dr Shakelton smiled again. 'I do beg your pardon, Flip with a "F". So, Casey? What do you think? You up for a bit of a medical trial?'

The answer was, of course, yes. Had to be, really. Dr Shakelton had been our family GP for many years. He didn't just know the job I did, and the kinds of kids I tended to look after – he'd been pretty active in supporting us in doing so. If he was suggesting something, I trusted him enough to know that he was acting in Flip's best interest. 'I guess we can do that,' I said, mentally crossing my fingers that the 'trial' went the way we both hoped. 'How long before we see any results, do you think?'

'We might not see any results,' he said, 'but then again, if she was misdiagnosed by any chance – and it can happen – we just might. Either way, I'd say to give it at least a month, and if things worsen in that time we can always try putting her back on it again.'

Flip was already up on her feet, clutching my hand and hopping from one to the other impatiently. I stood up as well. 'Right then, kiddo, let's go see what school has to say, then, shall we?'

Flip grinned and pulled at me. 'Yes, come *on*! I promised the brothers we wouldn't be late!' She then seemed to remember something. 'Mummy, could you ask the doctor man if I can have a poo in his toilet first? I don't wanna have no accidents, do I?'

This was fast becoming something of a thing with Flip. We'd all banged on so much about the importance of recognising you needed the toilet in good time to actually *get* to a toilet that we'd arrived at a place where Flip wanted the opportunity to use any toilet, anywhere, whether she needed to or not. There were points involved for using a toilet, after all. It had almost become something of a game to her.

'Do you *really* need to go?' I asked her, just as Dr Shakelton was raising a finger to point us in the direction of his. 'Could you wait five minutes till we get home, do you think? You'll still get a star on your chart.' It really was like dealing with a pre-schooler.

Happy now, she assured me she could wait and we hurried home – her chattering away in her usual manner about the first thing that caught her attention, and with me wondering what line the school might take when I told them she wouldn't be getting any medication for the foreseeable future. Which I absolutely had to do, even if it was tempting not to.

And Flip clearly did need to use the toilet. She was half-way up the stairs before I'd even closed the front door.

'Hang on, why don't you use the downst—' I began.

'Can't!' she said. 'It's already coming out!' Then she disappeared round the corner of the landing.

I shook my head as I went to find my car keys, ready to drive to school. That made no sense either, but the main thing was that I would need to have a word with her about her tendency towards the descriptive when it came to bodily functions; a social nicety that would be second nature to an average eight-year-old and the sort of lapse that would mark her out as odd. And I had no doubt she'd probably been a much-bullied child. I found the keys, then went to grab a couple of shopping bags to take with me, so I could pop to the supermarket as soon as we'd finished up in school – well, assuming they allowed her to stay. I had also promised Kieron that I'd drop in on Lauren – she'd been feeling under the weather since getting back from holiday and was taking a few days off work. I decided I'd get a few extra bits and drop them off for her. I'd just stuffed the bags into my handbag when Flip appeared again on the landing – this time with Pink Barbie in her hand. So *that* was why she was keen to use the upstairs bathroom.

'Uh-oh,' she said, her face taking on the expression of an exasperated mother as she came back down the stairs. 'Looks like this little princess doesn't know her manners. She was meant to wipe my bum for me, and she managed to leave the poo on my new knickers.' She frowned at the doll and then at me. 'She left *skidders*, Mummy!'

'Oh, *Flip*!' I said, dropping the car keys and my bag onto the hall table. 'Are you serious? Truth, now. Did you poo in the toilet or in your pants?' I turned her around and started walking her back up the stairs. 'Come on, back to the bathroom. Let's get you sorted out.'

'I told you! It was this little madam!' she cried indignantly. 'I wouldn't mess in my new school knickers! Not never!'

Though of course she had. And it wasn't just the under-wear. It was down the back of her legs, the lovely white school socks, and also smeared down the back of her cute pinafore dress. I could have cried. She'd looked so pretty a couple of hours ago, when I'd taken the obligatory first-day-at-school photo that I'd done with my own children, and every foster child since.

I'd been reading up on soiling and, with such a plethora of information on the subject (good old Google …), I felt no better informed about what might be at the root of Flip's behaviour than I had when I'd started. There just seemed to be so many factors that might be involved. It was clearly something that needed more professional interven-tion, and as a priority, because I couldn't really see much progress being made on the 'socialising' front till it was dealt with.

But it wasn't her fault, and I knew I had to keep that uppermost in mind while, nose wrinkling, I stripped her down and cleaned her up, ready to change into another set of clothes. I thanked the lord that I'd had the foresight to buy four of everything. If things went on like this, I'd struggle to keep up.

Fifteen minutes later – and ten minutes late for our appointment – we were sitting in the headmaster's office. Mr Stancliffe, the headteacher, had already introduced himself and was now introducing the friendly-looking woman who had also joined us.

'Selina Carter,' he said as I leaned over to shake hands with her. 'Selina runs our nurture group.'

I'd not heard of them having a nurture group, and it must have shown on my face, because Miss Carter was quick to explain. It was a new class, apparently, born out of the previous learning support group, and simply renamed to differentiate it. She smiled at Flip, who reciprocated. I had a hunch she was going to like Miss Carter. 'We decided that, while Flip gets used to her new surroundings, and we work out which groups she needs to be in,' she went on, 'she'll spend her first couple of weeks here in my class. It's just a small group – six other children or so, generally no more than that – and she'll be doing the curriculum, just the same as everyone else. Just in a less stressful environment, you know –' she smiled at Flip again – 'to help get her settled in.'

Flip didn't return the second smile. In fact, she immediately gripped my hand and wriggled herself closer to me. 'What about the *brothers*?' she whispered, as if discussing some obscure religious sect. 'Ask her, Mummy. Are the brothers going to be in my class?' She squeezed my hand tighter, her voice tight, and I feared the imminent arrival of tears followed by a meltdown.

'Sweetie,' I said, leaning towards her, hoping I could prevent it. 'No they won't, but that's because this is a special, *special* class, for *very* special little girls. It's because *you're* such a special little girl that you've been picked – you have been *hand*-picked – to go in with Miss Carter, just for a little bit. Because you're special. And I'm sure it's going to be lots and *lots* of fun.' I glanced meaningfully at the two teachers who were watching our exchange, and thankfully Mr Stancliffe seemed to know what to do.

'Mrs Watson ... um ... your mummy ... is absolutely right,' he said. 'In fact, Miss Carter's class is the most fun in the *whole* school, Flip, and you'll still get to play with ... um ... the brothers?' He glanced at me, confused.

'My grandsons,' I quickly supplied. 'Levi and Jackson. They're both here, and that's how Flip refers to them.'

'Because they *are* my brothers,' she added, her anxiety seemingly now forgotten.

'Ah,' Mr Stancliffe said, 'yes, yes, of *course*. Well, you'll get to play with them at playtime – and lunchtime, of course – and I'm sure you'll get to wait for them at home time.' He leaned towards her. 'I promise you, you will *love* it in Miss Carter's group.'

It was a lot to live up to, but Miss Carter looked equal to the task. She stood up and held out a hand towards Flip. 'Why don't you and I go and have a sneaky peek at your new classroom, eh, Flip? You can meet the other children, and do you know what? I bet you *anything* you make a best friend forever this very morning. Don't worry,' she added, seeing Flip's worried look. 'Your mum can come and see you before she leaves.'

I encouraged Flip to go by producing Pink Barbie, who, unbeknown to Flip, I had slipped into my handbag before we left. 'I'm sure Barbie will be allowed just for today,' I said, glancing at Miss Carter hopefully. 'Just to see your new school.'

I then had to force a smile as I watched Flip leave the office, glancing back at me anxiously as she left. Bless her heart. She looked absolutely terrified.

* * *

Casey Watson

I ended up spending the best part of an hour with the head-teacher, trying to give him a bit of insight as to what he might expect from Flip; what sort of background was involved, how she'd been since she'd come to us, the problems of lack of attachments, her meltdowns and her tendency to wander, plus the fact – and to his credit, he didn't look too traumatised – that as of tomorrow she was off her Ritalin for a month. I hurried on, then, to what long-term plans had been tentatively put in place.

'Essentially to get her placed with a long-term foster family,' I told him. 'Or, ideally, an adoptive one, obviously.' I smiled. 'Well, once we've managed to socialise her a bit, at any rate.' I paused then. Better I do it now than have it – literally – come out once I'd gone. 'There is one other issue I should make you aware of, Mr Stancliffe.'

He raised his eyebrows quizzically. 'Which is?'

'That it seems she's never been properly potty-trained.'

I could see his brain whirring, wondering perhaps if I'd delivered her in a nappy. 'Which means?'

'Which means we're working on it, but she does need reminding to go to the toilet and, to some extent, if it's feasible, er … accompanying. Which is why I'm so pleased that you've decided to start her off in your nurture group,' I rattled on. 'Because it'll make the process altogether easier, won't it?'

I mentally apologised to poor Miss Carter as I said that, but, again, Mr Stancliffe seemed to take it all in his stride.

'Right,' he said, scribbling down something on the pad in front of him. 'Right.'

He put his pen down.

'So she's effectively an unknown quantity as of tomorrow,' he said finally.

I nodded. 'Well, I suppose, yes. We're doing this blind. All I know is that her medication doesn't seem to have any impact on her. She's just the same with it as when it wears off. My GP is hoping that it's the meds that are making her so erratic, and that after some time off from them she might settle down a bit. That's the plan, anyway. We'll just have to see. You never know – it might even help with the soiling.'

I saw his nose wrinkle, almost imperceptibly, but definitely. 'Ri-ight,' he said again, then cleared his throat decisively. 'As you probably already know, Mrs Watson, we did tell the local authority that we were at full capacity here.' I nodded. 'And that, like yours with her medication, this is going to be something of a trial. If we can't fully meet her needs, we'd be doing her a disservice if we held on to her. I'm sure you'd agree.'

I did. On both counts. The word 'trial' had more than one meaning, after all. So after I'd gone and blown a kiss goodbye to Flip, who I could see through the classroom window now seemed be enjoying herself enormously with Miss Carter, I crossed both pairs of fingers on both of my hands. And then crossed my thumbs for good measure.

Chapter 7

I had a busy day ahead, and as I ran around with the duster and furniture polish I offered up a silent prayer that one thing wouldn't happen: that the phone would start ringing and that it would be the school. It was Flip's first proper day and I was mentally crossing everything that it wouldn't also be her last.

It was yet another stress to the checklist in my head; my mental 'to do' list, which currently included the fact that both Tyler and Mike had birthdays coming up in the next fortnight – within days of each other. Plus there had been Kieron, who I'd dropped in to see after I'd dropped Flip at school. He and Lauren had been back from Cyprus almost a week now, but what with her being poorly, I'd not really had a chance for a proper catch-up, and I knew he'd been dying to show me all his photos. One by one, as it turned out, having given me his smartphone – forgetting as he invariably did that, no, I *didn't* know how to 'touch, tap and scroll' – and giving me a blow-by-blow account of all the whats, whys and wherefores of every image. Safe to say,

Kieron had really enjoyed his holiday, which was a great relief.

'I wasn't one bit stressed out!' he'd enthused, as he showed me how to work the phone, and I was only too happy to hear it. For all that my mind had been on Flip, he and Lauren had never been far from it either, and despite the confidence I'd tried to instil in him I'd still had half an ear on my mobile, half-expecting to get a call telling me he couldn't cope and would have to come straight home. It was a source of real joy that it hadn't actually happened; that my little boy, all grown up now, had leapt such a major hurdle.

Not that I'd really had time to do justice to the seemingly endless parade of zoo and waterpark pictures and accompanying commentaries. I had Ellie, Flip's social worker, due to arrive at noon, so I had to curtail the slide show with promises that we'd go through them properly at the weekend – not to mention sampling the Zivania, apparently a wine-type beverage that was famous in Cyprus, a bottle of which they'd brought back for Mike and me. 'Though between you and me, Mum,' he confessed as I left, 'it's pretty strong stuff. I'm not sure it wasn't responsible for Lauren feeling so poorly. She only had a glassful and that was it. Barf! She couldn't touch a drop of anything for the rest of the week. So I won't be offended if you put it in one of your trifles!' he finished, handing it to me. Then, being Kieron, he did a helpful mime to illustrate.

* * *

Right now, however, my mind was very much back on Flip again; well, on the fact that now I had two less-than-tidy children in the house again, my cleaning anxiety had gone up a notch or two, my paranoia about hidden germs into overdrive. There was little time, however, for more than a quick flick-around downstairs and (telling myself to stop fretting – that the house was just *fine*) I was just going into the kitchen to put the kettle on for coffee when the phone did what it wasn't supposed to – started ringing.

One of the interesting developments that had happened once we'd been fostering a while was that I'd developed a kind of Pavlovian response to a ringing phone. It was a kind of gut-wrench that was more acute when a child was newly with us, born of several years' experience of it invariably being bad news, or at least news that would comprehensively derail my day. That was the nature of the beast. It was in the early days that the situation was most volatile, the child most unpredictable, the dramas and travails most likely.

I did what I always did – took a second to adjust before going to it; both wondering what it might be and at the same time wishing it away, almost subconsciously willing it to *stop* ringing. And if it wasn't going to, willing it not to be the school. I smiled to myself, even as I psyched myself up for battle. A psychologist would have fun with me, they really would.

I knew the answerphone wouldn't kick in for a fair few rings yet, so it continued to ring right up till the point when I picked it up, already half expecting to hear 'Casey, it's about Flip …'

It wasn't the school. It was a cheerful-sounding male voice, saying, 'Hi Casey, how's it hanging?'

Which meant only one person: Tyler's social worker, Will Fisher. I lowered my imaginary guard and let out a big sigh of relief.

'You sound out of breath,' Will said, as he chuckled down the phone. 'The new kid wearing you out already?'

I laughed. Will knew all about Flip joining us and I was grateful that he was so down to earth. I guessed it was the main reason that kids seemed to get along so well with him; that and of course the fact that he had such a wicked sense of humour. He definitely reminded me of the type of person who would be the first to pick you up if you tripped – well, as in *after* he had finished laughing his head off. He was the perfect social worker for Tyler and I liked him very much.

'Not quite,' I told him. 'But she is proving to be quite the challenge. It's going okay, though. You know how it is: a couple of steps forward, the odd one or two back. She's officially started in school today so I'm very glad it's you on the other end of the phone and not her teacher. Anyway, what can I do for you?'

'Oh, it's just that I'm in the area and I thought I'd see if I could scrounge a cup of your legendary coffee off you. We're due a catch-up on Tyler, and it seemed to make sense to stop by while I'm nearby. If you're not off out or anything, that is.'

I walked into the kitchen and glanced at the clock on the wall. It was only 20 minutes before Ellie was due, but I supposed that didn't matter. Come one, come all, and, besides, it might be nice for them to meet up. I said so.

It seemed Will agreed. 'Right then,' he said, 'I'll be on my way in ten. Be good to meet her. We'd have to get together at some point in any case, so it'll kill two birds with one stone. I'll see you shortly.'

It never failed to surprise me when the social workers I came into contact with hadn't ever met. Not that it should – after all, I worked for a private agency, so the children that came to me could be from any local authority, each with their own social services department, and each with their own set of staff. But it always seemed to me that they would all be in some way connected – graduates of some huge central 'social worker school' where they all got together for training, compared notes, networked with each other and so on. It seemed not, though – even if, to my mind, there perhaps should have been; well, in care system utopia, at any rate.

As it was, these two were about to make each other's acquaintance for the first time, just as had happened with their respective professional charges. And before that happened, there was the kettle to put on, biscuits to be laid out and – my lucky social service meetings talisman – my mother's old milk jug to rummage in the cupboards for.

In the end, though, it was Ellie who was the first to arrive, remarking immediately on how clean and fresh-smelling the house was (again, bless her) and expressing her wish that she wasn't so domestically challenged.

'Trust me,' I told her, 'it isn't so much a virtue as a tedious affliction. I'm like a Flash junkie, me.'

She laughed. 'Well, you're welcome to come round mine if you ever need a fix, then. My absolute dream is to earn enough one day that I can justify getting a cleaner – well, when cleaning occurs to me, which it doesn't very often. Most of the time I just don't see clutter. It's like it was bludgeoned out of me at a very early age.'

She followed me into the kitchen, and while I started on the coffee she told me a little about her background. Far from being the wet-behind-the-ears youngster she could so easily have been mistaken for, Ellie it seemed had come from a big boisterous family – 'and dysfunctional enough that you couldn't make it up, believe me!' she told me as she pulled out a chair. 'There was a time when I had dreams of being an artist, or a vet, or even a ballerina,' she went on. 'All the usual girly stuff. But there was no way around it. I knew what I was best qualified to do. Social work pretty much chose *me*.'

I was keen to hear more. I'd always been fascinated about why people would choose a career that was so hard and emotionally draining, and which, more often than not, got such a bad rap in the press. But there was no time; the doorbell rang again and, as I'd left it on the latch, ready, Will appeared in my kitchen just at the moment when I'd finished explaining to Ellie who he was.

He was dressed, as he invariably was when not required to look formal, in coloured jeans, denim jacket and a T-shirt with a slogan. Today's read *Ask me about my T Rex*. As Will shook his jacket off, I nodded and rolled my eyes, before dutifully asking, 'So, go on then – tell me about your T Rex.' Needless to say, I instantly regretted it. Well, sort of. Because Will grabbed his T-shirt from the bottom, pulled it upwards and over his head, revealing – as well as a difficult-to-miss six-pack – a design on the reverse of a silly grinning dinosaur which now, of course, entirely covered his head.

And as I watched his yet-to-be-introduced colleague collapse into a fit of giggles, I thought of Ellie's comment; that perhaps some social workers were born rather than made. Will was one such, without a doubt. And not just for his ability to 'get down with the kids'. I remembered vividly how passionately he'd championed and supported Tyler, how he'd stood up in court and fought his corner, taken on his dad and step-mum, been a confidant, mentor and much-needed older brother figure. I had more than once wondered if Ty's journey might have turned out rather differently had he not had the great good fortune to have been allocated Will. Children came and went for social workers; that was the nature of the job. But Tyler and Will's was a bond that I suspected would have endured even if we hadn't taken him on permanently.

The hero in question had the grace to blush a little when he pulled down his top to see Ellie smiling at him, and quickly ran a hand through his messianic blond hair – though without any discernible effect. He then sat down at the kitchen table with us, plonked his satchel on the floor and made a big show of inhaling very deeply. 'Ah, Casey,' he said, 'I was praying that you'd have some of that delicious coffee of yours already on the go. And chocolate biscuits too! You spoil me.' He turned to Ellie. 'She spoil you as well?' Ellie duly nodded. 'Thought so.' He sighed. 'I've always liked to think I'm special, but, sad to say, I suspect I might not be.'

Though formal introductions seemed a little superfluous by now, I made them anyway, and then sat back a little as they immediately began comparing notes; they *were* both from the same authority, and the only reason they hadn't met yet was because Ellie was so new, but they were soon at it thirteen to the dozen, talking about children they might have in common, and managers they had both worked and trained with. Meanwhile, I played mum and poured the coffee.

Having a brace of social workers in my kitchen wasn't a new experience, obviously, but having two entirely unconnected ones together was, and for a fleeting moment I wondered about the implications for the respective children's confidentiality. It was something I'd not even thought about checking: was it actually okay for me to talk to one with the other one present? I quickly dismissed my concerns, though. Of course it would be okay to do that. We were looking after both children, so it made sense to work as a team, even if Will's role was different from Ellie's. He was taking more of a back seat now with Tyler, of course; now he was staying with us there was no need for Will to prepare him for leaving, rather to just take him out from time to time, and to support me and Mike in supporting *him*.

Even so, another child in the mix had implications for Tyler too, so, in the short term, at least, while Flip was on our programme, Will would need to be involved a little more than he had been lately, to be sure that mix wouldn't jeopardise Tyler's future, hence him being briefed on her joining the family.

'So, who's first?' I asked, wondering how this already distinctly un-meeting-like 'meeting' would work. 'Either of you need to rush off first or anything?'

'I'm fine for a bit,' Will said, having made an enquiring face at Ellie. 'If you want to catch up with Ellie about Flip first, I'll just listen in and make any notes that might be helpful for me. If that's all right?' he added, reaching for a biscuit.

Ellie smiled and nodded with something that I suspected could be construed as shyness, if you were the sort of person who tended to notice such things. 'Thank you,' she said, reaching into her large leather bag and pulling out a floral fabric-covered A5 notebook. 'If you can just catch me up on how she's been generally, Casey, that would be helpful, and then I can update you on developments with her mother, plus a few ideas we've been discussing at the office.'

And so to business, I thought, pulling my log book towards me, more by instinct than need, because I didn't need to refer to it to sum progress up. It was all right up there in my head. 'Okay,' I said, 'well, it's been hard work, if I'm honest. Nothing we can't cope with,' I rushed to reassure her. 'But the toileting – or lack of – is proving to be more difficult to keep on top of than we'd anticipated; hence my concerns about what might be happening in school even as we speak.'

'She's still soiling regularly, then?' Ellie asked. We both saw Will grimace. I nodded. 'Though, on the plus side, the screaming episodes are becoming less frequent, and she seems to be less stressed; she's calmer now generally, but she's still quite erratic – you can't really ever second-guess when she might go off on one – but you know Flip. I think that's all a part of who she is.'

Both Ellie and Will scribbled notes in their respective journals. Then Ellie glanced up again. 'And you were saying on the phone that she's off the Ritalin for the time being? Do we know how long this might be for?'

I shook my head. 'No idea. We're in the hands of our GP. He wants me to try it for as long as she's okay with it, really. He's quite evangelical about it, to be honest. He doesn't like the idea of children being medicated if they really don't need to be and I'm happy to respect his judgement – we're certainly willing to give it a good go. I'm just hoping school will be able to cope with her without the tablets.'

Will cleared his throat. 'I agree with your doctor, Casey,' he said. 'Seems to me, some GPs are all too quick to offer medication as an alternative to anything else these days. And if it works without then it'll be worth the struggle of her coming off them.'

I tried not to roll my eyes and seem dismissive of his idealism, but it was difficult because I'd seen so much to do with it. I'd seen many children who really needed their meds, and the periods when they didn't have them were horrendous. I had strong memories of one child we'd looked after in particular, a little girl called Olivia, who'd been horribly and consistently abused from a very young age and who was almost feral when we'd taken her and her brother on. She *needed* her Ritalin, certainly in the early days; she could barely function without it.

And, in my experience, Ritalin was only given out in very small amounts – just exactly what the child needed and not one tablet more. And when it wasn't available, didn't I know it; more than once with Olivia, I'd gone to the chemist to pick it up only to find they were out of stock and we'd have to wait for a couple of days – days that were shocking and chaotic for all concerned. So, no, they definitely didn't give Ritalin out like sweets.

So I could see both sides of the argument, and tried to keep an open mind. But it did seem that GPs were increasingly divided with their decisions to medicate these days. Some gave out prescriptions willingly, whilst others were very much of the 'I blame the parents' variety. It was a debate that I knew would continue for some time and, in the middle of it all, we were very much a part of it, and I'd reserve judgement till we saw how it panned out.

'I agree with you,' I told Will mildly. 'It will be great if it works out. But if Flip actually *does* rely on Ritalin to help her feel normal, then this may make matters worse. I don't know.' I spread my hands. 'I guess it's just a case of "suck it and see".'

Ellie nodded and put her pen down. 'Speaking of which, Casey, my own news is also a bit "suck it and see", because it's that Megan – Flip's mother – is asking to see her daughter.'

I hadn't expected this. 'We've agreed to supervised contact with a family support worker present at a neutral location – shopping, lunch out, whatever – but she's out of hospital now and being rehoused in a flat near to where she used to live. I don't think we've got a choice at the moment but to allow it.'

I was surprised by that. Did they really have no choice? From what I knew, Flip's life with her mother had been chaotic, to say the least, and Megan had definitely been neglectful. 'I didn't expect that,' I said. 'I thought the long-term plan was to find permanent foster carers, or adopters?'

'Oh, it is.' Ellie went on. 'It very much still is. And if it turns out that we end up going down the adoption route, contact would obviously be suspended. Early days, though – and as she's going to stay with you and Mike in the short term, and investigations are still ongoing, we think that if Flip agrees, then some form of contact might have a posi-tive effect on her. Heavily supervised contact, obviously.'

'And you said you'd been "discussing ideas" at the office?' I prompted.

'Yes,' she confirmed. 'Just about pulling together a very comprehensive report to put forward to Panel. We thought that while we wait, and while she's with you, you could record everything that happens – to an even greater degree than you normally would – any thoughts you have, and insights, any positive changes you notice, her day-to-day habits and mood really, plus anything that school updates you on. Just so that we are really well informed when we are asking for a particular set of carers for Flip in the long term.'

'Panel' was the name for the body of professionals who were approached by social workers who were seeking a long-term family for a particular child. There were usually about ten of them, all with professional careers in social services behind them, and together their job was to do the final match-making between children and potential carers. It was a very important role; it was naturally best for all concerned that they get it right first time if at all possible. Few things were more depressing than a placement that failed, given the huge emotional investment involved.

But, as Ellie said, it was still early days with our little princess, and though I felt ambivalent about sharing it my private opinion was that Flip would be a hard child to place long term. As I'd already voiced to Ellie, so much of the way she interacted with the world was the result of her FAS – was who she was – and therefore not necessarily easy to 'train' out of her. And thinking that made my heart go out to her even more, and to hope there would be a special family for her somewhere.

In any event, we were up to speed – not least about the mum news, which I still needed to process – and while Ellie made her own move on the biscuits, and Will closed his book, we were able to have a quick catch-up about Tyler who, though you might not have known it from his eye-rolling and frequent Flip-related tutting, seemed to have assimilated her into his life very well.

'Pecking order,' Will observed when I'd finished, with commendable acuity. 'My guess is that he's loving taking on the role of older brother – not least of feeling that he's already part of the family; having that sense of collective familial responsibility to help take care of her as well. And that reminds me. Do you have anything planned yet for his birthday?' He turned to Ellie. 'He's 13 in just over a week, isn't he? Another pool party, perhaps, Casey?' he finished, turning back to me.

'Make that *two* pool parties,' I said, frowning at the thought of the work that was going to be involved – none of which I'd had a chance to start as yet. I loved planning parties every bit as much as I loved planning Christmas. It was just that this year my plans had been comprehensively derailed by a four-foot nothing whirlwind and her tiny pink sidekick. 'It's Mike's biggie – his 50th – two days before Tyler's. My master plan is to organise something for them jointly, but I haven't had the time to do anything yet.'

Will waved away my frown. He obviously knew me well now. 'You'll be fine, Casey,' he said, the words coming out almost like an order. 'I'm sure you'll rope in Riley to do the donkey-work for you. *Really*,' he added emphatically, leaning towards me. 'Casey, it will be *fine*. So stop being such a stress-head!'

Which, curiously, given just how preoccupied I was with it all, felt like a real shot in the arm. And with everything pretty much wrapped up as far as Flip was concerned, I went on to have another natter about Tyler, and how well he was doing, before leaving the two of them to get further acquainted while I washed up the coffee mugs. I glanced back through to the dining area as I heard them laughing about a particular manager they'd both worked with, and found myself smiling to myself.

Those two would make such a cute couple! I decided, and couldn't help but wonder if either of them had significant others, in that way one can't help but do when you see two young people getting on so famously. I might be a bit like the dinosaur on Will's shirt, I thought, and Mike, Riley and Kieron might roll their eyes if I told them, but I knew a spark when I saw one. I turned around, a mischievous thought cemented in my mind. 'And when I *do* pull those spectacular parties together, you're both invited,' I trilled. 'And I will be *very* offended if either of you fail to show!'

Chapter 8

Thankfully, the next few days went smoothly. Well, at school at least. Each afternoon, when I collected Flip, I made a point of having a chat with Miss Carter, who seemed to think that for a child just coming off Ritalin she was actually doing remarkably well.

'We had another new girl start a couple of days ago,' she explained to me at the end of Flip's first week. 'Just moved to the area and – this has been a *big* plus – definitely seems to share Flip's love of Barbies.' She smiled and ruffled Flip's hair as she spoke. 'So this little darling here and Scout have become best friends.'

Flip grinned up at her teacher, and I was struck, as I often was, at how sunny and loving a little thing she was, and how little you might guess at the challenges she faced. 'And guess what, Miss?' she said to her teacher, who she now also loved, of course. 'We both got the same wobbly tooth, look!' She then slipped a couple of fingers into her now gaping mouth to illustrate, wobbling it back and forth to prove her point.

'Well, that's lovely, sweetie,' I said, coaxing her hand away by tugging gently on her arm. 'It's great that you've got a new friend who loves Barbies as much as you do, but let's just leave that tooth to fall out by itself, shall we? Don't want you bleeding all over the place!'

Scout, I learned on the way home, was 'beautiful'. She spoke 'funny' because she came from another 'kingdom' called Newcastle, and like Flip she had no brothers or sisters at home. But that was okay, apparently, because Flip had very kindly offered her a brand new brother. 'She can have Jackson, Mummy,' she explained. 'Like, to borrow for a bit, 'cos he's the annoying one. I've told her I'm keeping Levi.'

I grinned through the rear-view mirror, and she laughed, knowing exactly what she was about. For all the stress inherent in looking after her, she could be a delightful, and very witty, little girl. Perhaps she wouldn't be so difficult to place after all.

With a first full week in school under my belt, I felt a great deal more positive about Flip's prospects, but, given the way yin and yang tend to work, the prospect of organising a full-on double birthday party extravaganza was one that was filling me with uncharacteristic panic.

I loved organising birthday parties; I was one of those people for whom the business of celebration was not just a part of life but one of its great joys – particularly if I was given free rein in making the arrangements. 'Over the top' was almost my mantra, and not just when it came to the little ones, where it was generally the order of the day, but

with pretty much anything involving cakes, balloons and
fairy lights.

Right now, though, I had less than a week to get something sorted for both Mike's 50th – which is a biggie in
anyone's calendar – and Tyler's 13th, which, even if he
didn't want any fuss, was, emotionally speaking, pretty big
as well. So much had happened – such a *huge* amount had
happened with Tyler – that it didn't seem quite possible
that it was only a year since he had said the words to me
that had changed everything.

He'd had a fine 12th birthday party, no doubt about that,
thanks to Will and his handy local leisure centre connections. An 'epic' pool party, to use Tyler's parlance. No, his
half-brother Grant hadn't come, and naturally there'd been
all sorts of angst about that, but it had been that evening,
once we were home, that he'd casually told me that he
knew full well there'd be no reconciliation with his dad and
step-mum, because they basically didn't love him, and
never would.

I thought about Flip now, and how readily she'd adopted
me as her 'new mummy'. Which was fine; whatever made
the transition work best for her. Falling 'in love' with
people was part of who she was. No deep attachments –
that was down to the damage wrought by FAS – but lots of
affection and physical contact, and I was more than happy
to be one of her mummies along the way.

Tyler had been different; he was older and wiser, and
remarkably intuitive – unlike Flip, he knew exactly how
badly life had treated him. He trusted no one, expected
nothing, didn't feel worthy of anyone's affection. His early

years had comprehensively seen to that. But then he'd asked me. Had said, 'Casey, can't *you* just be my mum?' And for some reason – maybe timing, but who knew, I tried not to over-analyse – those words had taken all our immediate futures down a very different road.

And here we were now, all that time passed, and sometimes it felt like Tyler's bad times had taken on the quality of a dream. A very bad dream, and there was no doubt his scars would travel through life with him, but we were travelling with him too. And that made a world of difference.

'You know what?' Riley said, as she wrestled with an indignant Marley-Mae. 'I think you should scale down a little bit. I know, I know –' she added, flipping up a free hand to stop me arguing. 'That's like telling Richard Branson to stop building spaceships, I *know*. But given the time constraints, it's the only way to go.'

It was Saturday morning, and, with the weather still gorgeous for early September, we'd banished the kids out into the garden so we could have a catch-up and make a plan. Well, all bar Marley-Mae, because we'd pulled out the garden toys from the shed and at 16 months she was far too young to be left with the gang outside, unsupervised.

Not that Marley-Mae was having any of it. She could rant for Britain, and if she got it into her head that she might be missing out on something it usually took both guile and effort to quell her screams and angry shouts. It was no different today. 'Honestly, it's like she's already a bloody teenager!' Riley huffed, finally managing to settle her disgruntled daughter in front of the TV, with a couple of colouring books for her to scribble on artistically. 'Speaking of which, Mother, as I say, I think you're worrying too much. He's a 13-year-old boy; he won't be wanting a big fandango, will he?' She grinned. 'Just that it's marked in some way. Plus you have "cool" on your side now. Remember Kieron at that age? When you suggested that superhero party theme? You'd have thought you'd suggested booking him and his mates into the beauty parlour for a makeover and full body wax, remember? He couldn't have been more mortified.'

I remembered only too well. And I knew she was right. Tyler was a tad too old for anything too OTT. 'I know, I know,' I said, 'but, to be fair, Kieron did and still *does* love anything remotely Marvel, so I can hardly be blamed for having suggested it, can I? Anyway, yes, you're probably right. I'm sure he won't want a big fuss. But he will want *some* fuss. And there's still the small matter of your father.'

'Dad? God, are you *kidding*, Mum? I'm sure if he had his way he'd shelve the whole thing till next year. Or the year after, if he could, don't you think?' She shook her head. 'I'm seriously thinking of getting him some of that stuff – what's it called? That stuff that "gradually blends in grey"? No, Mum, honestly, all you need is something low key at home. You'd never be able to book a room anywhere this late in the day anyway.'

I opened a packet of ginger biscuits, and after giving half of one to Marley-Mae we steadily got through a good half dozen with our coffee and sketched out what I had to agree was a much more sensible, much pared-down plan. Mike's birthday was the following Friday and Tyler's was on the Sunday, so I'd give Mike his personal present from me on the Friday, but tell him that we'd be having a joint celebration for him and Tyler on the Saturday – but also tell him to keep schtum about it so Tyler didn't twig. And as the two birthday boys would be at football with Kieron all that morning, it would give the rest of us the chance to do up the house and sort the food out before they returned. That would work. As Tyler wouldn't be expecting anything to happen till the Sunday, it would be a nice surprise when he got back.

'And get a couple of friends round for him, of course,' Riley said. 'You could secretly invite that mad Denver boy he hangs out with, and Grant, of course – he'd come along, wouldn't he?'

I nodded. One of the most edifying things that had happened since we took on Tyler was that no amount of coercion on the part of Grant's mother could keep the two brothers from each other. It had taken months, but she had finally come round to understanding that, while they as parents were no longer a part of Tyler's life, Grant very much was, and would continue to be so.

'And the family,' I said. 'Mum and Dad. Lauren and Kieron. And I think I'll ask Donna and the kids to come too.' (Like me, my younger sister loved a party.) 'Should be a proper little shindig. Oh, and Ellie and Will, don't forget,' I said, reaching for my pad and pen.

'Who and who?' Riley wanted to know.

'Ellie and Will,' I said again. 'Flip and Tyler's social workers? I told them both to come – insisted they both come, in fact. Thought it would be good for bonding and general good relations.'

'Bonding?' Riley wanted to know. I didn't tell her.

The weekend continued as set fair as the weather. With a plan of sorts in place – and I do love it when a plan comes together – it was really just a question of food and decorations, neither of which would tax me unduly. I even felt relaxed enough to suggest heading out for a walk and a picnic on the Sunday; it was just me, Mike and the kids, by then, and, after a mad kid-filled Saturday, it felt too big a production to make a roast just for the four of us. Instead we headed down to the local woods so that Tyler could show Flip the stream, and induct her into the dark and dangerous art of rock-hopping to cross it, plus show her all the places he'd previously fallen in.

'So you just be careful,' he told her, as she ventured across a particularly tricky crossing place behind him, 'because this is no place for girls, really. And before you ask, no, you can't go to the toilet down here, okay?' He rolled his eyes. 'I'd just die if any of my mates accidentally stepped into something you'd left behind.'

'Tyler!' Mike called across. 'Stop winding Flip up.'

'He's teasing me, isn't he, Daddy Mike?' Flip shouted back. 'If I need a poo, I can have one, can't I?'

Mike looked helplessly at me and spread his palms. There was clearly some way to go yet.

'No, Flip,' I told her firmly. Then, seeing her squatting down by the stream's edge, 'What are you up to down there?'

'Just giving Pink Barbie a hair wash. She's such a mucky little bugger, she is.'

I hopped across the stream and joined her. 'Well, just you be careful close to the edge there. I don't want you toppling in and getting a hair wash as well.'

'I'm *always* careful,' she told me, as she swooshed the doll back and forth, letting her hair trail in the water. 'Didn't you know? She could get deaded.'

'Dead,' Tyler corrected.

'No, deaded,' she insisted. 'A child can drown in two inches of water, you know.'

'Yes, I do know,' I agreed, and was just about to add that that was why it was important that she be careful when she spoke again. 'Two inches of water, Megan,' she trotted out, in a suddenly stern voice. 'Two *inches*, you understand?'

Mike was still on the other bank and our eyes met across the stream. We both knew all about that. A few years previously we'd looked after a little boy called Jenson whose difficulties, in part, stemmed from the drowning of a child. The secret he'd carried was that his two-year-old sister had drowned in a paddling pool, while in his 'care', while his mum had nipped out for a packet of cigarettes. He'd been five.

I pushed the flood of horrible thoughts away. We were having too nice a time. 'That's right,' I said lightly, as Flip squeezed Barbie's hair in her fist. 'They can indeed. Who told you that, sweetie?'

She stood up and flicked the doll so a spray of water hit Tyler. 'She didn't tell *me*. She told *Mum*,' she clarified.

'Told her *right* off. The horrible fat lady did,' she added, presumably seeing my confusion.

'Right!' Tyler roared, stopping to scoop up a handful of his own water.

I held a hand up to dissuade him. 'Flip, you know that's not a nice way to describe someone,' I said. 'Can't you think of any nicer way to –'

'But she *was* horrible and she *was* fat,' she said, with undeniable logic. Then she frowned. 'And she used to shout at my old mum all the time. I heard her.'

'Who was she, Flip?' I asked her.

'I told you. The horrible fat lady. The one who used to come round to tell my mum off.'

'Tell her off?'

'Don't do this, don't do that,' she said, her voice turning stern again. 'And don't do the fucking other, neither!'

I could hear Tyler's snort of amusement at this, but decided not to say anything. Flip lifted Pink Barbie to her face and spoke directly to her, waggling her finger. 'Even in the bath, you hear me? *Specially* in the bath! 'Cos she could drown, she could. In *two inches of water*!' She then turned to me and smiled. 'Can we have lunch now? I'm Hank Marvin!'

We dined by the stream, on cheese and pickle baguettes and still-warm new potatoes – a concoction Tyler assured us was perfectly acceptable for a Sunday dinner – and when we returned, mid-afternoon, settled down on the settees with *Charlie and the Chocolate Factory*. Again. Thankfully, Tyler didn't deem himself too grown up for a bit of Roald

Dahl; in fact he delighted in the opportunity to tease Flip once more.

'Look!' he said, when the character of Veruca Salt came on screen. 'That's you, that is, Flip. To a T. A little madam who never shuts up.'

For his cheek he got a rap on the knees with Pink Barbie; in Flip's hands she really was a very multi-functional sort of doll. And I smiled: their playful joshing was becoming quite a thing of joy for me, having such a reassuring flavour of normal family life; something neither child had experienced very much in their young lives.

'Um, we'll have less chatting and more watching,' I reprimanded anyway. 'I need quiet so that I can concentrate on Johnny Depp.'

Though not just on Johnny Depp, it must be said. I still had half a mind on the 'horrible fat lady' – which had almost certainly been a social worker – who apparently came round and shouted at her mum, and on the past I still knew so little about. It might be the 'same old same old' of life with an addicted parent, but it was important to remember that every story was different. And, as Willy Wonka himself might have said, the devil was always in the detail.

Chapter 9

In the meantime, however, we were in a positive place, and by Monday morning I was tentatively allowing myself to believe that we were making decent progress with our little charge. For all Tyler's admonishments, she'd not soiled in over a week, she'd not had a full-blown screaming session in longer than that and, realistic as I was about the chances of another accident or meltdown, there just seemed a general softening of the extreme edges of her behaviour. I'd been working with kids long enough to know not to get ahead of myself, but it did made me think Dr Shakelton might have been right in his theory about her possible adverse response to Ritalin. And I definitely felt a kernel of pride that, just perhaps, we were doing something right in the way we were handling her.

So far, at any rate. I ran Flip to school (Tyler only wanted a lift these days if it was raining), then did a trolley dash around the supermarket to make a start on the coming festivities, and by the time I got started on my various cleaning tasks I was feeling quite chipper. I even turned up the radio so I could jig about to some golden oldies in the privacy of my own kitchen.

I should have known pride usually comes before a fall; ten minutes later my attention was diverted by a rap on the kitchen window – it was the postman, grinning widely, presumably at the 'shapes' I'd been throwing, and brandishing a rectangular parcel that he couldn't manage to force through the letterbox.

'You go for it,' he said, as, cheeks burning, I relieved him of the package – which was hopefully the latest FIFA game I'd ordered online for Tyler's birthday. 'That's what they say, don't they? To dance as if nobody's watching?' Then he guffawed. 'Made my day, that, Mrs Watson.'

Yes, I thought, mortified at the thought of what he *had* seen. The quote also said 'sing like nobody's listening'. Thank God for the small mercy of double glazing.

I sent him on his way and, returning to the kitchen to hide the present, saw my mobile was ringing – I just caught the pulsing glow from it out of the corner of my eye, from where it sat on the worktop, attached to its charger. I heard it soon after; it was currently playing something called the annoying frog – well, that or something equally ridiculous. Tyler had altered my ringtone – as boys tended to do – assuring me it would make me laugh. It didn't. I made a mental note to get either Riley or Kieron to change it to something more befitting an almost 50-year-old foster carer, rather than an over-excited ten-year-old.

With that on my mind, and perhaps because of my positive mood, it was without so much as a whisper of a heart-lurch I picked it up and turned down the radio simultaneously, noticing that John Fulshaw's name was showing on the display.

I wondered what he wanted, instinctively checking the calendar in my head to see if I was due a call or a visit.

'Hi, Casey,' he said. 'I'm not interrupting anything important, am I? Only I wondered if you had five minutes – I need to run through some news.'

'Good news or bad news?' I asked automatically, crossing into the living room and perching on the arm of the sofa.

'Not bad, no, but not especially good news, I have to say. It's Flip's mother. She's demanding to see her daughter.'

'Don't worry. That's not news,' I said. 'Ellie warned me about that last week. So they're letting it go ahead, then? She thought that might be the case.'

'Very much so,' John confirmed. 'And apparently as soon as possible. She's been quoting her rights, by all accounts. Obviously done her homework.'

He went on to confirm that Flip's mother had now been rehoused in her new flat, and despite the fact that investigations had now proved she had been the one responsible for the fire (not to mention social services building a case against her, citing negligence and her inability to provide a safe environment) she knew that didn't impact on her right to see her daughter. Not as things stood at the moment, at any rate.

'That's interesting,' I said. 'I mean, given that they are actively considering adoption, I'd have thought they might want to make the separation complete.'

'And you'd be right, but our hands are tied, because she's only on a section 20, as you probably know. So we have no power to stop contact taking place.'

A section 20 care order is a voluntary arrangement; one in which the parent (or parents) have agreed that social services can take temporary care of their child. I'd fostered several kids on section 20 orders, and preparing children for contact was a routine part of what Mike and I did. Sometimes it was straightforward, sometimes it was anything but; I'd watched children have their hearts broken again and again as mothers, and sometimes fathers, got their child's hopes up with regular contact, then let it all slide, contact dropping off and then finally ceasing, break- ing their child's heart all over again. It was a common prob- lem with parents who had addictions. They would get clean and do their best but it was often only a matter of time before those addictions got their stranglehold around the parent again. That was why many kids ended up in care in the first place.

The next step down the line was a section 30 care order, one obtained by social services by going to court. In cases where section 30 orders were sought the parents lost their right to contact – if it was considered inappropriate or potentially detrimental to a child's well-being, then social services had the power to stop or deny it.

With Flip's mother Megan not long out of hospital and having so far co-operated with the social worker allocated to her, there had obviously not yet been a need to go for a section 30 care order. Though they were building a case, and working on the basis that Flip needed to go into local authority care long term, right now the issue of contact was still something under discussion – no one wanted to completely cut a child off from their natural parents unless it was absolutely necessary, say in the case of sexual, emotional or physical abuse, and even then contact in controlled conditions was sometimes granted. In matters of a child's care and emotional well-being nothing was ever set in stone. With help and support, people changed. People tried hard to be better parents. It didn't happen often, but 'bad' people *were* sometimes rehabilitated. So it was important to keep an open mind.

I also thought about what Flip had alluded to the previous day, about the 'horrible fat lady' and what she'd overheard her saying to her mother. It rang very true; Megan would have had regular visits from her social worker and a part of that would have involved trying to support her in her parenting. It had all painted a picture in my mind – albeit a sketchy one – of a young single mother who, yes, might have been alcohol-addicted, but who still might have been doing her level best to cope. I might be wrong, and experience couldn't help but tell me I probably was, but, whatever else was true, Megan was still a mother. And was presumably now a mother racked with guilt.

So my mind was fully open, just as I'm sure John's was. The only worry here, as it can't help but be when a child is in care and vulnerable, was about what sort of effect a meeting with her mum would have on Flip.

'So when do you want to arrange it for?' I asked John, already wondering how best to broach it with her.

'As I said,' John replied, 'they're keen to do it sooner rather than later, so is there any chance you can sort something out for this week? It can be near you if you like, and obviously supervised by a family support worker. It has to be on neutral ground; no chance of them going to the flat or anything.'

I knew how this worked. A family support worker would pick Flip up from either home or school and then take her to meet with her mother. The worker would stay with them for a couple of hours, and then bring her home, hopefully none the worse emotionally for her encounter. Though, again, experience had taught me that however such meetings went – good or bad – they had a way of tearing down and churning up a child's carefully constructed emotional defences. But what would be would be; and I couldn't second-guess it. In Flip, with her FAS, we were dealing with such a singular child.

'Yes, I'd prefer it were somewhere local,' I told John. 'Just makes it easier logistically. How about Wednesday after school? It'll give me the chance to prepare Flip.' Well, as much as I wanted to prepare her anyway. A long period of anticipation never helped in these situations. The child either dreaded it, or became over-excited. And I'd seen hopes dashed too many times to want that to happen. Though with Flip – well, how would she react to knowing she was seeing her so-called 'old mummy'?

Well, I hoped – and expected.

I was wrong.

* * *

I didn't waste any time. I decided to tell her what would happen on Wednesday while we chatted on our way across the school playground to the car; get it out of the way before Tyler got home.

'So I'll bring you home as usual,' I was explaining, 'and you can get changed out of your uniform, and then a lady called Debbie is coming to fetch you, and she'll take you to see Mummy – that will be nice, won't it? And then she'll bring you home to us at about six.'

'Seeing my mummy?' she asked me, looking up at me, wide-eyed and shocked. 'That's silly, Mummy. I see you every day.'

I stopped walking and knelt down in front of her. 'Now, Flip, you *know* I'm not your real mummy. Your real mummy was in the hospital because of the fire, remember? I'm just your foster mummy, and your real mummy wants to see you.'

I waited so she could digest that before continuing, not that I was sure she was. 'She *misses* you, you see,' I added gently. 'You're her little girl and she hasn't had any cuddles from you for weeks now, has she? I've been getting all the nice hugs, haven't I?'

She grabbed my shoulders so hard that, squatting as I was in front of her, I almost lost my balance and fell over. Her chin was wobbling and her eyes had filled with unshed tears. 'But I'm *done* with that other mummy!' she cried, her voice shrill and loud. 'You mustn't send me back there! She hates me! She *hates* me! You mustn't make me, Mummy! I'm too ugly!'

She threw herself into my lap then, and now I did go over, landing hard on my bottom with Flip flailing on top of me, all too aware of the spectacle we must be in the middle of the after-school playground rush-hour. What an idiot I'd been, I thought, as I scrambled us both back upright. Why hadn't I waited till I'd got her in the car?

I picked her up then and gathered her into my arms, cradling her like a baby, and hurried her to the car, her sobs growing more voluble and hysterical with every step; a sure sign that a screaming event might be imminent. With that in mind, I clambered into the back of the car beside her and held her tight till I could feel her calming down.

'Hush, sweetie,' I tried to soothe. 'That's nonsense, Flip, you *know* that. You're one of the prettiest little girls I've ever seen. Just look at that beautiful hair, and those beautiful eyes! You're like a little princess. Anyone can see that. And your real mummy will *always* be your real mummy, you know that, too.'

I pulled back from her slightly so I could meet her frightened eyes. 'But I'm not sending you back to her, you understand that? Not at *all*. It's just a visit. To have some tea. So she can chat to you, give you a cuddle.' She balked at this. 'To see how you're getting on at school and everything,' I hurried on. 'Just for tea. And the lady – the lady called Debbie I told you about? Well, she'll be there as well. All the time. Do you understand, love? She'll be there all the time, and then she'll bring you straight back home to us, okay?'

She rubbed her eyes. She had paint on her fingers; they'd obviously done painting last period. She now transferred vivid green in two smears on her cheeks. I was about to mention it, to lighten the atmosphere, but immediately thought better of it. Given her mood, her own face was the last thing she needed to see.

'You understand, Flip?' I said instead. 'You understand what I'm saying. Just a visit, that's all. Then home again.'

'You promise?'

'Cross my heart,' I said.

'And hope to die?'

'And hope to die. I promise.'

'Well that's all right, then.' She sniffed and drew a cuff across her nose. Then exhaled heavily, almost resignedly even, as if she'd been forced to accept some minor inconvenience, such as an inferior table at a restaurant. Sometimes, I really couldn't fathom her at all. I was about to say 'Good', but she carried right on. 'I don't mind seeing my old mummy – just for a bit – but she can't keep me. You have to tell the lady that, okay? Because what would poor Tyler do if I don't come back?'

An unexpected and unanswerable question. It never ceased to puzzle me, the way her mind worked; how quick she was to give herself an alternative, more practical, almost more *acceptable* set of problems, rather than to deal with the way things actually were. How quickly she seemed able to almost 'switch' the emotional part of her brain off and move on. Was that a protective measure, to make the emotional more manageable? I had no idea, but she was now dry-eyed and conversational, and I would clearly have to play the same game.

'Exactly!' I said. 'In fact, what would *any* of us do? So that's settled, then. You'll go see Mummy for tea on

Wednesday with Debbie, and then you'll be back home in time for bath and bed. Deal?'

'Deal!' she said, holding out her fist for her latest learned behaviour – a Tyler-style fist bump.

Bemused, I duly bumped it.

Chapter 10

By the time Wednesday morning arrived, I had no more idea of how Flip would deal with being reunited with her mother than I had when I first told her. She was no more easy to second guess than she had ever been, really, her moods as capricious as sunshine in August; one minute she could be as bright as the proverbial button, the next as gloomy as a thundercloud.

Still, one thing she didn't do was mention it again; not once. And though I'd alluded to it in passing when tucking her into bed on the Monday evening, her response had been almost offhand. She'd simply waggled Pink Barbie in my face and said, 'Yes, we *know*, Mummy,' with one of her world-weary (not to mention world-class) sighs.

I'd decided not to press it till I had to. It might just be a defence mechanism, after all. And there was nothing to be gained from building it up in her mind, in any case. Given her *apparent* feelings about it – that it was just now some tedious arrangement she had to comply with – perhaps it was better just to keep it light; throw it casually into the conversation here and there, and if she chose to acknowledge but not engage, that was fine.

I had plenty on my own plate anyway, with two important birthdays to celebrate the coming weekend, which were now at least 'themed' to some extent, because Riley had taken it upon herself to buy a huge football cake and I'd rustled up some cupcakes to match. Well, I say, rustle, but any implication that I actually made them is a lie. My mum and sister Donna had actually made some lovely matching cupcakes, and I'd rustled them in the same way a poacher rustles cattle, i.e. claimed them as my own. And then I'd sworn them to secrecy.

I knew I was probably on a hiding to nothing, given my previous forays into baking over the years, but it was a case of never say die, because you never knew, did you? Mike might just be fooled and Tyler definitely would. Well, or so I thought. My dad was round Donna's when I said this, and just as he'd done the previous time, when I'd suggested I actually try to make some, he spat out a mouthful of his tea.

Whatever the origin of the cakes, at least I could tick everything off my mental to-do list, and with the goodies all safely hidden at Riley's house, including the balloons and decorations, I could largely put it out of my mind. All that remained for me to do was buy presents for both Mike and Tyler, and do the party nibbles on the Saturday morning.

Which left me able to focus all my energies on Flip, who appeared in the kitchen with her hair neatly brushed and bound with a pink ribbon that she'd tied in a passable approximation of a bow.

'So,' I said as I poured milk over her cereal. 'You're meeting with Mummy after school today, remember? Debbie Scott, the family support lady, will come here and pick you up after you've changed out of your school uniform, and …'

Flip dropped her spoon back onto the table with a clatter. 'No, Mummy!' she said, shaking her head emphatically and sticking her lower lip out. 'I'm not taking my uniform off. I wanna keep it on.'

I put down the milk bottle and sat down across the table from her. 'Really?' I said. 'But I thought you'd want to put on a pretty dress and your nice pink shoes for when you have tea with Mummy.'

She shook her head wildly now. 'No! That other mummy'll just tell me I look silly. Anyway, I wanna keep my school stuff on so's I look like all the other kids.'

Again, I was struck by her train of thought, and tried to fathom what might have prompted it. 'Sweetie,' I reassured her, 'you can wear whatever you like. If you want to stay in your uniform, that's absolutely fine. Anyway, I'm sure your mummy will think you look lovely no matter what you wear.'

I half expected her to remind me that her 'other' mummy would do no such thing. She'd told me that often enough, after all. But she was still on the same tack and now I could make sense of it. 'That Debbie lady,' she said, picking up her spoon again and dipping it into her cornflakes. 'She'll *have* to bring me back if I've got my uniform on, won't she? Kids can't just sleep in their uniforms, can they? She'll know I have to come back home 'cos my jamas are here.'

If she'd said 'Simples!' next, just like they did in that insurance advert, I don't think I'd have batted an eyelid. As it was I nodded and, as she set about wolfing down her cereal, wondered how long it had taken her to work out that her school uniform *was* her insurance; well, in her head, at least.

Flip was a conundrum for sure. Her mind seemed to flit from one wild thought to another and I wondered if this too was a symptom of FAS. I didn't recall reading anything that specific when I'd done my research, but it did mention the attachment issues and the difficulty in retaining information. That certainly explained why I had to continually go over instructions for almost everything, and I had no doubt that by the time school was over, and I picked her up, I'd have to explain all this all over again.

I was right. True to form, as I collected Flip from her classroom, she skipped out to meet me as if she didn't have a care in the world. She certainly didn't look as though the business of meeting her mum was on her mind. 'Hiya, Mummy,' she trilled as she grabbed my hand and started to cast her gaze about. 'Where's Riley and my boys? Are they waiting for us?'

Jackson and Levi finished school five minutes before Flip, because the enrichment group stayed a little later. They did it that way so that there wouldn't be such a large crowd of demob-happy children running around and potentially unsettling them. Since Flip had been in the school, however, Riley and the boys had waited for us once or twice, when Tyler had after-school football or was seeing a friend, so that we could go for something to eat together.

'Not today, sweetie,' I said as we set off to the car. 'It's your day for having tea with your mummy, remember?'

She stopped dead in her tracks, just for a moment, then carried on again, swinging my arm as she walked. 'Oh, I've changed my mind about that,' she said conversationally. 'So can you let that other lady know that I'll go next week instead?'

I took a deep breath as I guided her into the car. 'I'm sorry, sweetie,' I said, 'but we can't do that, I'm afraid. It's all arranged now and your mummy will be expecting you.' I leaned in to help her with her seatbelt and kissed her forehead as I did so. 'And just think how disappointed she'd be if you didn't go.'

She shook her head. 'She wouldn't be. I told you. She hates me. Anyway, *you're* my new mummy now,' she said, spreading her hands. 'So what do I need to see the *old* one for?'

Her tone implied that it was a perfectly reasonable and rational question, which for her I guessed it must be. She'd never once wavered over her 'out with the old mummy and in with the new' approach to her circumstances, so why I'd imagine she'd be any different now, I had no idea. Perhaps just plain old wishful thinking; perhaps just a natural compulsion to try and imagine she had attachments to her kin that simply weren't there; that underneath her apparent lack of emotion was a normal, feeling child for whom a mother's lack of love really hurt. The evidence, however, was that it didn't hurt for Flip – not in ways I could yet measure, at any rate. Which was a depressing thing to accept, which was perhaps why I hadn't yet. The implications for the rest of her life were just so grim. 'Sweetheart,' I said gently, feeling like a stuck record, 'you *know* that I'm not your real new mummy. I'm just looking after you for a while, remember?' I started to buckle her into the seatbelt. 'You already *have* a mummy and she'll always be your mummy no matter where you live. You understand that as well, don't you?'

Flip sighed. '*Yes*. If you *say* so,' she said.

But understanding the facts didn't make Flip any more kindly disposed to the business of being dragged off almost as soon as she was home from school. By the time we got back she'd gone quiet, and seemed in such a sullen mood that I didn't even suggest swapping her school shoes for the funky new trainers we'd got her and which she loved. I just had a feeling it might provoke a scene. It was for the same reason that I also did an about-turn on the food and drink front, allowing her to sit and watch television with some milk and a couple of biscuits until the family support worker turned up.

I've had dealings with lots of family support workers over the years, and they were almost always really nice. The sort of people you knew would try to see the best in any person, however well hidden and small that best bit might be. It was in the nature of the job, I supposed, one of their main ones being to work with vulnerable families who needed support and guidance in order to hang onto their children. They also worked with parents who had already lost their children, supporting them in learning the skills they'd need to have a chance of getting them back.

Family support workers were also the ones who were usually called in whenever supervised contact was arranged.

They'd be responsible for the child, sit in and if necessary intervene during the meeting, then, having returned the child to wherever they were being cared for, report back to their social worker to let them know how things went.

I opened the door to find Debbie Scott was exactly as I'd expected her to be, warm-looking and friendly, with an apologetic smile already on her face. 'I'm so sorry I'm late,' she said, even though I hadn't even realised she was, and when I assured her she wasn't and commented on how puffed out she seemed, she explained that she'd just picked up her own two children from school and dashed to drop them off with a child-minder in order to be on time for us. 'Oh, I'm fine,' she said, refusing my offer of a cold drink and five minutes to gather her breath. 'Sure you know all about such juggling acts!' she added brightly.

I agreed that I did, and as I gave her some money for Flip's tea I quickly filled her in on how Flip didn't currently share her sunny mood, explaining the whys and wherefores as succinctly and quietly as I could before taking her in to be introduced. 'Don't worry about that,' she reassured me. 'I'm sure I'll be able to bring her round. And if I can't, well, we both know how these things can go, don't we?' and, again, I could agree that I did.

Needless to say, the child in question did her usual mercurial party piece, leaping up to greet Debbie as if she'd been hoping to bump into her all her life. 'Hello, lady!' she said, grabbing her hand and smiling happily. 'Are we allowed to go for burgers?'

I could only shake my head as I watched the pair head off to Debbie's car, best friends forever, it looked like, in just a matter of seconds. I wondered if there would be a similar turnaround when she saw her mother. For all that had happened and might have happened, I really hoped so, for both their sakes. Even if no more came of it, and Flip was ultimately adopted, surely no harm could come of it? And potentially some good, even if they never saw each other again. At the very least Flip would have a more positive memory of her mum to take through life with her.

I waved them off, consciously trying to will myself into feeling positive. It was, at least, a nice thought to think.

With Tyler off up the football field and having tea with Denver, and Mike not due home till seven, I did what little ironing was needed, then, having polished that off in no time, found myself in the rare position of having little else to occupy me till Flip was dropped home a couple of hours hence. Well, bar wrapping birthday presents. Which was galling, since I'd left the presents hidden round at Riley's and, as a quick call established that she was currently pushing a trolley round the supermarket, I calculated that by the time she got home there would be hardly enough time to make it worth my while.

'You've just got ants in your pants, Mum,' she deduced from the tea and coffee aisle. 'Stop stressing. They are probably having a whale of a time. And if they're not – well, in the words of Grandma, what will be will be.'

'That's what worries me,' I said, knowing it was a 'what' that might well involve a fall-out. But just as I'd started a 20-minute countdown, my mobile trilled. It was Kieron's

Lauren, wanting to know about the arrangements for the weekend.

I explained what we'd planned and that, if they were able to, I'd love it if they could come round for both birthday gatherings, but particularly for Tyler's, as I knew it would mean such a lot to him.

'Of course,' she reassured me. 'That's the plan. Who's going to be there, by the way? Everyone? All the family?'

'Pretty much,' I told her. 'All the immediate family anyway. My mum and dad. Donna and Chloe, Riley, David and the kids, obviously ... plus a couple of Tyler's school friends. Oh, and the absolute best news is that I've secretly invited Grant, and had him tell Tyler he's away and can't make it. I can't wait to see his face ...' I paused, the penny suddenly dropping. 'But that's it,' I said. 'No one else. No battalions of rampaging teenagers, or cousins, or elderly aunts, or second cousins ... And, of course, there's going to be *zero* fuss on Friday evening for Mike; just dinner. And that's just us, so tell Kieron there's no need for him to stress.'

Lauren laughed. 'You know your son *soooo* well,' she said. 'Which, of course, you *would* do. But, well, you know what I mean, Casey. He just wants to know what he's going to be walking into ...'

'A place of tranquillity and harmony with a side-order of cake,' I said firmly. 'And that's a promise. Not so much as a party popper to shatter the blissful peace. Well, come to think of it, *actually* ...'

Lauren laughed again. 'Oh, it'll be so great to see everyone properly,' she said. 'Specially the little ones. What with being away on holiday ...'

'And being ill …'

'And being ill, yes,' she repeated. 'Anyway, I'll let you go. I'm in work tomorrow and Friday morning, but if you need a hand with anything, just shout, okay?'

Bless her, I thought, as I disconnected the call. Forget about *me* knowing and understanding all Kieron's little peccadilloes – I was his mum, so I ought to. But in Lauren, who understood so well all the things that stressed him out – parties very much included – he had really found a gem.

And it seemed we'd also found one in Debbie Scott, who delivered Flip back to us just as I'd started preparing tea for Mike and myself. And who must have been doing something right, because Flip seemed to be in the same sunny mood as she had been when she'd skipped out to Debbie's car hand in hand with her.

'We had, like, *the* biggest burgers you ever saw, Mummy, *ever*!' she chirruped while I helped her pull her school sweatshirt over her head. 'And chips, too. With their skins on, which you have to do because it makes them better for you, and my old mummy said I can have a horse for Pink Barbie and she's got new hair and it's, like, *this* short!'

She placed her thumb and index finger together to illustrate exactly how short. 'Shorter than even *Denver's*!' she told Tyler, who'd rattled down the stairs now, maths book in his hand.

'What, like a number *2*?' he asked her incredulously, and then sceptically. 'Come on. *Really*?'

'Because she was *burnded*, stupid,' Flip was quick to respond. 'And it's not grown back all over yet. And I'm getting a Barbie horse, so *there*!'

I was conscious both of the time and the fact that I was keen to exchange a few words with Debbie before she left, just to get some sense of how things had gone. My eyes alighted on the madcap Jim Carrey DVD Tyler also had on him.

'I'm assuming you're hoping to talk Mike into watching that with you after tea, are you, love?' I asked him.

He smiled sheepishly and waggled the exercise book. 'Soon as I've done this lot, at any rate,' he confirmed.

'Right, Flip,' I said, turning to her. 'In that case, if you are a *very* good girl and go up to your room, get out of your uniform and into your jim-jams – and hang it all up tidily, mind – then once we've had tea and Tyler and Mike are watching their silly film you and I can get out the craft things and make a cardboard stable for that new horse you're getting. How does that sound?' I held my fist out for a bump, which Flip duly connected with. Tyler grinned.

'That sounds *epic*,' she said, thundering up the stairs two at a time, rather like a Barbie horse herself.

'Well, in a nutshell, that was ... interesting,' Debbie Scott said once Tyler was installed at the dining table with his homework while Mike read the paper, and Flip was busy getting herself changed.

'In what way?' I asked, eager to get as much of an idea about how things had gone as I could.

'In that it wasn't at all what I'd expected, I suppose. You know what it's like – you get the background details and you form a picture, don't you? Even if it's a sketchy one. And I suppose Mum – Megan – well, she just didn't quite fit, you know? Not from what I'd been told about her. She seemed terribly nervous, for one thing – though I'm told she's trying to get clean, isn't she? You know. Off the drink? So I suppose the sober her might be very different from the version that led us to this in the first place.'

She paused as if in thought. And I took the opportunity to ask her to elaborate. 'Pleased to see Flip? That's always been my biggest concern. Though, given that she was apparently so keen to see her, I suppose that doesn't make much sense, does it?'

Debbie was nodding now. 'Oh, yes, it does. But, yes, definitely. Shell-shocked,' she added. 'A bit awkward – well, you'd expect that, of course, wouldn't you? But, yes, without a doubt. She didn't say so to me, not in so many words – and, of course, I was anxious not to intrude too much – but yes, genuinely pleased to see her. Upset, even. She apologised to Flip a *lot*. There were even a few tears. Real tears. She wasn't in a state, or anything, but she was definitely a bit overcome. Rather more emotional than I think poor Flip knew quite what to do with, to be honest, bless her.' She paused again. 'Sorry – I've dealt with a child with FAS before, and there are definite things you tend to spot, aren't there? But she didn't appear too fazed; certainly hadn't lost her appetite, that's for sure.'

'So Megan was really quite upset, then?' I said, trying to digest this unexpected news.

'Oh yes. No question.' She nodded once and then glanced down at her watch. I needed to stop interrogating her and let her get home.

'Sorry,' I said. 'I'm holding you up. We can chat further when you phone to arrange the next visit – well, if there's to be one, of course, which it sounds like there might well be. But no rush if you're busy; I'll wait till Ellie has your report and she can fill me in with all the details.' I smiled wryly. 'I'm guess I'm just always a bit sceptical about such displays of affection when all the evidence suggests otherwise, aren't you?'

Debbie nodded. 'Believe me, it's easy to become a cynic in our line of work, isn't it? And I know there's been a lot of water flowing under this particular bridge, but – well, what do I know?' She smiled. 'But if I was made to take a line, I'd say she absolutely means it. I mean, we all know the score when it comes to long-term addicts, don't we? And actions speak much louder than words. But you never know, do you? Perhaps that house fire *was* the line that needed drawing in the sand.'

I thought about what Flip had said about her mother's burned hair, and tried to imagine just how terrifying the experience they had both been through must have been. 'Perhaps you're right,' I said. 'It's certainly interesting to get a different perspective. As you say, early days, and though the odds probably aren't brilliant, I agree – we can only be positive. It's great that there haven't been any traumas – well, by the sound of it, anyway. She could still react down the line, once it all sinks in, of course. But so far so good. From what you've said, it sounds like it's been a good experience, which is the main thing. She certainly sounds like she had fun.'

'Oh, yes,' she said. 'No doubt about that – not least because of the presence of the Barbie horse in the equation.' She grinned. 'So let's hope it materialises from somewhere at some point soon, because I suspect there will be hell to pay if it doesn't!'

Chapter 11

For all that Flip had seemed so happy to have seen her mother, it soon became evident that there was a significant negative buried in all the positives; the fact that it had triggered a renewed interest in her looks, and a return to her obsession with being ugly.

'She's so pretty, my real mummy,' she'd told me that night when I tucked her and her faithful dolly up in bed. 'See Pink Barbie's eyes?' she said, thrusting the doll into my face. 'My real mummy's got eyes like that. And when she cries they're all sparkly.' She sighed. 'She's so pretty. I wish *I* had pretty eyes. Mine are horrid.'

I had a lump in my throat as I stared into her own little eyes, set further apart than most children's and serving to set her apart too. I kissed her goodnight. 'You've got the sparkliest, most beautiful eyes I've ever seen,' I said, 'and don't let anybody ever tell you any different.'

Who had told her different anyway? Her mother, I presumed. Who else? I could see it all too easily; people with deep-rooted intractable issues were apt to get nasty when worse for wear on alcohol. Apt to feel resentful. Apt to lash out at those closest to them. Apt to blame …

It felt all too believable a scenario. The daughter she hadn't meant to have; the daughter she'd always struggled to accept? I'd gone to bed that night turning it all over in my mind and worrying. This sudden blooming of motherly concern and contrition was all well and good, but what if Megan *did* hit the bottle again? Much as I understood that Flip's mum was a victim herself (of her addiction, and the nameless demons that had presumably prompted it) it was Flip's welfare I was worried about, and the potential shift in her expectations. Though she hadn't articulated any interest in returning to her mother (she was much more fixated on the promised Barbie horse) what if she did end up back with this new version of her mum only for that version to be lost if she failed to stay sober? It would just create more damage on top of the damage already done. I just hoped social services would take their time in considering their next step.

'I thought you were a glass-half-full type of girl?' Mike commented when I shared my thoughts with him the following morning. 'Where's all this doom and gloom come from? You know, Casey, I think that Debbie woman hit the nail on the head. I think that fire would have been enough to bring *anyone* to their senses. I think she deserves a chance at least, don't you?'

So even when, that afternoon, I was horrified to see that Flip had hacked off almost all Pink Barbie's hair, I decided to bite my tongue and say nothing negative about it.

'She looks sweet, doesn't she, Mummy Casey? Just like my real mummy.'

I noted that 'real mummy' had now replaced 'old mummy' in her vocabulary. Noted but didn't know quite what to make of. Not yet. I simply smiled and patted Flip's head. 'Yes, she does,' I agreed. 'Sweet, just like you,' and made a mental note to add it to my log.

By the weekend, however, Flip's attention had been diverted. Always butterfly-minded, she was soon absorbed in the exciting here and now, just as any eight-year-old girl would be at the prospect of a party. As was I, once I felt I was properly on top of it, having secured Mike a killer present and given it to him on the Friday evening: a pair of tickets to see an apparently brilliant Madness tribute band who were touring locally in a couple of months. Yes, they were almost as much for me as they were for him, but he was over the moon, which naturally made me very happy, there being few pleasures in life nicer than surprising someone you loved and seeing that look that confirmed you'd got it absolutely right.

I'd also – a real spur of the moment addition – managed to book a bouncy castle for the back garden, due to arrive on the Saturday morning just after Mike and Tyler had gone off to watch Kieron play football – their weekly fix. I'd been particularly pleased to hear Tyler's parting words, too.

'Let's leave the women to it,' he said – he did love winding me up with all his 'women' schtick – 'because I expect a certain someone might need to go shopping for another certain someone. Know what I mean?' he added, winking, not an inkling of an idea that when he got home he'd find the party he had no idea about all set up and good to go.

Thankfully, I hadn't let slip anything to Flip either. But now I needed to, so I sat down and explained everything to her. 'And so you see,' I finished, once I'd run down who was coming and what was going to be happening, 'I kept it a *big* secret till the men left, but now we have to get everything organised. So, what d'you say? You want to help me make it extra special?'

Flip was over the moon, just as I'd imagined she would be. 'Oh, Mummy!' she cried, clapping her hands together as excitedly as if it had been arranged just for her. 'Oh, Tyler will be *so* happy! A birthday party! That's *epic*! You know, one of my friends at my old school once had a birthday party,' she babbled excitedly. 'I nearly got invited, too. She said I did. She just forgotted it at the last minute. She promised me she wouldn't forget again, though, so I'm going to be going to one, too. Well, if Ellie tells her where to find me. She will tell her, won't she? And – oh, I need to get Pink Barbie ready for this party, don't I?' She jumped down from the chair she'd been sitting at, eating her breakfast. 'I need to go dress her in her special birthday clothes!'

She went to skip off to her bedroom, but I placed a hand on her arm. 'Flip, you have had a party for yourself before, haven't you? You know – for your own birthday?'

She was still grinning at me even as she shook her head. 'Not yet,' she said. 'I haven't been old enough yet. But that's okay, Mummy,' she said, beaming at me as if I'd just given her the moon on a stick. ''Cos I can go to Tyler's party, can't I?'

I nodded, feeling sad not only for the lack, but for the fact that she'd simply accepted that fact, despite having seen friends – peers, presumably – having parties all the time. 'Of course you can, pumpkin,' I told her brightly. 'It wouldn't be a party without you there, now, would it? Off you go, then. Go and dress Barbie in her finery. Then you can come back and help me with the tidying before Riley arrives with the cakes and decorations.'

'And the magical fairy castle fit for a princess,' she reminded me.

'Yes,' I agreed, grinning at her girlish embellishment to what would in fact be a workaday lump of inflated rubber. '*And* the fairy castle.' Well, sort of.

The expression 'out of the mouths of babes ...' is a cliché for good reason. There can't be a parent alive who hasn't at some point been embarrassed by some undiplomatic thing a child has inconveniently said. Though, as these things tend to come at you out of left field, such truisms couldn't have been further from my mind. I had plenty of other stuff on my mind, for one thing.

Riley arrived with the boys only minutes after Flip had left me, Marley-Mae staying in the car with David, who was taking her to spend the morning with her other nanna, so we could get on with things without needing eyes in the backs of our heads. 'Go on, boys, run inside,' she said as she ushered them through the hall. 'Nanny needs to help me unload the car. And don't make any mess!'

I called up to Flip, to let her know that the boys were on their way up, then followed Riley out to help unload the party food and decorations from the car. It had just started to rain. 'Trust this bloody weather!' I complained as we hurried back inside with our booty. 'Why today of all days? Just what you want when you've got a bouncy castle coming, I don't think.'

'Don't worry, Mum,' Riley said. 'They'll have some sort of rain cover that can be fixed on it. They usually do. Besides, the kids won't care if they get wet anyway. They'll think it's more fun if they end up on their bums, I'm sure.'

Even as I pictured it I cringed. Quite apart from the health and safety implications of the added slip-and-slide potential, I couldn't imagine anything worse than to get wet and muddy and then bounce around getting even *more* wet and muddy after slipping around on other people's dirt. But I tried to look on the bright side. Riley was right. The children *would* love it. Even though Tyler was 13 now, both he and his friend Denver still liked to forget how 'grown up' they were and get down with the kids.

Thinking ahead, I had already set up an art and craft table in the conservatory for Flip, Levi and Jackson; something to keep them all occupied while I supervised the arrival and erection of the giant plaything and, once that was done, while Riley and I trimmed the place up and cooked pizzas and chicken drumsticks, and as I buttered mini bread rolls and Riley topped them with ham and cheese, I finally relaxed into my usual happy pre-party mode, not even complaining when Riley channel-hopped to some distinctly of-the-moment music station on the TV and turned it up to a ridiculous volume. 'Mum, it's not often I get to remember I'm still young,' she countered as I winced. 'So while Marley-Mae is away I'm making the most of it.'

I grinned, pleased to see her swaying in time to the music. She was right. Being 'Mum' could be an all-consuming thing. I even threw in what I hoped was a modern kind of wiggle.

She burst out laughing. 'Mother! *Please* tell me that you're not trying to twerk! OMG. I need my phone. I *so* have to capture this …'

I was just about to try another when we heard the screaming.

In fact, just a single scream. High pitched and piercing. 'What the *hell*?' said Riley, as I threw down the butter knife.

We both rushed into the conservatory to see Flip standing screaming at full throttle – arms stiffened by her sides, head thrown back, mouth gaping. She had more breath than a free diver sometimes.

Levi and Jackson, in contrast, were still on their stools and staring at her, their expressions mirroring hers, except minus the sound. 'What on *earth* is going on?' I asked, taking my usual position on my knees in front of Flip, and, grabbing her clenched fists, feeling grateful for a lack of accident or apparent injury. 'Take a big breath, Flip. A very big one. That's it.' I freed a hand and gently nudged her chin up. 'That's it. Breathe. So. Come on. Tell me what's happened.'

'I'm sorry, Nanny,' Jackson immediately said, tears pooling in his eyes. 'I think it's because of me.'

'Because of you?' Riley asked. 'Why? What did you do?'

Jackson looked to Levi for reassurance, then back to me and his mum. 'I only said I didn't like her Barbie's hair.'

I felt Flip's hand tighten in mine. She turned and glared at Jackson.

My heart sank. My poor grandson looked mortified, bless him. He couldn't have known that Flip had given her doll a haircut so she'd look just like her mum. 'It's okay, Jackson,' I told him. 'I know you didn't intend to hurt Flip. Flip, you understand that, don't you, sweetie?' I motioned to Jackson with a brief tip of my head. 'Boys don't really like dollies, do they? Most of them don't, anyway. And look, here he is, come to say sorry.'

Jackson slid from his stool and duly came over to give Flip a hug. But as he put his arms around her she suddenly unstiffened sufficiently to lash out at him. We could all hear the sound of her hand connecting with his face, and plainly see the weal reddening on his cheek. More tears began spilling from his eyes.

Riley was quick to grab him and sweep him up out of harm's way. 'Flip!' she snapped. 'We do *not* hit other children! Jackson was trying to apologise and now look what you've done!' She put a hand to Jackson's cheek and sat down on his stool with him, rocking him.

Great, I thought. Just as things were going well. I turned my attention to Flip, my expression stern. 'That wasn't a very nice thing to do, was it, love?' I said to her. 'I told you he didn't mean it, and he was trying to apologise. Now *you* need to say sorry for what you just did.'

She was as implacable as she invariably was in such situations, however. 'But he said Pink Barbie was ugly, Mummy! *Ugly!*' she screeched, then burst out crying herself, this time no screams, but just sobbing her heart out. 'She is *not* ugly!' she railed at Jackson. 'She's beautiful! I'm ugly, but Barbie is *beautiful*! Like a princess! Not ugly. Bad Jackson. Barbie hates you!'

Jackson knew better than to respond, bless him, and was too busy crying anyway. And now I understood the trigger, I understood Flip's over-reaction. That word 'ugly' exerted a terrible power over her life. I looked over at Riley, hoping for her own understanding, and, thankfully, she nodded it. I knew she understood what a big thing it was for Flip to have her beautiful dolly criticised; Pink Barbie (who to be fair now looked much more like Punk Barbie) had almost taken on the status of talisman – against a world she felt judged her, and harshly, on her looks.

But how were the boys to know that? How were they to know not to tease her?

'You're not ugly, Flip,' Levi said, loyally trying to make things better for his brother. 'Jackson just meant that he liked her better with her long hair. You're pretty, and so's your dolly. Marley-Mae has one just like it.'

Bless Levi. And, thankfully, it seemed to do the trick. Flip sniffled a bit, then went to pick up her beloved doll, which, from her location, I guessed she'd probably lobbed at Jackson. She kissed her. 'Okay, Levi,' she conceded, looking coy now. 'I'm sorry, Jackson. I didn't mean to hit you, it just happened. I promise not to do it again.' She glanced at me. 'I swear down I won't.'

'Good,' said Riley, as Jackson slid down off her lap and, children being children, the three were once again the best of friends. I could tell that she was still a little upset, however, as we went back to our work in the kitchen, so I tried to explain about how Flip had never had a party, and how powerfully and negatively the word 'ugly' impacted on her, and why she'd hacked the doll's hair off in the first place.

'Mum, it's fine,' Riley said eventually, and in a tone that made me realise I was probably sounding a bit too defensive, which addled me as well, so I was grateful when the doorbell went. 'Home from footie already?' she asked, as I wiped my hands to go and answer it.

I winked, the tension going now. 'No,' I said. 'That'll be our two social workers.'

Riley glanced up at the kitchen clock. 'Bit early for guests yet, isn't it?'

'Not for what I have in mind,' I said, grinning.

In truth, I'd told the pair of them to come a little early on the pretext that it would be nice for Ellie to spend a bit of time with Flip before the crowds arrived (which was sort of true) and that it would mean the world to Tyler if Will was already here when he and Mike returned from football. He was probably the closest adult in Tyler's life outside the family, after all. Mostly, however, I was keen on the business of getting *them* together.

'Throwing them together, more like,' Riley observed – with some acuity – after I'd refused all offers of help in the kitchen and insisted the pair of them take their coffees out into the conservatory to be with the kids. 'You have absolutely no shame whatsoever,' she finished.

* * *

After that, Grant and Denver arrived, each carrying a brightly wrapped gift, then my mum and dad, Donna and Chloe, and finally Lauren. The pile of birthday gifts got higher, as well as a small, separate pile that people had kindly brought for Mike, and pretty soon everyone was chatting together. I was super-pleased with my sneaky match-making efforts; it was as if Ellie and Will had known each other for years as they mingled with the family like a couple.

Just before Mike, Kieron and Tyler were due back, David pulled up outside with a very excited Marley-Mae. 'They'll be here in about 60 seconds,' he said as he ran inside, daughter tucked under his arm like a chunky carpet. 'Kieron just texted me. Are we all hiding or something?'

'No time for that,' I said, 'and besides, all the food and balloons are on show, so he'll know as soon as he walks in.'

'I'll just close the curtains then,' David said as he did just that, 'and if we shut this door we can just all yell "surprise" when they come in.'

I grinned. In all the years David had been among our family, he had got the party bug along with the rest of us. He was as excited as the kids were.

For all my anxieties, the party went like a dream. Tyler was over the moon when he realised what had been going on in his absence; which was more important than the gifts we got him, really, because it was just one of those signifiers that you are thought about and cherished. He was especially thrilled to see his brother Grant, and Denver had been roped into the surprise.

'I can't believe I never caught on,' he said, laughing as he ripped paper from his presents. 'I never even thought when Grant said he couldn't see me this weekend! You're all a sneaky lot, aren't you?' he said, his eyes shining with delight.

'I love *everything*,' he said, grinning from ear to ear, once he'd torn through his pile of gifts. 'And the cakes look *great*, Casey. What a turn up. I didn't know you could bake.'

Much guffawing followed; he'd obviously worked *that* one out, no problem. I chose to ignore it. Instead I cleared my throat and moved on to the next part of my cunning plan. 'Well, needs must,' I confessed. 'A girl has to do what a girl has to do when it's a special boy's special day, after all. But we mustn't forget our other birthday "boy", must we? Come on, old man,' I said, gesturing to Mike. 'I see a little pile of pressies here for you.'

'Nice change of subject, Casey,' he whispered as he passed me to reach for his gifts. Another round of 'Happy Birthday' followed as Mike began unwrapping them, while Tyler, I noticed, who was standing close by, was as ever busy fiddling with his phone. I didn't stop him. I knew he was just probably adding to his ever-growing collection of pictures of one or other of us in unflattering poses. And when you thought about it properly, just him being *able* to do that was pretty precious.

'Rule of thumb. Always save the smallest till last,' Mike laughed, holding up a tiny square package. 'And let's see, oh, look. It's from Lauren and my loving son.' He winked at Kieron. 'You should all know that he once wrapped up a pack of batteries for my birthday, so it's anyone's guess what could be in here.'

Everyone laughed as Mike carefully lifted the tape from the paper, and I worried about all eyes being turned towards Kieron. But a quick glance reassured me that he seemed to be doing okay.

'Hurry up, then,' I said, keen to divert attention from him anyway. 'Let us all in on it, will you?'

Mike had taken a small cube-shaped charm out of a jeweller's box and was now staring at it intently, rolling it over in his hand, while Tyler, unofficial film director, moved in for a close-up. I smiled to myself at Kieron's – or more likely, Lauren's – good thinking. It was the sort of charm that attached to the bootlace-style bracelet they had bought him the previous year. 'What is it?' I asked, unable to see properly. 'Is it a dice?'

Mike wasn't looking at me, however. He was staring at Kieron and Lauren in turn, as if seeing them properly – seeing something I couldn't. I followed his gaze, and saw Kieron slip his hand into Lauren's. They were both beaming as if plugged directly into the sun.

Mike dropped the charm into my palm, grinning now, then embraced the pair of them in a bear hug. Bit of an over-reaction, I thought. He hadn't made such a fuss over the new satnav Riley and David had bought him. But then I looked down at the dice and saw it was engraved with letters. Just as Mike had done before me, I carefully read each one; there were six of them, one on each face of the dice. 'G', I read, and 'M'. Then an 'A', 'P' and 'S'. Then finally 'R'. And that's when it hit me. Rearranged, they spelled 'GRAMPS'. They spelled Gramps! 'Oh my God!' I yelled. 'Does this mean …?'

Kieron nodded. 'Look, everyone!' I whooped. 'It says gramps! It says *gramps*!' I danced a little jig. 'They're having a baby!'

It was only then that I realised Tyler's phone was now turned towards me. He smiled and pressed 'stop' before being engulfed in a group bear hug, and I realised just why he'd been so intent on capturing it. 'You're right,' he confirmed, answering the question even before I'd asked it. 'Kieron asked me specially. See – you weren't the only one on a secret mission, Casey. I was in cahoots,' he finished proudly.

Chapter 12

I sometimes wonder if there's some big celestial balance sheet that requires every yin to have a yang, every positive to have a negative, every bit of good news subject to a short sharp reality check, just to keep the scales in alignment.

Probably bunkum, but, even so, perhaps I should have seen it coming. Should have seen that there had to be something down the line to wipe the dopey 'I'm going to be a gran again' grin off my face.

It was the following weekend. One of those balmy autumn days that everyone looks forward to. The sort of days I imagine they wait for when doing shoots for fashion magazines and catalogues, or for advertising out-of-season mini-breaks in country-house hotels. It was certainly a day to be glad, on the whole, that we lived in Britain and had our seasons to enjoy. The sky was an unbroken blue, bar a few dissolving plane trails, and the sun fell on everything especially lovingly: the heaps of coppery leaves, the drooping heads of the last of the late-summer roses and the perfect webs that festooned the hedge – and which never ceased to enchant little Jackson – still prettily strung with beads of morning dew, and with a fat and patient spider in every centre.

'This is such a treat, Mum,' Riley said, as we scraped and stacked the plates on the kitchen worktop between us, to add to the pile Mike had promised he would start tackling later. I'd decided to do our Sunday lunch out in the conservatory to make the most of the light and warmth; though it might be too nippy to actually eat in the garden, if you squinted just so it was easy to believe you were *al fresco* in the Costa del Sol, it was that hot.

'It's a treat for me as well,' I pointed out. 'Nice to continue the celebrations. I can't seem to stop smiling to myself.'

'I know,' she said. 'Me too. Not to mention doing a double take. Kieron. A *father*. It still hasn't sunk in.'

I laughed. 'I know. But, you know, I think it might just be the making of him. After all, babies thrive on routine, and routine is *everything* to Kieron.'

'Oh, I'm sure that'll be a *big* help, a screaming baby,' she said, guffawing as she opened the fridge door and pulled out the trifle I'd made earlier – trifle being something I *could* make. It had also been lightly accessorised with a drop or two of Kieron's killer drink, which had been blamed for Lauren's dicky tummy. I smiled to myself. It obviously hadn't been the culprit after all. And Lauren hadn't been checking who was coming because Kieron was anxious, for that matter. They wanted a full house for their announcements, cheeky so and so's.

'Oh, I know,' I said. 'But he'll be fine. They both will. I just *know* it. And they'll have all of us to help them.'

'Absolutely,' she said. Then shook her head bemusedly. 'It blows my mind, even so. I still can't quite *see* it, you know? He just doesn't seem *old* enough, bless him.'

I grabbed the serving spoon and bowls, picturing Tyler's face when he saw what we were having for pudding. In Tyler's book, trifle was *epic*. Bless him – he, too, was in a particularly happy place. Having been secret official photographer for the Important Announcement had put a real spring in his step. Honestly, I'd thought, for all people go on about people with ASD lacking social skills, my son had shown emotional intelligence and then some. He really was all grown-up now. And routinely confounding expectations.

I knew what Riley meant, though. 'That's because Kieron's your baby brother,' I whispered to her as I followed her back out, mindful of not wanting to disturb Marley-Mae. She'd conked out for a nap almost as soon as I'd begun dishing up lunch, and Riley had parked her up in her buggy at the foot of the stairs, away from the worst of the noise. With any luck she'd be down for an hour, perhaps more. She certainly should, I thought – she'd been running around like a whirling dervish since she'd arrived.

I turned to Riley just before we stepped back out into the conservatory. 'He'll never seem quite as grown up as he really is to you,' I finished. 'That's the way it works. Even when you're both old and grey and chasing your own grandchildren around, like me and old Gunga Din here.'

'Old? Who said old?' Mike wanted to know, catching the tail end of it. 'Enough of the "old" if you don't mind, Mrs. *And* the Gunga Din!'

'Dad, shush, will you?' Riley hissed at him, nodding back towards her sleeping toddler. 'I'm trying to enjoy five minutes' peace here!'

'It that trifle?' piped up Tyler. 'Yesss! OMG, that's epic!' Then he frowned. 'Sorry, Riley ...' he whispered.

All had been relatively calm with Flip since Tyler's party. And though Debbie had called to arrange a second meeting with Megan, she'd apparently become less of a fixation in Flip's mind – well, bar the odd mention of the forthcoming Barbie horse. Which was fine by me; be it emotional or practical, we'd cross each new bridge as we came to it. In the meantime, I was happy just to concentrate on Flip's programme and celebrate each increment of progress she made.

And she was, little by little, making progress. It certainly felt like it when she popped Pink Barbie up onto the table and asked if they could both get down.

'What about your pudding?' I asked her, as I placed the bowls on the table.

'Oh, we still want our pudding,' she told me. 'But we both need a wee.' She jiggled the doll to illustrate, having her hop up and down. 'So can we get down, please, Mummy?'

'Good girl,' said Mike, nodding his approval. I praised her too, because this was another welcome development in a week of welcome developments. With a child who'd had such a complicated start, simple things like asking for permission to leave the table were anything but second nature – just sitting eating a meal at the table had been a big enough hurdle; I don't think it was something Flip had ever really experienced outside of school. It would also mean a valuable point on her chart.

'And don't forget to wash your hands,' I reminded her, as she slipped from her chair and came around the table.

'We won't, Mummy,' she assured me, smiling brightly as she skipped away. For all that was going on under that pretty head of blonde waves (not to mention all those episodes of screaming) there were times – increasingly common now – when Flip was an incredibly easy child to have around, particularly when we were at home and it was just the family around her; as if she became simply absorbed into the general fabric of the household, flitting from person to person and activity to activity, with nothing more stressful on her mind than the next thing she was doing, dispensing hugs and smiles to all.

I carried on dispensing trifle and everyone started chatting about the various merits of various puddings – trifle I could make, and the liqueur was deemed a very good addition, so much so that I was glad I'd dug out portions for the little ones with only tiny amounts of the devilishly soaked sponge.

It was only when I realised Tyler was pretty much scraping the pattern off his plate that I also noticed that there was a full bowl next to him and still an empty seat at the table. 'Flip's been a while, hasn't she?' I said, to no one in particular, frowning and automatically pushing my chair back.

Mike's expression told me he understood why as well. Though the episodes of soiling had become markedly less frequent in recent weeks, it was by no means a thing of the past. 'I'll go and check on her,' I said, feeling slightly queasy at the thought of the joys I might potentially find in the downstairs cloakroom.

But it was less a case of what I did find and more of what I didn't find, because the first thing I saw when I stepped into the hallway was that Marley-Mae's buggy was empty.

I shook my head and sighed. Typical. *How* many times had I told her? 'Flip?' I called up the stairs. 'Have you taken the baby up there?'

We had gates permanently fixed at the top and bottom of our staircase – with little ones around so much, it was the only sensible thing to do. The bottom one was locked shut, but that meant nothing. All the kids knew how to open them; you just had to pull them back on a spring-loaded clip. The important thing – the thing I'd always drummed into all of them – was to make sure you clicked it shut again once through. I looked up as I opened it; the gate at the top was locked too, and I was just headed upstairs – there'd been no answer from Flip, of course – when my movement was arrested by the sound of the front door swinging open and banging against the wall. I turned around. *What the …? I thought*, eyeing it, confused.

I went back through the stairgate, clicking it shut almost on autopilot, as I tried to compute what had happened. The cloakroom door was open too, but I didn't need to peer in to know that it was odds on I wouldn't find Flip or Marley-Mae in there.

I went right past it, therefore, and stepped out onto the doorstep, because if the front door was open then it seemed pretty obvious that both my granddaughter and Flip had gone outside into the street. I felt a sick feeling in my stomach.

'What's up, Mum?' Riley said, coming up behind me with the dirty bowls. 'She's not run off again, has she? God, you need eyes in the back of your –' She stopped then, just as I turned around. She looked into the empty buggy. 'Mum, where's Marley-Mae?'

'Uh-oh.' This was Tyler's voice, loaded with the usual knowing nuance he always adopted where Flip-related matters were concerned. He was carrying the trifle bowl and Levi was hot on his heels with what was left of the cream. 'She's run off with her, hasn't she?' he added, looking at me.

'It would seem so,' I said, trying to swallow my anxiety as I reached back into the hallway for my old boots.

'Oh, for God's *sake*,' Riley said, pushing past me as I wriggled my feet into them. 'Tyler, send Levi back to dad and come back with David to help us look, will you please? Honestly, Mum,' she added as I followed her down the path, hopping as I finished wriggling my right foot into its boot. 'This is getting beyond a joke, it really is!' I could almost feel the hum of anxiety coming off her. 'Flip!' she bellowed, when we reached the open gate. 'Flip! Jesus, Mum – where do we start?' she wanted to know. She spread her arms wide. 'She could have taken her *anywhere*!'

I could hear the rising panic in her voice too, even above the rush of blood pounding in my temples. There are few things more scary than the knowledge that a toddler – *your* toddler – is out on the streets unsupervised, and the feeling was one I knew depressingly well. I'd looked after two regular absconders in my time as a foster carer, and a couple before that, when I'd worked in the local high school, all of which memories were still fresh in my mind; the sort of gut-churning recollections you never forgot.

I tried to push them from my mind and keep a semblance of calm, expecting to lay eyes on the pair any second. I didn't. Neither did Riley. There was no sign of them anywhere. In fact, the sleepy Sunday street was completely deserted, so there wasn't even anyone we could ask if they'd seen them. We could only hope that they hadn't got very far. But she'd been gone from the table for, what? I mulled. At least 15 minutes, it must have been. Maybe even more. My stomach flipped again at the realisation.

'You go left, and I'll go right,' I suggested, because those were really the only options; left down the footpath to the park and woods beyond it, right to the bigger road off which ours was a spur; though it was odds on she'd go to the park – and God, I hoped she had – I felt a powerful need to be the one sprinting towards the main road, where the greatest danger lay. I then dashed off without waiting for an answer.

Not that I expected Riley to offer one. She'd broken into a run every bit as quickly as I had, and I didn't doubt she was as furious with me as I was myself and imagining all sorts of horrible things. And if my own mind was already teeming with unthinkable scenarios – which it was – it certainly wasn't helped by Tyler's take on the possibilities as he caught up with me, moments later, even if that had been his intention. 'It'll be okay,' he told me, breathing hard as we hurried up to the end of the road. 'I mean, what are the chances?'

'Chances of what?' I said, as I scanned the area in front of us, already knowing the sort of distance Flip could cover if she was on any sort of mission. Marley-Mae, on her wobbly legs, wouldn't hinder her either; Flip might have been slight, but she was also strong and wiry. She'd simply plonk Marley-Mae on her hip. *Damn* her, I thought distractedly. No, I corrected, damn *me*. Whatever had possessed her to hare off, her being able to do so was entirely my fault.

Tyler was still on more prosaic matters, however. 'Chances of there just happening to be a paedo hanging around, of course – you know, *just* at this moment and *just* in this place. I'd say it's pretty unlikely, Casey, wouldn't you? You know, statistically. And, like, it's not like Flip's stupid, is it? I mean, she's *pretty* stupid, but she's not *that* stupid. Not about the Green Cross Code and all that kind of stuff, anyway. Shall I go down to the main road and you go the other way?' he suggested as we reached the junction.

'Yes, *go*,' I told him. 'Hurry. And mind the road!'

I wished I could share Tyler's pragmatism and seeming lack of fear. But it was nigh on impossible. And he was spot on, of course. Abduction was all I could think about because the words 'stranger danger' kept jangling in my head. *No fear of strangers. Apt to wander. Falls in love with everyone as soon as she's met them*. And as soon as I did banish the thoughts, new ones rushed in to replace them. Flip was eight. That was all. Marley-Mae not yet 18 months. So if a bogeyman didn't get them, how about a speeding car or truck? Abduction or being run over – the twin evils that every parent dreads; and the main road was now a mere two streets away. I quickened my step further, breaking into a proper run now, cursing myself as I went. I'd been lulled into complacency and I was furious with myself – probably because my head was too full of Kieron and Lauren and the excitement of a new baby in the family. None of which excused me at all. I should have bolted the front door without even having to think about it. Why hadn't I done that? *Why?* I knew enough to know that I should always expect the unexpected. Was my mind really *that* far into fluffy bunny baby land?

I ran along the top street, where I finally saw someone I could ask – a middle-aged man who was out walking a small yappy dog. 'Excuse me!' I called, crossing the road diagonally in order to speak to him. At least I had yet to see a car driving past. Thank goodness for the small mercy of it being a Sunday afternoon, however confident Tyler had seemed about Flip's health and safety.

But it seemed he'd not seen them. 'Pretty sure I'd have noticed if I had,' he said, reasonably. 'How old d'you say the older one was? *Eight?*'

I nodded and thanked him, feeling chastened, not to mention judged, by his expression. I might have been over-sensitive, but had he narrowed his eyes at me? Did the set of his mouth reveal how careless I'd been in misplacing them both? Possibly, but it made no difference. I *had* been careless. Riley had every right to give me hell, and I didn't doubt she would. Only before *that*, there were still two small girls out there somewhere, missing and vulnerable …

I mentally regrouped. I couldn't allow my thoughts to stray any further than that.

But where should I head next? I turned around and ran back to the junction with the street I'd just come from. There was no sign of Tyler now, but then I knew there wouldn't be. He would have headed off to the warren of streets that ran adjacent to the main road further down. No, probably better that I just try to think like Flip. Where might she have gone? What route might she have taken? To the doctor's? To the local shops? We'd walked both those routes more than once now. I'd go that way. And if I didn't see them in the next five or ten minutes, I'd head back the other way; try and find Riley. Hope I was right, and that they were both safe and well.

I set off again, joined the main road – scarily heavy with traffic – and almost immediately saw Tyler in the distance, jogging along in my direction, his gaze swinging left and right.

'Casey!' he called, waving, as soon as he saw me, and as I waved back I realised he had his mobile in his hand. I cursed myself anew for being so bloody *stupid* – why had I torn off without grabbing mine?

He obviously had news. And as he approached I felt the anxiety drain from me in a welcome stream, only to be replaced by a stab of love and gratitude – the kind that hits you entirely without warning. I threw my arms around him and hugged him tight, unable to even articulate why I needed to so badly. It was no biggie, as Tyler himself would say; just ten minutes of panic; 15 at most. And all he'd done was have the foresight to pick up his phone and bring it.

But it wasn't just that. Though some might consider me wet, I felt his own love very keenly; he was a steady, supportive presence amid the maelstrom of our challenging new child, when he could easily have been a force pulling in the opposite direction, feeling sidelined by Flip's need for my attention.

'Casey, calm *down*!' he said, extricating himself from me.

'Sorry,' I said. 'Sorry. God, I'm just *so* relieved. Where did they find them? Did Riley say?'

He blinked at me. 'Casey, they *haven't*. Well, not as far as I know.' He lifted the phone. And in that instant I realised he hadn't been waving it; it had just been in his hand. I felt another whump of fear in my gut. 'David told me he'd call me if they found them,' he added. 'And he hasn't, but I *have* had a brainstorm. I bet I know where they are, Casey. I *bet*. I bet they're at the stream.' He turned and pointed back where he'd come. 'It just hit me, back then. Going past that little shoe shop. I remember last week. Flip going on about the wellies. Those pink and white spotty ones, remember? The ones like Marley-Mae has?'

I was nodding like a nodding dog on some sort of amphetamine. The *wellies*. Flip saying she wanted the same ones as Marley-Mae had – and which I'd subsequently bought for her. Some rambling story or other that she'd told about jumping in puddles with the next-door neighbour when she was little ... Mrs Hardy, was it? Oh, God ... And her turning to Tyler as we walked home and telling him he should get some new wellies too ... so they could jump in ... oh, *God*. 'The *stream*! Oh, God, Ty,' I said, turning tail and not even bothering to finish the thought off.

138

'And Riley brought Marley-Mae's wellies with her today, didn't she?' he said, falling into step and now jogging along beside me. 'So I just thought … Well, it's logical, isn't it? So I reckon they'll be there. Don't you think?'

But I could only think one thing. One all-consuming thought. That you could drown in two inches of water.

Chapter 13

Tyler was right. Just as we'd belted towards the house again (Mike, Levi and Jackson out front, just in case the girls reappeared there) his mobile buzzed with a text from David. *Got them.*

It had taken us just four minutes to run the distance from the high street back to home and they'd been a terrifying four minutes, too, because it had come to me that what had preceded our unexpectedly balmy weather had been two days of almost biblical quantities of rain. Rain that swelled the stream. Made it run fast. Submerged half the stepping stones. Made it too treacherous to cross.

No wonder, then, that Riley was beside herself. There's no feeling quite so terrifying as the fear that your child might be in danger, no emotion so urgent and raw. And as we started across the park I could see the pink spots blazing on her cheeks from some distance away.

She had Marley-Mae on her hip now. She'd presumably plucked her swiftly away from Flip, who was still clutching Pink Barbie in her hand. I took in both pairs of wellie boots, mud-smeared but present. And while my grand-daughter wriggled and complained (she'd obviously been having a high old time, whatever they'd been up to) I could see Riley was berating Flip for doing something so danger-ous – I could almost make out the words as Tyler and I ran across the grass to them; see the anger in the set of her jaw.

I watched Riley then hand Marley-Mae over to David, and as her daughter kicked and bucked and managed to get mud all down her front – just to compound everything – saw her anger notch up yet another gear. David, ever the calmer presence, hoisted her straight up to his shoulders, from where she could now watch proceedings from her imperial throne.

'Nanna!' she squealed, pointing at me and waving the other chubby arm around. But Riley only had eyes for Flip.

In an ideal world, I think I would have acted differently. In an ideal world, on another day – one unfettered by such heightened emotions – I might have seen things rather more objectively than I did. Might have more readily seen the state Riley had obviously – and understandably – gotten herself into. But the truth was that I, too, was so relieved to see them both safe and well that I couldn't seem to rein myself back into some sort of order – much less take charge and try to calm everything down.

Which was crazy – nothing had happened, no one had been hurt, no harm had evidently been done to anyone, and it wasn't as if I didn't know there were extenuating circum-stances, because I did. Of *course* I did. I'd even been reminded of that fact not a minute and a half earlier, when passing Mike. 'Calm down, love,' he'd said to me, as Tyler and I had hurried past them. 'Panic over. All well. No need to call out the cavalry!'

But such was the power of the adrenaline that was still coursing through me that now I'd seen the girls for myself, rather than pour balm on the close-to-boiling emotional temperature, which was what I should have done, I marched up and joined in.

I couldn't seem to stop myself, and it wasn't just a knee-jerk reaction. There was a conscious part of me involved as well. Every child needed to make the connection between actions and consequences and, in some cock-eyed way, I remember even thinking it was important that Flip make that connection *now*, while the relationship between what she'd done and the implications of it could *really* be impressed upon her, the better to help her think twice before ever doing it again. 'What on earth were you *thinking*, you silly girl!' I barked, echoing Riley's own staccato dressing-down. 'How many times have I *told* you? You must NOT wander off on your own!' I waved towards the sky. 'Look! It's getting dark, Flip! What do you think might have happened to you both if it *had* got dark before we found you? What then, eh? What if you'd got lost and couldn't find your way home? What if one of you had fallen in the *stream*, for heaven's sake?'

Flip's eyes were like milky saucers in the gloom. 'What on earth *possessed* you, Flip?' Riley added. '*Anything* could have happened to you! I can't believe you did something so stupid, Flip! So *dangerous*!' She wheeled around towards David and stabbed a finger in the air. 'Look, she hasn't even got a coat on, for goodness' sake!'

David placed a warm hand over each of his daughter's knees. It was certainly getting cold now the sun was setting. 'Come on,' he said, firmly but mildly, looking at Riley. 'No point standing here, is there, love? Let's head back, shall we?'

I agreed. But, like Riley, I couldn't seem to stop myself berating Flip. Probably because I felt I had to. Not least because relief – and the gathering dark – had brought such a big side-order of fresh guilt. 'Flip, you know how dangerous it is in the wood. In the stream. You *know* all that. What were you *thinking*? And what about *strangers*?' I added, taking her hand, as another horror ambushed me. 'You *know* about strangers. I've *told* you about strangers. I've even told you, when we've been in this very *park*, not to talk to strangers! You could have been picked up, and …' I couldn't even articulate the 'and' part. 'Flip, you must promise me you will never, *ever* do *anything* like this again! I don't know what possessed you, I *really* don't. I –'

'STOP IT!'

The words hit me like a train, such was their strength and authority. But this wasn't David. He'd already started back off across the park ahead of us, little Marley-Mae a bouncing silhouette above his head.

No, it was Tyler, and he said it a second time. 'Casey, *stop* it!'

And it was only then, in the half-light, that I properly took in Flip, whose hand was curled in mine and who had so far said nothing, her only reaction the tears that were silently rolling down both her cheeks. I glanced at Riley. She looked back, then sighed and stomped ahead to David.

She was still furious – still beside herself; I could still feel it radiating from her. She was still unable to speak rationally about it. And she wasn't the only one. I didn't know quite what to say.

Tyler did, though. 'Stop shouting at her,' he said, though he said it quietly. 'You don't even *know* if she went in the stream. You don't *know* if she spoke to any strangers. Can't you just let her *speak*?'

But it seemed she could not. No more than I now could. Not immediately. She could only gaze up at me, wide-eyed and – I could see now – very, very frightened. Tyler put an arm around her, and as he did so I felt her grip loosen in my hand. She kind of fell against him then, allowing herself to be enclosed by his encircling arm, and only now it was obvious – so *blindingly* obvious – that she *was* properly frightened now, of *me*. She leaned up to whisper something in his ear.

'It's all right, Minnie Minx,' he said. 'It's all right. It's *okay*. Everyone's upset, that's all. Course they are. *Shhh*. Come on. No one's going to kill you, silly. Are they, Casey?' Directing those last words to me.

I felt terrible. Punctured. Like a burst balloon at a party. And I still, uncharacteristically, didn't know quite what to say. I was just so struck by how Tyler had leapt to her defence to stop Riley and me shouting at her (and, at the thought, shame washed over me now, as well as guilt). To stop us bludgeoning her with our anger and our raised, ugly voices. 'Flip, *no*. No, of *course* not,' I finally managed to reassure her. 'And I'm sorry I shouted at you,' I added as we left the park and trudged back up our street. 'I didn't mean to shout – like Tyler says, we were all just so *worried* about the pair of you. I know you didn't mean any harm … and I know no harm's been done, either, but you can see why we got upset, can't you? It's …' I stopped then, because I could tell she wasn't really responding – either to me or my excuses. Instead, she was reaching up again as she walked, cupping her free hand round her mouth so she could whisper again to Tyler.

'What?' I said. '*What*, love?' Then to Tyler, 'What's she saying?'

He nodded to Flip before turning to face me. His expression was hard to read in the gathering dusk. His words weren't.

'She said she was just trying to give Riley five minutes' peace,' he answered quietly.

There are always going to be flash points. That's how it works with children – whether they are your own or your own children's or, if you foster, the ones you care for. As an adult, you need to set boundaries on behaviour, which is bound to cause conflict at times. And no one's perfect. None of us are saints; few of us blessed with endless patience and understanding. Most of us are all too aware that there will always be occasions when we fall short of our own standards.

So it was ridiculous for me to keep beating myself up, as Mike had been reminding me all evening. I'd forgotten to lock the door again after Riley and David had arrived – such a simple, forgivable, ordinary mistake – and, with my nerves jangling with terror about what might have happened to Flip and Marley-Mae, I'd overreacted, as had Riley, and we'd both lost our tempers. It wasn't the end of the world. It really wasn't. So, as Mike also said, it was hardly a hanging offence.

But as I lay wide awake in bed at getting on for three in the morning, it still felt like it, almost.

With the day comprehensively hijacked, Riley and David hadn't lingered. We all had a cup of coffee and a de-brief, finished clearing up the dinner things, tried to forget about it, tried to put it to bed, but I knew Riley was still agitated – if I'd felt that terrified, what must have been going through *her* mind? And though she kept telling me not to blame myself, that she should have been more alert to the possibility too, the feeling that I'd let her down just wouldn't seem to go away. Back it came, as it always did, to the question of choices. I'd *chosen* to foster – and, yes, she was choosing to follow in my footsteps and do likewise – and it was a choice that would always have an impact on my family, potentially put my grandchildren at risk.

Then there was Tyler, whose 'Stop it!' still ricocheted around my head, like a stray assassin's bullet. Tyler, who'd been the first and perhaps the only one to take proper stock of the situation. To realise there was no point in shouting at Flip; that, as I'd done on countless occasions with *him*, it was so much better to calm down and find out the reason – because, as had been Mike's and my mantra when we'd got him, there is *always* a reason.

It was also Tyler who'd managed to flesh out the details, Flip having attached herself to him both bodily and emotionally, correctly recognising him as being her best shot at a safe port in the proverbial storm. Wet-cheeked and on his lap now, as we all sat round the conservatory table, she had haltingly explained what had happened.

'She was awake,' she told us. 'Waving her arms about, like this.' She demonstrated with Pink Barbie. 'An' she wanted to get out of her buggy and go and play. An' it was her,' she said, without recrimination. 'It was Marley-Mae who wanted to go and play – "Garden! Garden!" – so as you was all having five minutes' peace out the back, I thought I'd put our wellies on and take her to play in the park instead. An' the woods. But I *knowed* not to play in the water!' she added, hotly. 'I *did*, Mummy,' she added, turning to me. 'Please don't be cross, Mummy! We just went to play to give Riley five minutes' peace!'

Her eyes had pooled with fresh tears and I instinctively reached my arms out to her, but she turned her face from me, and instead burrowed closer into Tyler's chest.

'Which is a *good* thing!' Mike's later words came back to me now too. 'Don't you see? It's a big thing that she's formed a bond with Tyler. It's a *bond*, Case – a real attachment. That thing that she struggles with, remember? Look, I know you feel bad, but try to grab the positive here – she's integrated into the family, and that's a huge thing to happen. It means she's not the lost cause everyone started off thinking she was. It means she *is* capable of forming attachments, of having – what's that thing you're always on about? That's it, empathy. She *does* have empathy. Look how she was with Riley when she went – she looked genuinely sorry for the trouble she'd caused. That's a *big* thing. You've got to be pleased about that, love.'

And, of course, Mike was right, but a 'nearly' thing – a potential terrible thing – leaves a long tail of agitation. Not post-traumatic stress exactly (that would just be melodramatic) but as any parent who has ever mislaid a child for any length of time knows, the horrible, stomach-clenching 'what if' feeling persists, sometimes for hours, sometimes for days, sometimes for years. And if I felt bad about being so cross with Flip, letting Tyler down, having been an idiot for not locking the bloody door, I felt equally bad, if not worse, about Riley – my little girl, who'd had that 'what if' feeling foisted upon her. By me.

Moving as quietly as a mouse – Mike would have to be up for work in less than three hours – I slipped out from beneath the duvet and padded down to the kitchen. My mouth was dry, so I did need to run myself a glass of water, but mostly I wanted to send Riley a text. She wouldn't see it till the morning, I knew, and I'd already apologised, like, five or six times, if not more. But I also I knew I'd sleep better if I did.

I went into the kitchen and closed the door behind me before putting on the light and going across to where my phone sat, beside its charger. I then unlocked the screen, ready to text, and it immediately glowed brightly. One new message. Of the best kind. I felt stupidly tearful.

'It's okay, Mum. Sleep tight. Love you xxx.'

Deep breath. Back to bed. Tomorrow was another day.

Chapter 14

I wrote Sunday's débâcle up in my log the following morning, once both the children were installed in school. I'd tried to put it out of my mind, but once I got under way I realised that sitting down and getting it out of me was cathartic. I scribbled it out in a single lengthy session – barely pausing for breath, really – and as I did so I found I was able to focus much more on the positives. As Mike had kept reminding me, yes, I *could* dwell on the fact that I'd forgotten to lock the front door if I wanted, but wasn't it much more sensible to concentrate on what had been the unexpected silver lining? Which was that not only had Tyler leapt so stoutly to Flip's defence, but that Flip herself had shown she *did* have the ability to form strong attachments; her relationship with Tyler was clearly evidence of that. It was a strong pointer towards that happy state of affairs at the very least, and might make the business of her being fostered long term or adopted a more likely proposition, because it would widen the pool of prospective carers considerably.

Well, I thought, as I finished, that was if finding a long-term carer was still going to be the plan. Which, after the meeting with Megan, and what Debbie had said, it seemed might no longer be the case, a state of affairs I was still turning over in my mind.

And which it seemed had caused someone's ears to be burning – John's. He called me only minutes before I'd pressed 'send' to dispatch the email, and, as per usual, he got straight to the point. 'I'm calling to canvas your opinion,' he told me. 'Your honest opinion. About whether the plans currently in place for Flip should now be put on hold.'

'In terms of seeking a long-term carer?' I asked him. 'No, I'm not sure they should, to be honest. I mean, it's brilliant that Megan's keen to build bridges with Flip, obviously, but I don't know, John. I think I'd still be cautious.'

'That was my thinking too,' he said. 'But you're the one who's toiling at the coal face, so to speak. Though the family support worker – Debbie, isn't it? – was apparently pretty positive about it. And as the most desirable outcome is always going to be to get a child back to the family wherever possible, I think they're keen to give it the best shot they can.'

I had thought long and hard about my conversation with Debbie after the meeting, and had been slightly shocked to find myself so full of reservations. I didn't want to be a cynic – *ever* – but I'd been round the block enough to know that, even with the best will in the world, leopards didn't change their spots that often. And if repeated, such a cycle of acceptance and rejection could have really damaging and negative repercussions on Flip's progress, which would be a terrible shame now she was making some at last.

That said, this was her mother, and if she was genuine in her remorse, who was I to cast doubt? 'I don't know, John ...' I began.

'Thought that might be the case,' he answered immediately. 'So how are you fixed if I try to get a meeting organised for tomorrow or Wednesday? Megan is apparently pressing for another contact visit – later this week if possible – and I think everyone is keen to make a decision on where we think we're going with this before it takes place.'

'Of course,' I said. 'Here?'

'Only if you're particularly keen to. Might be easier to have it at the agency offices, since Megan's social worker knows where we are. Her name's Hayley Groves, by the way. Have you come across her?'

'The name's not familiar. But that's not to say our paths haven't crossed at some conference or seminar or suchlike. How does *she* feel? Do you know? She presumably knows Megan better than anyone else in the equation.'

'Sadly not,' John corrected. 'She's new to the area. Was only assigned her caseload in the last couple of weeks. Though there'll be notes, of course ...'

And we both knew how often notes told you almost nothing. Or, in some cases, led you barking up entirely the wrong tree. 'Blind leading the blind then,' I joked.

John laughed. 'Yup. That's about the size of it.'

* * *

In theory, a person with a long history with social services would have a comprehensive record that would follow them wherever they went, which would aid those responsible for supporting them or, in some cases, having to make decisions about removing their children, sometimes permanently.

In reality, however, the system wasn't perfect; sometimes there were gaps in a person's history; other times their file was stuffed full to bursting. And it could work both ways. A person keen to turn their life around could be dogged by a lack of a joined-up history to support them or equally dogged by a long tail of damning accounts, which could so easily colour how they were viewed in the present.

I'd not been much involved with social workers who supported adults, as it was the social workers attached to children with whom I tended to form the closest relationships, obviously, but I certainly knew, through my connections with them, that a bad history could follow a child around like a bad smell. That had very much been the case with Justin, the first child we'd ever fostered, and such negative baggage accompanying a child – not to mention the information black holes – had been a feature of my working life ever since. As it would be; after all, when money is tight, no system is ever going to be perfect.

It was worth remembering. I certainly had to be mindful of how little I really knew about Megan before putting in my sixpence worth.

When I got ready for our meeting, which we'd arranged for the Wednesday, that was the thing that was uppermost in my mind; that I must avoid trying to pre-judge what

Megan might do in the future, based on hearsay about what she'd done before.

I buttoned up my blouse – for some reason, a meeting in an office always meant I felt obliged to truss myself up in 'office' clothes – and wondered if Megan's social worker was trying to do the same, when deciding whether to run with Megan's assertion that she was keen to make amends and sort her drinking out.

I knew Debbie was keen to accept that she was – at least for the moment – but what about Ellie? What was her take? I realised I had no idea. Which meant going into the meeting without a clue what the outcome of it might be. 'Which is surely the best way, isn't it?' Mike had counselled before leaving for work that morning. 'If no one goes in with their minds already made up, you've surely got the best chance of reaching a rational decision?'

Which was absolutely right. But even so, I felt I should at least have a position. Did I feel Flip would be better off with her mother or didn't I?

But as it turned out, it was a position that I wasn't going to have to voice – well, not in person, anyway. I'd just run into the kitchen for a last slurp of coffee when John called to let me know that Hayley Groves was running late, as she'd had to deal with an emergency removal of a child out of town and was unlikely to be back till after lunch.

'So we're talking about rescheduling for 3 p.m., instead,' John explained. 'Which I realise won't work very well for you, will it? But I think we're all agreed we need to get this sorted today, because there's another contact visit to sched-ule for this week, isn't there?'

John was right. It wouldn't work for me. I had the school run to do and, though I could ask Riley to pick Flip up for me and take her home to hers, I'd already promised to pick Tyler and Denver up and drive them to a football match at another school. Which I couldn't ask Riley to do as she wouldn't have room in her car.

'That's fine,' I said, decided. 'Go ahead without me and report back. You know my feelings on the matter anyway.'

'Optimistic but *extremely* cautious,' John said. 'That's about the size of it, isn't it?'

'With emphasis on the "extremely" bit,' I said, unbuttoning the hated blouse. Which was some compensation.

At the centre of all this, of course, was Flip. Flip who, when told Debbie would be coming the following afternoon to take her to see her mum again, responded firstly with a non-committal shrug, closely followed by a whoop. 'D'you think she'll bring me the Barbie horse? That'll be epic!'

The news from the meeting was also much as I'd expected, the consensus being that it made sense to take Megan at face value; to trust in her assertion that she wanted to work towards getting Flip back – a process that could (and *should*) take several months, during which regular contact between mother and daughter would be put in place.

Of course, while this was happening, there'd be no search for a long-term family, but, provided we were happy – which we were – we'd continue with the programme, working with Flip on all the aspects in which her childhood had been deficient while, at the same time, Megan's social worker worked alongside *her*, supporting her in learning the skills she'd be required to have in order to become a better parent – and that she stayed off the drink obviously being a given.

So perhaps the future looked more rosy than I'd previously imagined. And when Debbie returned with Flip it seemed clear to both of us that Megan *had* made an effort with Flip. No, she hadn't bought a horse, but she had bought some felt tips and a Disney Princess book for colouring in. 'An' I told her I'd do one for her and take it next week,' she explained. ''Cos she's in a horrible flat with mould on the walls.'

Be that as it may, things felt positive – and Flip herself seemed positive. So perhaps I shouldn't have been so quick to fear the worst. It had obviously had an effect, that enforced stay in hospital; at least sobered Megan up sufficiently (as far as everybody assumed, anyway) for her to be able to see her situation more clearly. And, who knew, perhaps that line in the sand Debbie had alluded to had been drawn after all. Perhaps, sobered up and faced with the reality that she might have lost her, she realised how much she loved Flip after all.

But, whatever else was true (and we all really wanted it to be true, of course) there was one truth that was inescapable: we'd just have to wait and see how things panned out. In the meantime, it would be full steam ahead now, trying to build on what had been started and, who knew, it might well be her own mother Flip ended up being placed with when Mike and I had done what we could with her. So it was a case of sleeves up and make progress, on both the home and the school fronts – or rather, try and build on the progress already made. Because on both fronts it seemed she was doing okay.

Life can be a tease like that, though, can't it? Which is why the quote – that it's what happens while you're busy making other plans – is one of my favourites. It was definitely the case that my notion of 'okay', in *this* case, was misinformed. It was around 11 on the Friday morning when I got the call from Ellie. I'd been out and about since dropping Flip at school, on an errand for my mum collecting some parcels from the post office that she'd ordered for Christmas. It was a stark reminder that, even though we were almost into November, I hadn't so much as given a thought to Christmas as yet.

I'd just put my key in the front door when my mobile buzzed. 'Ah, you're there!' Ellie said. 'I tried the landline, but no joy. Sorry, is this a good time to chat? I wondered if you might already be up at the school.'

'At the school?' I said, pushing the door open and dropping my bag on the hall floor the better to speak to her. 'No, not at this time. I've not long dropped Flip off. I've been round at my parents. Why? Is something up?'

'Ah,' she said. 'So you've not had the email then?'

I was still stuck on why she'd thought I'd already be at school. Forget home time. It wasn't even lunchtime yet. And Flip didn't come home for lunch. 'What email?' I asked her, confused now.

'The email from Mr Stancliffe?' she said. 'Last night?'

The penny dropped. So *that* was why she thought I might be up at school. But that didn't answer why she thought I might have gone there in the first place. 'Nope,' I said. 'Should I have?'

'Or a phone call, at any rate. He said he was going to be calling you.'

I glanced automatically, then, to see what the house phone might have to say for itself. Sure enough, the LED display was winking the number 1 at me. Which meant one message, which meant a missed call. 'Why do I suddenly feel as if I'm not going to like what I hear next?' I asked Ellie, with a sinking feeling. 'Go on. Tell me the worst. What's happened? What's she done?'

It was at that point that the penny should have dropped even further. But it didn't. I was too fixated on what I *thought* I'd be hearing – an account of some sort of incident in the classroom or the playground. Some altercation, or tantrum or accident – I truly hoped not an accident – which, whatever the details, would mean a step back in progress, and the loss of some precious points on Flip's chart. Which was a stupid thing to think, once I thought about it properly. Since when did schools inform parents and guardians of such incidents via email?

'Ah,' Ellie said again, and I could hear the re-calibration in her voice. 'Ah, that's just it,' she went on. 'It's not so much a "what's she done?" situation. It's more a "what are we going to do with her" kind of thing.' She paused then, as if in thought. 'You know, I can't believe you didn't get the email. He said he was going to phone you, but I'm almost certain sure he also copied you in. In fact, I *know* he did. I remember seeing your email address there. Typical!'

Ellie's frustration at this digital hiccup was genuine but misplaced. I could hear Kieron's voice in my ear as it began to sink in properly that Flip's headmaster had sent an email and I'd yet to read it. 'Mum, that's the whole *point* of having a smartphone. So you can access the internet! Go on Facebook! Go on Twitter! Check *your emails*!' As far as Kieron was concerned I had no business rattling around with a smartphone in the first place. Not if the 'smart' bit was never deployed. In his eyes, it was a crime against technology itself. One possibly punishable by excommunication.

'But I don't want to check my emails every five minutes!' I'd bleated. 'Why would I want to do that?' And all sorts of stuff along the same lines; lectures about work–life balance and how important it was for one's soul.

'He might well have emailed me,' I told Ellie now. 'In fact, I'm sure he did. It's just that I've not checked my inbox since yesterday. Anyway, *what* email? Why did he email? What did he say? Why is it a "what are we going to do with her" situation?'

Ellie sighed. 'You want the short answer?'

'If I have to,' I said, the sinking feeling now going into free fall.

'Okay. So, they're excluding her,' she said.

'*Excluding* her?'

"Fraid so. As of the end of today.'

'But it's half-term next week!' I blurted out, before my brain could catch up with my mouth, the question I *should* have been asking obviously being 'why?'.

'Exactly,' Ellie said. 'They thought if they did it today it would be the least disruptive option. They were thinking of you, at least – thinking you'd have already been expecting to have her home next week anyway. I'll give him that. He was keen not to put you out too much, and it'll at least give us time … Look, since you've not read the email, maybe it's better that you go away and do so. Not that there's much in it –'

I was still a step behind. 'What *is* in it? *Why* are they excluding her? What's she done?'

'He doesn't really say, Casey. It's just been delivered as something of a *fait accompli*. That they've had a meeting with the governors' – I groaned – 'and they've given it a good deal of thought,' she carried on, 'They just feel – this is pretty much all he says, really – that they are "not able to fully meet her needs". That's the nub of it. But I'm sure his plan was to clarify everything on the phone to you. Have you up to school to discuss it. Go into more detail.'

'Too bloody right!' I said, feeling myself beginning to bristle; now it was properly sinking in, I couldn't stop myself. How could they exclude Flip just like that? Without any warning? And more to the point, why hadn't I had any inkling things were anything but fine?

But I was getting ahead of myself. If the message on the answerphone *was* from Mr Stancliffe, what I really needed to do was call him back and find out for myself what was going on.

'I know,' Ellie soothed. 'Which is why I was ringing. I'm going to get onto the school myself now and see if I can get them to change their minds.' She laughed. 'I have a right of appeal and I fully intend to use it! Well, I'm not sure I really have anything that fancy, but I'm definitely going to ask them to reconsider. Because if they don't I'm not sure what else we're going to do with her. Not in the short term, anyway. You know what it's like with places in special schools.'

'Indeed I do,' I said grimly. 'The words "hens" and "teeth" spring to mind.'

'Exactly,' Ellie said. 'Which is why I'm going to be bull-ish. It'll take a miracle for anywhere to be found for her this side of Christmas – locally, anyway. And the last thing anyone wants is for us to have to move her out of the area. Not now she's settled with you and definitely not when there's a chance of her going back to mum. So I'll do my best, okay? Tell you what. Why don't you go and read the email, and in the meantime I'll get onto the school and see what I can do. I'll call you back, okay? Just as soon as I can. In the meantime, best start praying for that miracle.'

Chapter 15

The miracle didn't happen. Well, not that day, anyway. Ellie did her best, but Mr Branchlite was like the proverbial mountain. He was sympathetic, but he wasn't going to be moved.

'I'm sorry,' he told me, when I called him myself, after Ellie had tried her best and got nowhere and I'd decided to at least see how the land lay. 'I know it's going to cause you all sorts of headaches,' he went on. 'But it's not a decision we've reached lightly, as I'm sure you'll appreciate.'

I could tell how the land lay just hearing his tone. It was barren and hilly and impassable. A major blow. I'd still been clinging on to the hope that I could persuade him to give Flip a second chance; that once half-term was over he could perhaps be persuaded to give things another go – especially if I played my ace: the Ritalin card. It had come to me suddenly that maybe that was key; that if I could persuade Dr Shakelton that Flip needed to return to it, she might prove more manageable by the time school went back.

I was clutching at straws and I knew it. The whole point of trying her without the drug was that its benefit to her was questionable. But I felt so keenly that this new disruption to her life could be catastrophic, given everything, that it seemed a risk worth taking. If it kept her in school – which she loved – surely it would be worth it?

But it seemed the question of whether Flip was medicated or not was largely irrelevant. No, there were other forces at work, mostly of a political variety. The school was full to bursting, it had inadequate trained staff and pressure was being brought to bear to ensure precious resources were allocated in ways that benefited all the pupils, which meant a child like Flip was essentially getting more than her 'share', by remaining in the nurture group, and there was no way she could be moved on to a regular class. One thing seemed clear: this was about policy more than particulars, and though I couldn't lay the blame at whichever governor had been most vocal about it I got the sense (partly from Mr Stancliffe's apologetic tone) that there was a strong lobby of the opinion that complicated children such as Flip should be educated in separate, specialist schools.

Which took us back to when we'd taken her and Mr Stancliffe's original words – that they would make no promises, but rather take her in on trial basis and 'see how things went'. And, to my dismay, it now seemed the trial was over, leaving me to break the news to Flip as best I could.

* * *

'Yesssssss!' she whooped, thundering down the stairs on the Monday morning, causing me to wonder quite how I'd deal with her surfeit of energy once we lost the routine of school every day. And for how long? Ellie's estimate of 'early in the New Year' seemed a world away. 'Half-term! Half-term! Half-terrrrrrmmmm!' she chanted, bowling into the living room, Pink Barbie swinging from her hand, in search of Tyler.

Our adopted son was currently sprawled on the rug in front of the television, watching *iCarly*. It was a programme I'd assumed was for teenage girls, but had been assured by Kieron – who knew all about such things through his youth work – that *everyone* young loved *iCarly* (Kieron dealt in absolutes only) whatever their gender.

Tyler had grown a good two or three inches in the last couple of months, and was wolfing down food at a terrifying rate of knots. He'd grown lanky, too – a long streak of tawny adolescent limbs. He was growing up and I was expecting his voice to break at any minute. And then he really would start breaking hearts.

Flip aimed a toe in his direction and batted him lightly on the shin, then straddled him and sat down on his back. He growled at her, though mildly. His tolerance with her was a joy to watch. 'Gerroff me, you madhead!' he told her, wriggling to shake her off. And, presumably finding the TV show not to her liking, she quickly obliged, turning her attention to the kitchen and me.

With no school run to do, I was still in my pyjamas, operating on a temporary 'can't beat them, join them' philosophy, which I knew would last for no more than a day. Flip skipped across and slung both arms around my middle. 'Half-term!' she said brightly, as if it was a newly discovered gem. Which perhaps it was, because we'd already made all sorts of standard half-term plans, all of which were fallen upon in raptures. 'Going swimming?' 'Going bowling?' 'Going to feed the ducks in the park?' Each suggestion was greeted with rapt, wide-eyed wonderment – as if I'd told her we were going to Disneyland every day. It tugged – really tugged – at my heartstrings to know how little everyday childish joy she'd had in her young life.

'You want something cooked, sweetie, or just cereal?' I asked her.

'I'm a madhead!' she told me, ignoring the question. 'Look, Mummy! I'm a madhead!' She shook her head wildly, to demonstrate.

'You'll be seeing stars if you keep on like that,' I told her.

'But I am!' she persisted. 'Look at my madhead, being mad!'

I smiled and leant down to plant a kiss on her cheek. 'Yes, I think you are, lovey, but you're an adorable little madhead. Now plonk your bottom on that chair and I'll get you some breakfast. So, which is it to be? An egg, perhaps? Cereal? Or how about some porridge?'

'Ooh yes!' she said. 'Porridge, porridge, porridge! We love porridge! And lots of that sticky stuff in it, please.'

I sorted out Flip's breakfast largely on auto-pilot, while she rattled on about this, that and everything in between. Chief among my own musings – and I felt terrible for it – was the one thing that had weighed heavily since I'd spoken to Mr Stancliffe; that no school meant being around her

24/7, and, with the best will in the world I wasn't sure how that would pan out without me needing medicating too.

For all that their decision to exclude Flip had dismayed me, I had sympathy for the ever-patient, gentle Miss Carter. I could see it in her face when I'd gone to collect Flip that afternoon and, having sent her off to help another child look for some gloves, in her voice, as she expressed her reluctance to let her go. 'It's just …' she'd begun. 'Well, you know what she's like. And much as I'd love to give her all my attention, I have all the other children … I'm so, so sorry,' she finished. And I believed her. Not to mention getting an inkling that perhaps she was toeing a line; that the decision to let Flip go hadn't been one she'd approved.

But perhaps the school was right. Perhaps the governors had a point. Perhaps Flip did need to be in a school for children with special needs, where the staff-to-pupil ratio was better. And it was complex because, on its own, FAS wouldn't be such a problem. I knew that, because I'd read up on it extensively; lots of FAS children were educated at normal schools. But add in the ADHD, the anxiety, the mood swings, the volatility, and, in fairness, the school did have a point. Looking after Flip put me a little in mind of having one of those life-like, computer-programmed, demanding baby dolls; the ones they gave teenage girls to look after for a weekend, to remind them just how bad an idea it would be to have unprotected sex.

But there was no more handing Flip back on Monday mornings. I put her porridge in front of her – Tyler, up early, had already eaten – and hoped either John or Ellie *could* magic up a miracle, because the prospect of having

Flip by my side morning, noon and night was one that already felt too much to cope with, not without some sort of back-up. And it wasn't just to alleviate the extra work-load heaped upon me; it was because an eight-year-old child really needed to be in school. She needed to learn and be stimulated and have her monumental levels of energy directed.

There was also the not inconsiderable matter of Tyler, who needed my attention as well. He needed to feel impor-tant too; deserved to have a bit more of us, not feel pushed aside by the constant clamour of Flip's needs. So, as Flip slurped her porridge, I made a mental list. I would call the surgery and ask for an appointment with Dr Shakelton, so I could ask if he thought our 'no meds' trial had gone on long enough. I'd then telephone John and ask him for some help. It might well be that miracles did happen and that a school could be found swiftly, but I was too much of a real-ist to expect that to happen, so it made sense to get support sooner rather than later. This week would be fine; with all the kids around there would be plenty to keep Flip occu-pied – including a third visit to see her mother – but after that, if she and I were to be rattling round while everyone else was in school, then I knew it would be nigh on essential for both of us for a support worker – Debbie, hopefully – to take her out a couple of times a week on top of that, so I could recharge for a few hours and have some valuable time with Tyler.

'Oh, and she said she'd get me a brand *new* Barbie! Isn't that amazing, Mummy? One with *extra*-long hair! *Mummy*!' Flip whined. 'Are you even *listening*?'

I belatedly realised she'd been rattling on for a while, which was another thing; this tendency I was developing to unconsciously tune out, lost in my thoughts while she twittered on thirteen to the dozen. It was a bad habit to get into and I mentally berated myself for it.

'I'm sorry, love,' I said, checking myself. 'What?'

She sighed melodramatically. 'I *said*. I said that my *old* mummy is going to buy me a *new* magical Barbie, with hair that comes down all the way to her bottom!'

'Is that right?' I said, wondering at Megan's motivation to keep promising her daughter all this booty. Money was obviously tight, so why promise what she couldn't deliver? Without the expectation, the colouring book and pens would have been more than enough.

'Yes,' Flip said irritably. 'So she can be friends with Pink Barbie. Pink Barbie's lonely. She has no friends in the world 'cept for me. Poor Barbie,' she cooed, stroking the doll's shorn head.

With all the drama of Friday's revelations, I'd been somewhat preoccupied, but it now occurred to me that Flip had really said very little about her last contact visit, either positive or negative. As with most things in her life, it seemed to be just another 'thing'; a new routine, which, this second time, she'd soon seemingly assimilated – more concerned about the promises of burgers and dollies than with the fact that she was bonding once again with her mum. It was almost as if she'd put her in an 'old mummy' box. And once she'd closed it and returned home, she could get on with her week. She'd not so much as looked at the colouring book since she'd brought it home.

'That's nice, love,' I said as I picked up her bowl.

She sighed a second time. 'Mummy, it's not *nice*. It's *epic*!'

It seemed Megan didn't want to remain in her box too long, however, my call to John throwing up at least one new activity: the promised third contact visit. He'd been about to call me to arrange it when I'd phoned. 'Is Thursday okay again?' he wanted to know. 'Only I think the plan is for them to get into some sort of regular routine.'

'I'm all for that,' I told him. 'Would she like it to be twice a week, by any chance?' He laughed.

'Seriously, Casey,' he said. 'I will bring *huge* pressure to bear re the school situation. I know how all this is going to impact on you, and I'll make sure social services do too. We both know how these things can drift once we start heading towards Christmas.'

I groaned. 'Don't even *mention* the C word,' I told him sternly.

He laughed even more. 'What, to *you*?' he asked incredulously. 'The little Christmas elf made flesh? You've got the C word running through like a stick of Blackpool rock,' he said. 'With added fairy lights!'

'Hmm, well, yes,' I said, smiling despite myself. 'And I dare say I'll be getting into the Christmas spirit at some point and start decking the halls. But right now all I can see is me climbing up them!'

'Message received and understood,' he said. 'Promise. Anyway, can I call Debbie and let her know she can pick Flip up on Thursday? Say around 3.30? By the way, what's the school position? Does she know she's not going back yet? How do you think she's going to react?'

I told John yes to the pick-up, then 'no' and then 'I don't know'. Because the truth was that I had no idea how Flip would react. All I had was the strong conviction that I shouldn't rush to spell it out to her that she'd been excluded from school. Why give her an anxiety to deal with that she could do nothing about? And who knew? Perhaps a suitable school with a vacancy would appear out of the ether, just at the point when I couldn't pretend any more.

I didn't think that would happen, but it might. And if it didn't, so be it. I'd tell her, with Mike, at some point on the Sunday and we'd just have to roll with the fall-out. One thing was for sure, though: that I would couch it in terms that made it easier to digest. Because the last thing I wanted was for her to feel rejected. She'd had enough of that to last her a lifetime. And in that sense the visit to see mum was a real plus, however reluctant I was to join in with the general optimism about the possibility of Flip returning home down the line.

Down the line wasn't today, though, and with my list complete I came off the phone feeling quite chipper. I could have kissed John, in fact, for being so reliably reassuring and helpful, which was ridiculous; when had he ever not been? But that's just how I am – sometimes I hate to ask for help, even though it's available, and I know how my reluctance to get some can pan out; and sometimes you don't realise just how tired you are until it's too late.

Which was not going to happen, because my team were on the ball, and even if we did have a gap between schools I knew I could handle it.

I looked across into the living room where both Tyler and Flip were now sprawled, side by side, noting that Flip had obviously talked him into changing channels, because we were now back with cartoons. They both had their lower legs up, feet crossed at the ankles, and looked just like a scene out of a children's storybook. The sort of storybook where the kids go on 'adventures' rather than just play, always accompanied by a small dog and lashings of lemonade.

I couldn't help with the dog, and I wasn't sure I had any lemonade, but it was crisp and dry out and the week might as well be got under way.

'Right,' I called. 'First one dressed gets to choose what we have for tea! And that includes me …' I added, as the pair of them scrambled up from in front of the telly and almost cannoned into me as we all made a bolt for the stairs.

'Where are we off to?' Tyler wanted to know as he deftly slipped past me, via the underhand tactic of yanking on the back of my dressing gown.

'Branch and twig gathering,' I said, having only just settled upon it. 'It's Bonfire Night next week and I've just decided we're going to have one in the back garden.'

'Yeah, right,' Tyler laughed, as he darted into his bedroom. 'Like Mike's *really* going to let you do that and ruin his lawn.'

'You just leave Mike to me,' I called, diving into my own room to grab some leggings and an old hoodie of Mike's to throw over my head. 'Flip? How are you doing in there? Chop chop!'

She was first out, having opted just to put her clothes over her pyjamas. Which showed great initiative, so I over-ruled Tyler's appeal. Which wasn't a huge one in any case, because she immediately chose my homemade chicken curry, exactly what he would have chosen himself.

'Will we be chop-chopping all the trees in the woods down?' Flip asked excitedly.

I shook my head. 'No, you silly sausage,' I said. 'Chop chop means hurry up.'

'Ah,' she said, the penny dropping 'So chop chop's a spression.'

'*Ex*pression, you noodle,' Tyler corrected, as was his way.

'I know what a spression is,' she said, batting him with Barbie. 'I know because we do spressions with Miss Carter at school. She always says to get your skates on when we don't have any skates. An' guess what, Mummy?'

'What, love?'

'I really love Miss Carter. She says I'm special 'cos I'm jet propelled, and *that's* a spression too.'

Miss Carter, who Flip would probably now never see again. Well, except fleetingly, in the playground, if I was picking up the boys.

I swallowed a sigh. Just like ships that passed in the night. Another 'spression' to throw into the mix.

Chapter 16

'She didn't turn up.'

It was Thursday afternoon and I'd literally just walked in the door; I had actually been in the act of closing it behind me when I saw Debbie Scott's car pull up outside, a full hour before I was expecting her. And that was because it had been less than an hour since I'd waved her off.

Flip had already pushed past her, apparently desperate for the loo, her expression telling me little. But with her still close by in the cloakroom, Debbie took care to keep her voice down.

'I'm sorry,' she said. 'Were you just heading out? Only I can call you later with a debrief, if you prefer.'

I shook my head. 'I've just got in. I just dropped Tyler round his friend's house.'

Debbie frowned apologetically. 'So you were hoping for five minutes' peace, no doubt. God, I'm sorry. How typical is that?'

I wasn't sure five minutes' peace was a term I'd look at in quite the same way again – not since the last débâcle with

Flip. 'No, it's fine,' I told Debbie. 'But go on – just a no-show? No call or anything? No explanation?'

'Nope,' she said. 'Nothing. Though Flip doesn't know that. Once we'd been waiting 40 minutes I ordered her some food, then feigned a call –'

'You don't have a number for Megan then?'

'Sadly not. Well, there's a number, but it's a friend's phone – she's never got any credit on hers, apparently. I did try it. But no joy. And no voicemail to leave a message on either. So I pretended to take a call –' She lowered her voice further. 'Pretended it was from the office. And then told Flip her mum had had to go to the dentist's because a filling had fallen out. Hope that's okay. First plausible thing that popped into my head. It just seemed better – well, you know. Than leaving her dangling.'

'Yes, yes, that's fine,' I said, impressed by her quick thinking but also aware of the sound of the toilet flushing behind me. 'Really. And full marks for such inventiveness. Flip,' I added, turning towards the closed door just down the hall. 'Don't you forget to wash your hands, okay?' There was a muffled 'Ok*ayyy*', then I turned back to Debbie. 'So what now? I'm assuming someone will try and get hold of her?'

She nodded. 'I'll call the office once I'm back in the car. Course, it could be that there's a perfectly good reason – you never know. Perhaps even the dentist! But ...'

'But on the *other* hand ...' I finished for her, knowing we were both thinking the same thing.

'Precisely,' she said. 'So we'll just have to wait and see. I'll call and let you know as soon as I hear what's going on.

Later on this evening, with any luck. And let's hope the excuse is credible.'

Flip emerged at that point, waving wet hands in my direction. 'Towels carry bacterias,' she announced to both of us. 'Did you know that?'

I couldn't help but smile, trying to work out where she might have heard that. 'Not my towels,' I told her. 'They wouldn't dare. Go on – go back and dry those hands off properly.'

In answer – or rather not, as was her way much of the time – she put a hand on each hip first, and harrumphed. 'Did Debbie tell you about Mummy?' she asked. 'And her fallen out tooth?' She sighed again, theatrically, and tipped her head to one side. 'Typical! So I've *still* got no horse!'

Debbie called around nine the next morning, just after we'd finished clearing away breakfast, with the news that Megan had been in touch with her social worker first thing.

'Mix-up with the dates,' she said. 'Well, apparently. She thought it was today.'

'Really?' I asked her, sceptical. My antennae had been twitching ever since Flip had come home and the long silence subsequently had done nothing to still them. Not that Flip seemed that bothered. She'd still had the biggest burger on the planet *and* an ice cream. As she'd kept telling Tyler all night.

'It's plausible,' Debbie said. 'Because there was some discussion. What with half-term and all, I did mention preferring to do it today rather than yesterday – my mum usually has the kids for me and she had something on.'

'But it was definitely arranged for Thursday?'

'Oh, yes. I called back to confirm it. As it turned out, my two had been invited to a party anyway. So, yes, definitely rearranged, and Hayley called me back to confirm it once she'd called and confirmed with Megan. But I guess we have to give her the benefit of the doubt.'

I guessed we did too. Which was not to say I necessarily believed it. Well, that I necessarily believed it was a simple mistake. No, there would be a complicating factor – there invariably was. Was that complicating factor to do with alcohol?

'Anyway, *can* she do the same time this afternoon?' Debbie asked me. I didn't see why not, so we went through the routine once again. And this time Megan *did* show, albeit late.

We were once again on the doorstep, and I had a keen sense of déjà vu, only this time, as Flip was right there, her hand clutched in Debbie's, there was little opportunity to find out very much. 'Just 15 or 20 minutes or so,' she said, keeping it light. 'So you had another ice cream, for being so patient, didn't you, chick?'

But Flip wasn't to be mollified.

'Yes, but she *still* hasn't brunged my horse!' she huffed crossly.

With no horse on the horizon, and Sunday night looming, I had half a mind to jump in the car and go and buy one myself. Anything, I'd decided, that might help the medicine go down. What I'd have given to snap my fingers like

Mary Poppins and have it sorted. It wasn't a conversation I was looking forward to at all.

I'd suggested as much to Riley on the Saturday morning. 'It might sweeten the pill just a little bit, mightn't it?' I'd said as the two of us mooched around the shops with Marley-Mae, Mike and Tyler, bless them, having elected to take both Flip and the boys off to football.

'Have you any idea what they cost, Mother?' she said, laughing. 'But seeing as you're obviously flush, tell you what, while you're at it, d'you think you could throw in a bottle of Chanel No. 5 for me?'

We'd laughed, and, in truth, it would have been ridiculous for us to get the horse for Flip, the whole point being that the flipping animal was supposed to be a part of the bonding process with her mum – however inappropriate such blatant bribery might be.

But having to tell Flip she wasn't going back to school was one of those jobs I just had to do. So I needed to get on with it. Heaven knew, I'd imparted worse news over the years.

It was early evening. And Tyler – who we'd already briefed – had nabbed the bathroom. He was keen to watch one of the motorway cop shows with Mike, once he was in his PJs, which would leave us upstairs, and me able to sit Flip down and explain why we didn't need to get her uniform out ready.

I did have one sweetener. I might not have bought the eye-wateringly expensive horse but I did bag a bargain; I'd nabbed an eye-popping candy-pink Barbie bed-set in the market, which she was helping me put on her bed while Tyler showered.

'This is epic, Mummy,' she said, once we'd wrestled the duvet into the cover and popped the pillowcase on. 'I'll be snug as a bug in a rug in this, won't I?'

'You will indeed,' I agreed. 'You'll be a snuggled ruggled bug!'

She giggled, and it struck me as it did every time that the business of beauty was such a sad and shallow thing. It was a truism precisely because it was true; the impostor we called beauty really *was* skin deep, and you didn't have to look far to see that the real beauty lay within, because a face was a movable, malleable thing that could be transformed entirely by the emotions that controlled it. And Flip's, at that moment, was joyful to behold; her obvious delight in such a simple thing infectious.

'Can I go straight to bed?' she asked, throwing herself on it.

'Not just yet, poppet,' I told her. 'You've still not had your bath.'

She wriggled off the bed again and dashed across the landing. 'Ty, chop chop! It's bath-time for *me* now!' she yelled before trotting back and plonking herself back down on the duvet. 'I've membered,' she added. 'I'm going to tell Miss Carter about chop chop. An' snug as a bug in a rug.' She paused. 'And … hmm, what's that other one about bugs you learned me, Mummy?'

I sat down beside her and put my arm around her shoulder. 'It's "Night night, sleep tight, don't let the bed-bugs bite." Remember. But listen, sweetie,' I added, squeezing her arm and holding her tighter. 'There's something important I have to tell you.'

With hindsight, Flip responded exactly as I'd imagined. With shock and confusion – why wasn't she allowed back? Had she done something naughty? Then tears because she wouldn't be able to put on her uniform, then, slowly but surely, with her own inalienable logic. Because, just like her old mummy (her current interest in rekindling relationships forgotten), Miss Carter no longer loved her. She no longer loved her because she was ugly.

Where to start? How did you explain to an eight-year-old child that decisions made by schools and governors were not about love, but about politics. About policy and expediency and other things like that? Difficult, with the best will in the world. For Flip, that touch more challenged than most eight-year-olds, impossible. School was Miss Carter; everything else was peripheral. Miss Carter, who'd loved her and now didn't love her. Why else wouldn't she want her in her class?

'Sweetheart,' I consoled as she wriggled and railed against me, 'Miss Carter *does* love you. You know what she said to me? She said she was so sad, because she knew she'd miss you terribly. But just like you must go and clean your teeth when I ask you, Miss Carter has to do what she's told as well, and –'

'*You* told her to do it?' she gasped, pulling away from me. '*You* did?'

I cursed myself. What an idiotic choice of analogy to use! I gathered her up again and held her very tight. 'No, no, no, Flip! Of *course* not! I would never do that! It was the school. The group of people who are in charge of running the whole school. They had a meeting, and in that meeting they all discussed it and agreed that they aren't the best place to bring out the *very* best in you. They think you'll do even better – because you're already doing so well, *so* well – in a school where there are lots less children to look after, and your new teacher – who will *also* be lovely and who'll be *so* happy to have you – will be able to spend so much more time with *just* you.'

'But Miss Carter spends loads of time with me, Mummy. She does! She calls me her little shadow and says I'm her little mini-me!'

I felt a lump rise in my throat, visualising Miss Carter saying exactly that. Knowing all too well what realities lay behind those words. That there was only one Miss Carter and, fond though I knew she was of Flip, I also knew how hard it must be for her to give *all* her kids attention with a child as full-on as Flip in her care. How could she possibly be moved to a regular class?

'I know, popper, I know,' I said. 'But she also wants what's best for you. And what's best – what they decided at their meeting at school – is for you to go to a new school that's just right for *you*.'

'Tomorrow?' She was suddenly animated. 'Have you got me a special uniform?'

'No, not tomorrow,' I said gently. 'It's going to be a few weeks yet. Ellie's working on it right now and being very, *very* thorough. Because she's spoken to Miss Carter so she knows exactly what you'd like, and she's not going to rest until she's found one that's perfect. So, for a bit, you're going to stay at home and be my little shadow. Same as always, but in the daytimes as well as the nights and weekends.'

I planted a kiss on her head and waited while she sat and digested it, conscious of Tyler emerging from the bathroom and hovering by the door, his expression questioning. I blew a kiss in his direction and mouthed the word 'okay' at him, feeling a familiar rush of love at his concern. It must be hard for him, I reasoned, all this emotional upset. He was secure in our love, I knew, but when life deals you cruel blows in early childhood, as his had, I think it's hard to feel truly emotionally secure, and I knew it was a journey that was still ongoing.

I felt Flip pull against me. Her face was wet with tears. 'I just thought,' she said, her chin puckering. 'I just remembered something. What about my *drawer*?'

'Your drawer? Oh, you mean your pencil case and everything? Don't worry, poppet, we can fetch that tomorrow. I tell you what else,' I began, blessed by a sudden inspiration, 'how about our first project tomorrow is to make Miss Carter a card?' Come to that, I suddenly realised, why couldn't I get some proper structured work for her? Find out what they'd been working on and continue some of it at home? *Christ, Casey Watson*, I told myself sternly. *You spent all those years working in school with challenged children. Get your act together. Make a plan. Sort her out!*

But Flip had dissolved into hot distressed tears again. 'My picture!' she wailed. 'My picture that's not done yet! My picture of fireworks! It's hung on the peg on the string at the ceiling to dry out over half-term so it isn't all soggy! And now I won't never finish it! *Never!*'

I sighed as I pulled her close and began to rock her back and forth. It was going to be a long Sunday night.

Forget the painting on the ceiling – duly unpegged and retrieved, that very Monday – what I should have had my eye on was the writing on the wall.

Though it was another dispiriting reminder of how tenuous Flip's hold was on all the usual emotions, from a practical point I was secretly relieved to see how quickly she bounced back from her distress. In fact, once she adjusted to the new temporary rhythm of her life – which seemed to have happened by around Wednesday – she embraced it with her usual energy and enthusiasm, particularly enjoying the bits of impromptu home-schooling I was doing with her. So when Ellie called to discuss the next contact meeting with Megan I was able to tell her truthfully that it was 'so far so more than good'; that, while I very much wanted a school to be found sooner rather than later, me and Flip, in the short term, were going to do just fine.

'That's great news,' she said, 'and – urgh – I hate to dampen your spirits, but just a heads up re Debbie's feedback about last Friday's meet-up. You know Megan was late, right?'

'I did,' I said, sensing I was about to hear something more.

I was. 'Well, she obviously couldn't mention it with Flip being in earshot, but Debbie's pretty sure she could smell alcohol on Megan's breath.'

I groaned. 'I know,' Ellie said. 'Bit of a bitch, that, isn't it? Though – well, we always knew it was going to be a rocky road. *However*. We've taken swift action to address it. Confronted her. Talked to her. Established she'd had a wobble. And it seems her counsellor has spoken up for her. Spoken up very strongly. So, for now, we keep going.'

'We do?'

'Yes, we do. There's obviously no talk in the short term of anything happening. Dancing off together into the sunset they ain't gonna be, for sure. But yes to weekly contact, closely supervised and closely monitored. Bottom line is the ball is very much in Megan's court. If she proves she can stay off the bottle, we continue. As long as – and that's where you come in, obviously – you don't think it's having an adverse effect on Flip.'

For all that I lacked confidence in Megan keeping off the bottle, on that front I could answer without hesitation. 'No,' I said, 'it's really not. At least, doesn't seem to be. I really do think she has her in a well-defined pigeonhole. She might have deep-seated self-esteem issues with this whole "ugly" thing she has – which, as you know, we're working on – but in terms of the reality of spending time with her mother, it really does seem as if it's just a chance to go for tea, have a bit of attention —' I laughed. 'As much from Debbie as Megan! Be made a fuss of and, hopefully, get given presents. So, no, from Flip's point of view I don't think it's doing any harm.'

'Good,' said Ellie. 'In that case, is Friday going to work for you? Only Debbie can't do Thursday and we'd like it to be Debbie.'

'Makes no difference to me,' I said. 'Only it would be good if it's slightly earlier. We're having a little bonfire party in the garden – I've got the grandkids coming over – and it would be good to have her back in time for the fireworks.'

'Aww,' Ellie said. 'I do love a proper Bonfire Night. Proper old-school, at home. All this rampant health and safety stuff has all but killed them off now, hasn't it?'

'Not in our house. Fireman Mike runs it all like a military operation. No one burned to date bar Guy Fawkes, I'm glad to say.' I had a thought then. 'Why don't you join us?' I suggested. 'I'm sure Flip would *love* that. And as it happens, I was already thinking of asking Will ... You know, for Tyler,' I added, just half a heartbeat later. 'And we'll be all done by eight if you've Friday night plans.'

'Oh,' she said. 'Right,' she said. 'Oh!'

In hindsight, it was perhaps because I was too busy smiling at myself that I *didn't* see the writing on the wall.

Chapter 17

What a difference a week can make. By Friday evening it was all change *chez* the Watsons and, by and large, in a positive way. No, we probably wouldn't be fixed up with a school for Flip before Christmas, but once I'd made my own mental adjustment to that I felt much more positive about it. After all, I had plenty of support promised and I had begun to feel focused; which was important because I needed structure every bit as much as Flip did. Thankfully, Selina Carter had been an absolute angel, providing me with all sorts of material with which I could cobble together some sort of daily learning plan. We'd also been to see Dr Shakelton and had a really positive meeting, after which he agreed that perhaps it would be prudent to put Flip back on her meds, at least while her school situation was up in the air, not least because I'd be able to monitor her so closely.

And in the midst of all this, I had the lovely warm feeling I got every time I remembered that, come the late spring, I was to be a grandmother all over again.

Though, in the short term, for Lauren, things weren't quite so rosy, to the extent that she had to phone in advance to do a recce of the bonfire party, to be sure she could cope. 'I just can't go near barbecues,' she told me on the Friday morning. 'Just a sniff of a barbecue and I heave – I *really* heave. Isn't that mad? I'm completely over the morning sickness. Not a sniff of it now. But the other day Kieron and I were out in the car and all it took was a whiff of someone's barbecue through the window, and I really thought I was going to throw up!'

'So we won't have a barbecue,' I told her. 'That suits me fine. To be honest, I'd rather just keep it simple anyway – jacket potatoes and beans and hot chocolate and so on. We'll have the bonfire to keep us warm so there's really no need to go to the fag of lighting the barbecue as well, is there?'

'Are you sure?' she asked anxiously.

'Certain sure,' I reassured her. 'Oh, and tell that son of mine to bring his apron. This seems to me to be the perfect excuse to put on a united cooking-embargo front. So let's do that, shall we? Insist it's all down to the menfolk.'

I *do* love it when a plan comes together.

As everybody expected, but still made us sad to discover, Flip had not only never been to a Bonfire Night party, she'd never seen a firework in her life. Her painting – which we'd finished and was now proudly displayed on the fridge – was imagined through fireworks she'd only seen on telly, or from far away, obliquely, through her bedroom window.

So as she skipped off with Debbie for her two hours with her mum, all she could talk about was what was going to happen when she got back, and how we must, must, must *not* light so much as a single sparkler until she got home.

Only Mike was allowed the small dispensation of being allowed to get the bonfire up and running, so that it was a decent-sized blaze ready for her return.

But it was a blaze of another kind that greeted us two and a half hours later. I was out in the garden with the little ones when Debbie and Flip returned, helping Levi and Jackson put marshmallows on the ends of a pack of wooden skewers, ready to be toasted later on. And with David on Marley-Mae duty (he was at the point of changing her nappy) Riley and Lauren were in the kitchen mulling Ribena, while Tyler and Mike supervised the fire.

The first I knew of their arrival therefore was when I heard my name called. My name. From Flip's mouth. Which was odd. I turned around.

'Casey! Casey!' Flip yelled, flying out through the conservatory doors. I tried to take it in. As far as I could remember, it was the first time she had addressed me by just my name. Prior to that, I had always been 'Mummy'. But what she followed it up with shocked me even more.

'You need to pack my stuff, Casey,' she said, hands planted on hips, gasping a little as she tried to catch her breath and speak at the same time. 'I have to go back to Mummy's and I have to go very quickly.' She turned then and jabbed a finger towards Debbie, who had followed her out back and was now looking on helplessly. '*She* won't take me back an' I told her it's 'portant that I go *now*!'

Mike and Tyler, both standing watching, looked as confused as I felt. There seemed nothing for it but to ask what was going on. 'Can you enlighten us?' I asked Debbie, trying to speak lightly, because I could see Flip working herself up into one of her rages. The boys and I had been sitting round the patio table and she was trying to clamber up onto my knee, even as I was trying to stand up. I changed my mind, sat down again and put a firm arm around her. 'What's the matter, love?' I asked her instead. 'What's going on?'

Flip wriggled her arms free and placed a hand on each of my cheeks, just as Kieron had done when he was little and keen to get my full attention. Her eyes were filled with unshed tears and, unusually, I could tell that she was trying hard *not* to cry, rather than just letting rip. Did she have a sense that this required her to keep as calm as she could to make us listen to her? I didn't know if her thinking was that sophisticated, but it certainly felt that way.

'I'm sorry, Mummy Casey,' she said, staring intently at me, just as I often did to her when trying to make her understand an instruction, 'but I have to leave you now. My real mummy has lost a lot of money 'cos I'm not home with her, and she's afraid she'll never get it back.' She turned towards Mike and Tyler, who were both still standing there, bundles of twigs in hand, as if it was important that she include them in this too. 'Casey, she will *starve* if I don't go back home. She might even *die*. She *needs* me,' she finished dramatically.

I could feel the fire crackling behind me and see the reflection of the flames dancing in her eyes. 'Sweetheart –' I began, but her hot little hands pressed even more firmly against my cheeks. 'Casey,' she said. 'Guess what as well?'

'What?' I asked her.

'Casey, she called me her pretty girl.'

'I've tried to explain,' Debbie said, just as I was digesting the earnestness with which Flip had spoken. 'I've already told you, haven't I, Flip? I'm sorry, chick, but you can't go home to Mummy yet. There need to be meetings, remember? Lots of meetings to decide where you would both live.' She stepped out onto the decking and ran a gentle hand over Flip's curls. 'I know it's hard, but we can't just take you home, chick. Not just like that. It would be – well, it would be like breaking the law. And you wouldn't want to be doing that, would you?'

Flip raised an arm to bat Debbie's hand away, and now the tears did fall from her eyes. Tears of frustration, I could tell, at our refusal to listen. 'You don't know nothink!' she screamed at Debbie. 'It's not your business anyway! You and the other horrible peoples have tooked my mum's monies! And now she might starve!' She was shrieking the words out. 'Can't you *see* that?'

Mike threw the twigs he was holding on the fire and motioned for Tyler to do likewise. Then he walked across and put his arms out towards her. Whether it was from surprise or simply because she was too disgusted to stay in our company any longer, she made not the slightest objection to Mike plucking her from my lap, hoisting her up on to his hip and taking her back inside the house, Tyler taking her hand and following close behind.

'Boys,' I said, turning to Levi and Jackson. 'Pop back inside with granddad for a minute, will you? You can help him sort out his special fireworks box. See which ones you want him to do first.'

They duly trotted off, and I patted the seat Levi had just vacated. 'Oh, Casey, I'm so sorry,' Debbie said once she sat down in it. 'Look at me,' she added, splaying her hands. 'I'm actually shaking. Can you believe that? I'm actually *shaking*. *Me*. Oh, I am soooo – grr. You won't believe it. I mean, you will, but – *God*, it makes me mad.'

'Believe what?'

'Believe the – pardon my French here – the *merde* she came out with! You know, you always tell yourself – you know, people like you and me, in the jobs we both do – that you're not going to let it make you negative and cynical, right?' I nodded. She was right. That was certainly true for me. 'But sometimes, God, it's hard, isn't it?' I nodded again. 'And you know the worst of it? That I didn't see it coming. I *so* should have seen it coming!'

Debbie went on to explain that everything had started out okay; that Flip had been in buoyant mood, chatting on about this and that. 'Particularly about whether today might be the day that she got her Barbie horse,' Debbie added wryly. 'Which, needless to say, was nowhere to be seen. Just these –' She pulled a set of Barbie clothes from her bag and placed them on the table. They looked worn and grubby. 'Which went down like the proverbial lead balloon,' Debbie finished.

'Anyway,' she went on, 'the food duly came – we went back to the burger bar Flip said she wanted to go to – and talk moved around to the flat, and how nice it was – so Megan said, anyway – and about how much she was looking forward to having Flip go there and how nice it would be when she moved back in. And, of course, I was already thinking – whoah, hold your frigging horses, missus – that sort of talk's not in the programme. Certainly not yet.

'Anyway, so Flip trots out the line I expected her to trot out – that she wasn't sure she wanted to, because she was happy where she was, thank you very much. Bless her, Casey, she started telling Megan how you were being her "ficial" teacher and how she was learning lots of "spressions". Bless her. There was also much mention of Tyler. *Lots* about Tyler. And how, though she liked *meeting* her real mummy, she didn't want to live there. Just go for tea and get presents.'

Debbie drew breath and smiled then. 'I think "come for tea and get presents" were her very words. And, of course, she brought the horse up again – she is *dead* set on getting that horse – and the thing is that I could see that Megan was getting agitated about it, though, of course, I was thinking she was upset because, well, because she *was*. So when she burst into tears I genuinely thought it was because she *cared*.'

She shook her head, as if genuinely bemused at what she was saying. 'So off I go, off up to the counter, to wrap the whole thing up – time was marching on and, given the increasingly emotional tone of things, it felt best. I also thought I'd better go and get Megan a handful of tissues to blow her nose on, and when I came back I just *knew* that the atmosphere had changed. Megan busy drying her eyes, Flip looking anxious. But neither of them forthcoming about filling me in. It was only once we were back in the car that Flip started up with what her mother had said.'

'Which was?' I asked.

'Pretty much what she said to you. That if she doesn't agree to go back to her she's going to die of starvation, because they won't give her any money unless Flip moves back in.'

Debbie glanced at her watch. 'You need to get off,' I told her, rising from the table, conscious she had kids of her own to get home to and that Kieron and Lauren would be arriving at any minute, not to mention Ellie and Will. I decided in that instant that now was not the time for a social services meeting. It would be the last thing anyone would want on a Friday night. No. Deep breath. Get Flip calmed down and distracted. Deal with the repercussions as and when.

'I've got the gist, I think,' I said. Then I shook my head. 'You know, I would never have believed she'd be that calculating. Well –' I consciously reined myself in. 'I say that. We don't know for *sure* that she's being calculating, do we? We don't know for sure that the money thing actually came from her lips, after all.'

'Oh, don't doubt it,' Debbie said, rising also, and shouldering her handbag. 'After the last time … And when I *did* broach it, as we were leaving – you know, just as in "Are you struggling to make ends meet, Megan?" – her response was unequivocal. It was "What do you fucking think? You live on benefits, do you, love?" Which will be going in my report, of course.' She glanced back towards the house. 'I'm just sorry you've got to deal with the fall-out.'

I shook my head. 'Don't be. Really. It's my job. And knowing Flip, she'll be over her whole moving-out plan just as soon as she finds something new to fixate on, i.e. the fireworks. You get off. Though it sounds like a rethink is on the cards now, doesn't it? She's clearly only angling to get Flip back so she's got some money coming in.'

Debbie nodded. 'And if anyone asks *me*, I know what I'll be saying. Get a section 30 order and suspend contact forthwith.'

I would have smiled at the irony of it being our Bonfire Night gathering. Except listening to the banshee wailing I could hear coming from upstairs as I let Debbie out, I doubted there'd be anything to smile about just yet. Seemed the fireworks had already begun.

Chapter 18

I woke up on the Monday morning freezing. I realised Mike must have forgotten to put the heating on before setting off for work and it was so chilly that when I looked out of the bedroom window I half expected to see a blanket of snow.

There wasn't, but for early November it was a bitterly cold day and I decided I'd let the house warm up for half an hour before waking Tyler up for school, and went down to make my ritual morning coffee using the lightest of fairy footsteps. Most of all, I didn't want to wake Flip.

It was perhaps only to be expected but it was still incredibly dispiriting to deal with the nightmare she had been all weekend. She'd lost the plot – Megan's plot – in spectacular fashion, and, despite my trying every trick in the book to bring her down again, the pair of us ended up spending almost the entirety of the much-looked-forward-to fireworks party holed up in her bedroom, with her completely inconsolable; even Tyler, who could work wonders with her, couldn't coax her out. Not even with a full-frontal assault (he'd been ably coached by Mike) about how terrible it would be for him, Levi, Jackson and Marley-Mae if she did leave.

Things barely improved over the weekend. It was as if a button had been pressed in her brain and had now been stuck in the 'on' position, or as if she was a record with the needle stuck in a groove. 'She'll die and it'll be *your* fault!' was her default expression, and when she wasn't railing at us she was screaming, the piercing high-pitched noise that we had half-forgotten but were now remembering with a vengeance.

I had also returned to being Mummy Casey, rather than Mummy. It was as if she was anxious to find every way possible to underline her point – that she shouldn't be here any more – and, to that end, Mike had similarly become Daddy Mike.

Not even the little ones – normally so good at it – had been able to deflect her from her anger, when Riley had agreed to come over with them on the Saturday afternoon. She'd broken toys, been horrible to Jackson, shouted at Marley-Mae, and smacked Levi and stormed to her room. If we'd had a cat, she'd have kicked it, no question.

It was such a full-on masterclass in how not to win friends and influence people that by Sunday afternoon I'd begun to think she was more focused than she appeared. That she wanted us all to hate her so we'd feel more inclined to let her go.

Coffee soothing my troubled soul – well, firing up my cylinders, which amounted to the same thing – I pondered as I popped two slices of bread in the toaster, ready for Tyler.

If that was Flip's intention, it wouldn't work, but it did make me sad. I'd seen it before: kids with self-esteem issues brought about through desperate, loveless childhoods often acted in ways designed to turn people away from them, almost as if anxious to confirm that they weren't worthy of love and were right in their persistent self-loathing. That's why one of the things that was always drummed into us during training was the need to be mindful every second of the day to punish the behaviour, not the person; 'that's a naughty thing to do', rather than 'you naughty girl'.

I tiptoed back up the stairs, carefully using the edges of the treads, like an assassin, but my hopes for another hour of peace (she must, after all, be shattered) were quickly dashed. I could hear her talking. In fact, I could hear her and Tyler talking. He must have gone into her bedroom. So, like an assassin, I grabbed the unexpected opportunity to gather intelligence, and stood still on the top step and listened.

'*Course* I belong here,' Tyler was saying, with an edge of defiance in his voice. 'I'm just like one of their real kids. It's like I'm adopted or something.' There was a pause. Then he lowered his voice very slightly. 'I might even change my name to Watson,' he added. 'Stop being so ridiculous, Flip. You know they love you too.'

'No they don't!' Flip snapped back at him. 'They don't love me. No way. You don't know nothing. They kidnapped me and now they won't let me home.'

'Oh, for God's sake!' Tyler hissed. 'I *told* you. That's rubbish. Anyway, how'd that work? Why'd they kidnap you if you say they don't love you? How does that work? That makes absolutely no sense!'

'You're the stupid one!' Flip huffed. "Cos of the money! I told you! If they keep me they get all the money off my mummy! They get the money she should have. And now she'll starve to death!' There was a low thud – perhaps Flip jumping down off the bed. 'They prob'ly kidnapped you as well. That's what they *do*!'

Tyler laughed out loud. 'Christ,' he said. 'What are you *on*?' Another pause. A creak of bedsprings. Was Tyler going to emerge? 'Look, Flip. I get what you're thinking, but your mum is talking bollocks. I know you don't want to hear it, but she's no good for you, Flip. I mean – don't pull that face. You *know* what she's like. You're the one that told me! An' I know what you're talking about because my step-mum was a bitch.' I heard his sigh. 'Flip, honestly. Trust me. You *haven't* been kidnapped. You're staying here with Mike and Casey for your own *good*. And I'll tell you something else,' he added. 'I felt just the same as you do. I hated everyone. Trusted no one. Thought everyone was out to get me. But they're not. Casey and Mike only ever wanted to look after me. And you're an idiot if you don't realise they're looking after you too. So stop being so horrible and – Ow! That hurt! – bloody grow *up*!'

I swallowed the lump in my throat, conscious that either of them might appear at any moment. Especially if Flip had launched herself on Tyler, as sounded probable. He was patient, but not that patient. I needed to intervene.

I rounded the corner of the landing and pushed Flip's bedroom door open. 'Morning, Flip!' I said brightly. 'You're awake bright and early!' Then, turning to Tyler, who was already dressed for school, 'Oh, you're in here as well, love. I was wondering where you'd got to. Ready for your breakfast?'

He glanced at Flip with an expression that I'd translate as 'Take note of what I've said, okay?' then nodded. 'I'm starving. I could eat a whole woolly mammoth.'

'Do you want to come down as well, love?' I said, turning to Flip now. 'If so, grab your dressing gown. It's really cold today.'

In response, Flip merely scowled and stomped back to her bed. Then she climbed in and pulled up her duvet. 'I'm watching telly,' she said, returning Tyler's glare with her own one. 'But if that woman calls 'bout my mummy, just shout me.'

'She's still really angry, Casey,' Tyler said as he sat down to his toast. 'She called me into her room – well, you saw, didn't you? She reckons she's going to run away.'

I rolled my eyes. An absconding was something I could really do without. 'You think she meant it?' I asked. 'That's all we need, isn't it? For Flip to go on the missing list once again.'

'I don't think so,' he said, wearing his 'learned sage' expression. 'She was just ranting,' he said. Then he grinned. 'As she does.' He swallowed a mouthful of breakfast and swallowed. 'Tell you what, though,' he said. 'You know what she thinks, don't you?'

'What?'

'That the whole being excluded from school thing is all a part of it. That you've stopped her going to school so she's locked up with you. So her mum can't come and get her. All part of your dastardly plan …'

I couldn't help but smile at that. Of course. It was logical enough. Well, using Flip's brand of logic, at any rate.

'And there's no talking her out of it, neither,' Tyler continued. 'She's convinced it's some wicked plot that you've cooked up together, and that now her mum's rumbled you, you're going to keep her locked up.' He smiled again. 'Casey, she is bonkers *beyond*.' He paused again. 'And she reckons I shouldn't be here either.'

'Well, that's just ridiculous,' I said, conscious of the change in his tone. Furious to think he, too, might now feel insecure. It could be incredibly destabilising, all this shouting and upset. 'Just you ignore her,' I told him. 'She's not thinking straight, is she? You are as much a part of this family as Kieron and Riley are. You know that, don't you?'

Tyler popped the last piece of toast into his mouth and chewed thoughtfully. 'I been thinking about that,' he said. 'You know, an' about the baby.'

'The baby?'

'The one Kieron and Lauren are going to have.'

'What about it?'

'Well, I just realised that it won't know any different, will it?'

'I don't follow.' Well, I sort of did but I still wanted Tyler to articulate it.

'I mean it won't know a time when I *wasn't* here, will it?' he clarified.

'No, it won't,' I agreed.

'Which is pretty epic, isn't it? Well, for me, anyway …' His cheeks coloured. 'I'll just be Uncle Tyler. Like, you know, it'll have an Aunty Riley and an Uncle Tyler, won't it? And it won't know any different. We'll both be the same. And then I will be really, *really* one of you.'

'Love, you already *are*.'

'Yeah, but still. You know what I mean.'

I threw my arms around him before he had time to escape and held him tight. 'Yes,' I said, kissing his hair. 'I know *exactly* what you mean.'

There are few things more uplifting than an expression of unconditional love from a child, so after I'd waved Tyler off and retraced my steps back upstairs, I was feeling both buoyant and determined. Whatever Flip threw at me, bless her – us as devious kidnappers! – I could, and most definitely would, handle it. My spirits were not up for being deflated.

To be fair, though, she had tried her darndest. I'd barely mouthed the words 'So, how d'you fancy coming down for some breakfast?' before what I saw dashed them from my lips. Now silenced, I scanned the room and took in the chaos. I had no idea how she'd managed it without either of us hearing her, but she had. The room looked like a hurricane had blown through. All the drawers in her chest had been pulled out and upturned, their contents strewn all over the floor. She'd ripped up several books: story books, school books and colouring books, and – her *pièce de resistance*, as it must have taken quite a lot of furious digging – smashed a palette of poster paints all over the carpet.

The architect of the destruction was standing by the window, hands on hips, unrepentant. 'Why, Flip?' I asked as she glared at me. 'Why would you do this?'

'I want my *real* mummy!' she screamed at me, as if she'd held sufficient breath specifically for the purpose. 'We can't just leave her to starve! She's going to die and you don't even *care*!'

I'd brought up a tablet and a glass of juice for her and I now placed both calmly on the drawer-less dresser. Then I sat down on her bed and patted the space beside me. She ignored it. 'Flip, sweetie,' I told her quietly. 'Your mummy *isn't* going to die. I don't know what she's said to you, but she's not going to die. I promise you she isn't. She has a social worker taking care of her and making sure she is okay.' I swept my arm across the room as I let that sink in. 'And all this – none of this is going to change things, is it? You should know that.'

'*You* don't know that, *Casey!*' she spat, emphasising my name. She jabbed a finger towards me. 'Pack my things right this minute, 'cos I'm going, and that's that!'

Where did you start? How did you explain to a child so young and so innocent that her mum wasn't capable of taking care of her? And in asking myself the question, I realised I already had the answer. With some children it might be different, but with Flip perhaps I shouldn't even try. Her butterfly mind had enough trouble grasping such simple concepts that perhaps I should stop trying to help her make sense of things. Perhaps I should just focus on that brilliant word 'boundaries', and then apply some. Because a child with too much power was a child out of control. And an out-of-control child was an unhappy child. A distressed child. And I knew I was looking at one now.

My mind made up, I stood up and picked up the juice and pill. 'Flip, I'm not having this conversation with you right now,' I said calmly as I walked back to the door. 'I'm too angry at the moment because of all this mess.' I gestured to the things I held. 'I will be back with your drink and tablet in precisely one hour, by which time I expect you to have tidied this mess up.' I held her furious gaze with a stern one. 'We'll talk some more then.'

Back downstairs, having checked the time and made a mental note of it, I decided to call Ellie and update her on developments; something I'd pondered doing over the weekend but decided against; it had hardly been an emergency after all.

She was laughing out loud as she answered her phone. 'You have second sight or something, Casey?' she wanted to know. 'I'm literally about ten minutes away from your house!'

'Really?' I asked.

'Really. Less than that even, maybe. An unannounced visit for John.' She laughed again. 'And now you've gone and spoiled it!'

I smiled, feeling my mood lifting again, just knowing that she'd soon be round to chew the cud. Even if the 'knowing' bit didn't quite fit the protocol. An annual 'unannounced visit' from someone was standard procedure, the key being in the word 'unannounced'. It was a standard check – and an important one – on the state of play in a foster home when the 'powers that be' turned up at times when they weren't expected, and prepared for.

In my case, it made no difference. Bar the odd deployment of my mum's posh bone china in the early days (something I'd long since given up) what you saw in my house was what you got; overlaid at all times by the faint whiff of furniture polish. I was a clean freak; it was never done for show. And, by and large – and the irony of Flip's theory about us kidnapping her didn't escape me – such visits found us in a state of either reasonable harmony, or otherwise; because that was the reality of fostering.

In reality, I always had an inkling when to expect such visits anyway, because they invariably took place at the same time of year. Which suited me just fine; though an unannounced visit was the last thing on my mind, the timing couldn't have been more perfect.

'So is she here?' Ellie asked as I let her in ten minutes later, causing me to grin. Where else did she think Flip might be?

'Upstairs,' I said as I led Ellie to a seat at the dining table. 'I'll make some coffee and then we can catch up. I don't have the best news to report, though, I'm afraid. She's taken what happened on Friday very badly.'

Coffee made, I updated Ellie on everything that had happened, up to and including the room-trashing performance I was hoping she was busy addressing as I spoke. 'So I'm hoping you have something – *anything* – up your sleeve to help me, Ellie. With everything so up in the air – both with her mother and with school – I'm really not sure what I should tell her.'

Ellie frowned. 'Oh dear,' she said, 'Well, then, I'm about to make things worse. I've had Debbie's full report through and it seems mother dearest has been putting some serious work in, promising Flip pretty much the world to go back. I mean *literally*. Trips to Disneyland, Barbie castles – forget the horse; we're talking the whole catalogue. Everything up to and including running off in the sun together. Every childhood dream she could conjure up, basically, all wrapped up in a big shiny pink bow.'

I shook my head. How could she be so cruel? Even in the best-case scenario, with her drying out and stepping up to her responsibilities, Megan wasn't going to be able to provide such things. She survived on her benefits, for a start, and most of that usually went on alcohol. And, sad to say, I suspected they'd continue to do so.

'But you can see where she's coming from, can't you?' Ellie reasoned. 'Without Flip she'd have been on less than half her usual money – a reality that obviously started kicking in around, well, right around the time she first got in touch with her whole "change of heart" schtick, I reckon – don't you?'

'What a piece of work,' I said. It wasn't strictly professional, but I couldn't help it. 'And, meanwhile, poor Flip believes that her mum really loves her. Can't bear to be without her. What a total piece of work.'

Ellie nodded. 'I know. So we're back with plan A now. Long-term fostering, or adoption – God willing, we'll find someone – and severing contact with mum for the foreseeable future.'

'And you've told her?'

'We have. And she's responded as you'd expect. Bitter and cross, but at the same time she's nothing if not pragmatic. She's been rumbled and she's not bothering to sweeten the pill. She even told her social worker she wasn't bothered because she could always have another one.'

It was a testament to Ellie's worldliness that she didn't bat an eyelid. As for me, I'd heard such words spoken more than once before. The old 'have a kid, get a council house' wasn't just a depressing headline for the tabloids. For a few it was a lifestyle decision.

Even so, I was, as ever, saddened beyond belief to hear it said. What child deserved to be born into such an emotional black hole?

'Why don't you get Flip down?' Ellie suggested. 'So I can tell her what's going on. She deserves to know the plan and it's probably better if it comes from me – particularly under the circumstances. She obviously needs putting straight.'

'Why don't you go up and fetch her?' I suggested. 'Or even talk to her up there if you want to. She's very angry with me currently, so she might be more amenable if I'm out of the picture.'

Ellie pushed her chair back. 'Good idea. I'll do that, then.'

While Ellie headed upstairs I prepared a fresh drink and put out Flip's pill, reflecting that I still had not the slightest idea whether it was doing her any good. To find that out, of course, you needed routine and continuity; something that was in painfully short supply right now. Finding out what was Flip's 'normal' felt every bit as likely currently as finding the proverbial needle in a haystack, given everything that was going on.

They both trooped back down 30 seconds later.

'Have you come to take me home?' Flip was asking Ellie. Then, to me, 'Has she?'

Ellie shook her head and pulled a chair out, which she gestured Flip to sit on. I could tell by her face just how much she'd been crying. Her cheeks were puffed up and the whites of her eyes red. I put the drink and pill in front of her. She took it obediently. I could see something else in her eyes then. Hope.

Hope which was soon to be crushed. 'I'm sorry, kiddo,' Ellie told her, 'but I'm afraid I haven't. I know you can't understand that, but I'm afraid you don't have a choice, chicken. You have to trust that we grown-ups are trying to do what's best for you.'

'My mummy needs me, Ellie,' Flip said, all the fight gone from her voice now, her tack completely changed. 'She said so. Said she'll have nothing without me. She said I'm her whole life.' She glanced across at me then. 'She says I'm pretty.' Her eyes pooled with tears. 'She says I'm *pretty*. Why are you spoiling everything? *Why?*'

Ellie moved in her seat a little. And I knew why. It was one of the hardest things to do, to tell a child who so wants to be loved that, in fact, they're not. Not to tell them in so many words – that would be too cruel, too visceral – but enough so they understood that such vestiges of hope as they'd worked so hard to keep alive had, for their own good, to be extinguished.

'Flip, listen,' Ellie said softly, but with that all-important air of authority. 'It doesn't matter what Mummy told you, because she wasn't being honest. Your mum has got lots of problems – problems that little girls shouldn't have to be around. You already know that she drinks a lot, don't you?' Flip nodded. 'Well, I think you also know that what she drinks isn't medicine, sweetie. It's something called alcohol, and it's very, very bad for her. And when she drinks, she can't look after you properly. Which is why –'

'No, Ellie,' Flip cried, 'you're wrong! I can *help* mummy. I know how. I used to do it for her before. Hide the bottles. I was good at it. I hid them away so she couldn't find them.' Her chin wobbled then. 'I only gived them back when she really, really needed them, honest I did. I promise. Only to make her better. An' it did make her better.' She gave a huge gulping sob. 'Sometimes it did, it *did*.'

Ellie tried to reach out to place a hand on Flip's arm but she snatched it back immediately. 'Sweetheart,' she said, 'it's not your job to do those things and you shouldn't be doing them. Mummy is a grown-up and it's her who should have looked after *you*, not the other way around. Look, Flip,' she went on, 'I've explained to you before what being in care means, haven't I? So I know you understand what that means. You're in care so we know you're safe. Safe from things like that terrible fire ever happening again to you. And ...' she paused again. 'The thing is, Flip, that we've decided the best thing for both you *and* Mummy is for you to stay in care while you are growing up. If we do that, Mummy can get the help she needs without having to worry about you coming to any harm, and you will be living in another family, somewhere where you will be loved and safe.'

Flip's eyes never left Ellie's face as she said this; her face a mask of porcelain stillness while inside the storm undoubtedly raged. 'So not *ever*?' she asked, her voice now tiny. 'I'm not *ever* going to see Mummy again?' She looked across at me. 'Mummy Casey, please tell Ellie that she can't do this. *Please!*'

I remembered back then. To the doll-like child who'd first appeared on my doorstep. The seemingly indifferent child who could so blithely shrug off one mummy and replace her with a shiny new one, seemingly entirely unaffected by the seismic change in her life, able to exist on that strange shallow plane. Where had that emotionally challenged, almost emotionally indifferent, child gone? The one who could forget about her mother and fall in love with strangers? Had she ever really been there? Did that version of her exist? I could certainly no longer find her in the little girl who was sobbing at my dining table now.

'I'm so sorry, baby,' I whispered, holding my arms out, hoping she'd want to be encircled by them, willing her to accept that small crumb of comfort. 'Listen,' I added, 'when you're bigger, *much* bigger, you might be able to start seeing Mummy again. But for now, sweetie, this is how it must be.'

I lowered my empty arms then, feeling helpless. Whoever she was now, I knew I couldn't reach her.

Chapter 19

Just after Ellie left she did at least play a modest ace, in the form of what was potentially much more positive news – news that, in the midst of all the upset, she'd forgotten to tell me.

'It's about that Mrs Hardy,' she explained, speaking to me hands-free, from her car, on her way to her next appointment. By this time, Flip had taken herself off to lie on the sofa to watch *Finding Nemo*. It was at my suggestion; she loved the film and watched it endlessly (she had found an icon in the scatty Dory) and it formed a kind of emotional time-out, which seemed the best thing for both of us.

'The next-door neighbour. I remember,' I confirmed to Ellie. 'What about her?'

'Well, it seems she's been in touch and has a whole lot of Barbie stuff to give Flip, bless her. I don't know if there's a horse in the mix – I didn't like to ask for an inventory – but it certainly sounds like quite a haul.'

She went on to explain that it all belonged to Mrs Hardy's grand-daughter, who'd outgrown it long since and was finally happy to let it go; apparently the family were moving abroad for a couple of years, hence the clear-out. She'd gone to some lengths to track Ellie down, by all accounts.

'But not Mrs Hardy herself?' I asked, a plan suddenly forming in my brain. 'She's not moving away, is she?' I didn't know much about Mrs Hardy, but Flip mentioned her often; she had clearly been a constant for much of her life. And a positive one, too. She was obviously a thoughtful and loving woman.

'No, I don't think so,' Ellie said. 'Why?'

'Because she's the only person to connect to Flip's past that we've so far had contact with,' I clarified. 'Well, but Megan. So I'd very much like to meet her.'

'And she's almost like family to Flip,' I explained to John Fulshaw, who asked the very same question the following day.

By now, I'd spoken to Flip about the Barbie things Mrs Hardy had put by for her and I knew the light in her eyes wasn't just about the toys. So I'd called John to run my thoughts by him – he was charged with making the arrangements, apparently, and I wanted him to know just how much I thought it would be of benefit if they could be handed over in person. 'She told me that herself,' I explained. 'She even used to call her Nanny Hardy, apparently, and I just have this strong sense that seeing her again will give Flip a real boost. I certainly don't see how it could do her any harm.'

'I'm not sure about that,' John said, reminding me why I sometimes go off half-cocked without thinking things through. 'I don't know if you've seen pictures or anything, but I'm told that their house – Flip and Megan's, I mean – is in a terrible state. I checked with Hayley and it seems the council haven't done much to it since the fire. There were investigators in there for weeks, and well, since then it's just been left.

'Not only that, but Hayley tells me vandals have been in there as well. She was back there with Megan, seeing what they could salvage, and there are apparently some pretty nasty things spray-painted on the exterior. Threats, basically. Of the "and don't frigging come back" variety, only using rather more colourful vocabulary.'

'Oh dear,' I said. 'Sorry, John. What was I thinking? Nope, correction. I just *didn't* think, did I? Too busy getting excited about what Flip might get out of a visit with Mrs Hardy. You know – touching base with the familiar, getting some more background and so on. I just thought it would be helpful for all of us. I still do.'

'And you're right,' John said. 'It probably *would* be a help. Mrs Hardy might just be the key that unlocks that complicated little mind. Tell you what,' he said. (I always liked it when John said 'Tell you what.'). 'How about if *I* pay a visit to Mrs Hardy to test the water? I could ask her if she's prepared to come and see Flip at your house – or somewhere else if you'd prefer?'

'Oh that would be great, John, and no, no. My house would be fine. Oh I hope she agrees. Flip will be *so* happy about it, and believe me, we are sorely missing Happy Flip right now.'

* * *

Flip remained fragile and intermittently tearful for several days, but that was only to be expected, and there was no doubt the thought of the promised toys was a distraction from her conspiracy theory about Mike and I 'stealing' her from her mummy. I wasn't sure if that was because the potential contact with Mrs Hardy might have made her think there was an opportunity to state her case again, but, equally, instinct told me it was just Flip being Flip; desolate as she'd seemed about contact ceasing and her not being able to go home and save her mother's life (and I didn't doubt the intensity of her emotions) it was almost as if her capacity for such feelings enduring was so compromised that she simply couldn't keep it up. And much as it compromised her ability to form deep, meaningful relationships, as adaptive strategies went, it had its benefits.

Indeed, by the end of the week, and with December on the horizon, she seemed much more in the same zone as I was, i.e. with Christmas very much on her mind.

Most people 'do' Christmas around the middle of December, and a determined few hang on till the final week itself. Others start thinking earlier, making lists and planning parties, while a die-hard few spend most of November wishing it was December already. Well, if it's going to be dark, cold and dismal outside, why not cheer it up with a few decorations, right?

'So that's your excuse this year, is it?' Kieron laughed when he came round for tea with Lauren and immediately found himself sent up to the loft to get all the boxes down. 'That you've got to crack on so you'll cheer Flip up? Yeah, right, Mum.'

'It *is*,' I insisted, leaning round the loft ladder to wink at Lauren, who was helping me pile up the boxes he was handing down. 'It's all part of the programme,' I went on. 'The poor child's barely so much as pulled a cracker, let alone had any sort of proper Christmas.

'Anyway,' I went on, 'it's something to keep her busy. It's a long day when you haven't any school to keep you occupied. She needs something to focus on, and I've decided this will be it. And just you wait,' I added. 'Give it a couple of years and this will be you two as well. Christmas starts much earlier when you've got little ones in your lives.'

Kieron's guffaw from above shook the rafters. 'Or you as a mother!' he called down. Cheeky tyke.

In reality, I'd not so much made everything about Christmas as about getting the house decorated in case Nanny Hardy was able to come and pay us a visit soon. I reckoned I could risk promising Flip that much – that she'd see Nanny Hardy – because John had already confirmed it. Though, with her daughter's move, it was just a question of pinning her down to a 'when'.

It was with that in mind, then, that I announced that, when she wasn't busy doing some sort of school work, Flip was officially now my personal assistant Domestic Engineer. Which news she greeted with joy, for all of five minutes. Then she reconsidered. 'Oh, *Mummy*,' she said (which was a joy in itself), 'that doesn't mean we're going to have to do one of your dip clean sessions, does it?'

It took me a moment to work out what she was on about. Then the penny dropped. 'It's not a dip clean – it's a *deep* clean,' I corrected, both amused and, at the same time, slightly concerned that she'd formed the impression that I routinely made my foster children scrub my house. 'Of course not, kiddo,' I reassured her. 'I'm talking Christmas! The trees, the lights, the tinsel, the decorations, everything. We have a mission to transform this house into something that Santa Claus – and Nanny Hardy, don't forget – would be thrilled to visit. So, how about it? How do you fancy being my little helper?'

'What, like an elf? Like in *Elf*?' (All the kids loved the film *Elf*.) 'Like I'm Santa's little elf? Oh yes, yes, yes!' She paused, to think again. 'Is that the time, then? Is it almost time for Christmas?'

I felt a little pang then, thinking about all that she was missing. The normal seasonal cycle of things they'd do at school: something she'd been snatched away from half way through her firework picture. No making Christmas cards, no practising for an upcoming nativity, no parties and mince pies and trooping down to the local church for the carol service. All the usual routines that served to bind communities together, all denied her. And in a life where so much had been denied to her already. I made a mental note to try and do all those things with her; perhaps I'd even find out when the local carol service was. I would certainly make sure we had a card-making session with Jackson and Levi, and that I took her into town to see Father Christmas. Had she even done that? She'd never said so and I doubted it.

'Not quite yet,' I said, 'but it will be in no time at all. And I like to be prepared.' I nodded towards the ceiling.

'You have a tutu up in that in that bedroom of yours, don't you? And a wand and a crown, too, if my memory serves correctly?'

She cottoned on, her eyes shining with excitement, her smile a picture. 'So I won't be an elf – I'll be a beautiful Christmas fairy!'

She needed no further encouragement to hot-foot it out of the kitchen and up to her bedroom to transform herself.

We were in luck, as I found out later that same day. Mrs Hardy apparently loved the idea of seeing Flip again, and it had been arranged that Debbie Scott would drop her off at ours that Thursday morning, and leave her with us for a couple of hours before collecting her.

I decided not to tell Flip. There was no particular reason to surprise her, and perhaps I was doing it mostly for myself, but I just couldn't resist the chance to see the expression on her face when she opened the front door and they were reunited.

In the meantime, the simple application of a tutu and some plastic bling seemed to have worked something of a minor miracle. From the moment my fairy helper came back downstairs, it was as though a magical transformation had taken place. She seemed to have forgotten about running away in any case, but now she chatted away about things that seemed to make it very clear that she'd forgotten we were the enemy as well. She certainly seemed to have forgotten she was cross with me; another bittersweet reminder that I tried to view as a minor positive – that her intellectual challenges sometimes worked in my favour.

For the next two days we danced around the house to Christmas tunes and movies while we trimmed up every available corner. I've never been much of a TV person really, but I found myself overjoyed to learn from Riley that Sky – bless their cotton socks – devoted one whole music channel and one whole movie channel just to Christmas, 24/7, every December. It was a red-letter day, and one Mike particularly cherished, because it was the day I officially stopped moaning on about the cost of a monthly TV subscription.

By the time Thursday came around, I was nigh-on exhausted, but Flip – still dressed in the same Chief Fairy uniform – was not done with seeking things to be blinged up, and on the hunt for any remaining pockets of less-than-twinkly house.

'Hmm,' she was saying, scrutinising my kitchen cabinets with a keen eye. 'We could do around the kitchen cupboards, Mummy, couldn't we? We still have some tinsel.'

She stood there, sucking the end of her wand thoughtfully, and looking for all the world like some tiny, camp scientist surveying her work and studying the results. She then used the same wand as an impromptu laser pointer and traced around the outline of my pan cupboard. 'This one would look *lovely*, all sparkly and flashing, wouldn't it?'

'Erm, I think we have enough fairy lights up, Flip,' I told her. 'Besides, the wires'll get tangled every time I need my frying pan, won't they? Not to mention that when Riley comes you know what she'll say, don't you? That we have already gone *way* over the top.'

Flip looked at me and then back at the cupboard. 'Will she? But this cupboard is under the bottom, not over the top.' She grinned, and I wasn't sure if she was ribbing me or not. 'So maybe we could just do the bottom ones?'

I glanced at the clock. It was almost 10. Debbie would be arriving with our surprise visitor at any moment, and I decided a distraction was in order. 'Mince pies and milk,' I said. 'I think that's what's called for. Mid-morning snack. We deserve a treat after all our hard work, after all, don't we?'

The doorbell rang on cue just as I was opening the mince-pie packet. 'Go get that for me, love,' I said, pretending to be struggling with the cellophane. 'It's probably the postman.'

Flip slipped from the chair she'd just sat on and danced out to the hall. I followed. 'Nanny Hardy!' she yelped, moments later. 'Nanny Hardy! Mummy –' she whirled around to find me right there behind her. 'Mummy, it's Nanny Hardy come to see me!'

Right away I could see why Flip had been so attached to her. Not to mention feeling sad that the fire and her subsequent removal had meant this one source of warmth in her life had been denied her up to now. Bless the woman for taking the trouble to track her down.

She was only in her late sixties, I judged – only just over a decade and a half older than me. But she oozed that indefinable quality of 'nannyness' – neat grey hair, a warm smile, a big handbag – and that no-nonsense way of speaking that never fails to remind you that while nannies are around all will be right with the world. And as I shook her hand, I half expected to hear her break out into a rendition of 'A Spoonful of Sugar', but instead, once released, she simply scooped Flip into her arms and parked her on her hip, where she clung happily, like a baby orang-utan.

'It's so lovely to meet you,' I said as I went out to help Debbie bring in the two large black bags and cardboard box she'd brought with her. 'Go through and I'll be back in to pop the kettle on.'

'She's just lovely,' Debbie confirmed as we gathered up the goodies to take back into the house. 'Whatever happens now, we must *not* let this woman escape!' Which left me musing that my reputation as a master-kidnapper might have already got around.

Back inside, Flip had already parked our guest on the sofa and installed herself on her lap, only to shimmy back down once I came in with the bags. 'Go on, sweetheart,' Mrs Hardy said. 'Get stuck in. They're all for you. Why don't you have a go-through while I speak with Mrs Watson.'

'Oh please, it's Casey,' I corrected as Flip started rummaging in the bags and gasping. 'Look, Mummy, look!' she cried, opening the first of the bags wider so I could see the contents. 'It's like all the Barbie things in the whole *world*!' she enthused. 'Can I take them upstairs, Nanny, so I can show them to Pink Barbie?'

'Good idea,' I said, thinking on my feet. 'Let's do that. I'll help you carry them up, then you can arrange them all in your bedroom. I think there's a Barbie house in the box, isn't there?' I asked, looking at Mrs Hardy.

'And a caravan, I think,' she said, standing up to help.

'Wow,' Flip said. 'Wow. That is epic *beyond*, Nanny!' Then she smiled at Mrs Hardy's momentary confusion. Another Tylerism to add to Flip's repertoire.

'I'm so glad you've come,' I told Mrs Hardy once we were alone in the living room, me with my coffee and her with a proper cup of tea. Sometimes, Mum's cups and saucers still came in handy. 'It's so obvious what a bond you have. She thinks the world of you.'

'I'm not surprised,' she said, with an edge of obvious anger in her voice. 'I'm the only thing she's ever had in her life that resembled any sort of loving parental figure. I'm sorry,' she finished, checking herself. 'But it still makes my blood boil. She was no mother, not really,' she said as she sipped her tea. 'Many was the morning when I'd have to bring Flip into my house after seeing her playing in the garden in her nightie. Absolutely no awareness of the time of day – or time of year, for that matter – and certainly no idea when she was supposed to be in school. It's a miracle they let her stay with her. I *still* don't understand it. She must have been good at acting, is all I'll say. Oscar-winning standard. Because whenever I asked Flip where her mummy was, the answer was always the same. She was either in bed or on the sofa, busy "sleeping". Poor little love was half starved most of the time, too – and there's nothing of her in the first place, is there? Ate me out of house and home, she did, whenever I took her inside.'

'The poor thing,' I sympathised. 'You're right. It's a miracle she didn't end up in care earlier, isn't it?'

'Well, not so much, maybe,' Mrs Hardy mused, 'the way things tend to be these days. There was the gran around – for a bit, at least – though she was long out of the picture by the time Meggie almost burned the house down. No, I think that's the way these days, isn't it? That there's so much reluctance to take kids away. Too much fear of being sued. Damned if you do, damned if you don't. The whole world's gone litigation mad, hasn't it?' She shook her head and tutted. 'Ugly business.'

Which reminded me there was something I very much wanted to ask her. I explained about Flip's obsession with being ugly. And how she'd told me that was what her mother called her once.

'Told her *once*?' Mrs Hardy gasped, shaking her head. 'I'm afraid that's the understatement of the year. Casey, the woman would scream obscenities at her on a daily – *hourly* – basis. The filth that came out of her mouth – and you could hear her right down the street. And you know how these things get picked up – I'm sure you do, in your line of work. Local kids.' She rolled her eyes. 'Some of those little so-and-so's wanted locking up, they really did. Monkey-face. That's what they used to call her. All the time. Used to hang around outside and pretend to be flipping gibbons or what-ever. *So* cruel.' She shook her head again. 'You'd think their parents would want to wash their mouths out. I certainly would have if I'd been able to get hold of them! I certainly gave them a piece of my mind – every blinking time. And that *ruddy* woman – standing there on her own doorstep, grinning like a flipping loon. Mother? Not a single maternal bone in her body, that one. And not an ounce of shame, either. The times I called her out on it! Oh, I couldn't count them, I really couldn't. And the same response every time. To mind my own dot dot dot business.'

She paused, as if in thought, then brushed at a speck of something on her lap. 'Oh, I know it's the drink talking. I *do* know that. And I'm not stupid. I know all about walking a mile in someone else's shoes. But there's only so many times you can excuse a person, isn't there? Only so many times you can pick up the pieces without expecting some sort of *responsibility* to be taken. I came *that* close to telling her social worker – oh, the things I could have told her. *That* close. But you try to keep hopeful, don't you? So I suppose I'm no different from the rest of them. No one likes to think of a kiddie being taken away from home, do they? And at least I was always close by to keep an eye on her.'

Mrs Hardy took another sip of tea, then placed the cup back in the saucer. 'But when it comes to it, that fire was the best thing that could have happened, really, wasn't it? Well, even though I've got to live next door to it for good-ness knows how much longer. Ruddy council. Bloody useless lot. Never get anything done. Oh, I'm sorry,' she finished, a hand flying to her mouth. 'I suppose you work for them, don't you? I do apologise.'

'Absolutely nothing to apologise for,' I assured her. 'I'm just so grateful you've come, I really am.' And also grateful for all the good people in the world, of which there were so very many. In my line of work it was sometimes easy to forget that.

* * *

'Nanny Hardy is like an angel come to earth, isn't she?' Flip told me that night, when I tucked her into bed, in the midst of her new Barbie kingdom. It was a quaint expression and I wondered where she'd heard it.

'Some angels are already born here,' I told her. 'But you're right. Mrs Hardy might just be one of them.'

I reached down to kiss her goodnight and as I did so I noticed that the framed photo on her bedside table was lying face down. It had been the last thing Mrs Hardy'd given her, just before she left: a picture of Flip with her mum, plus Mrs Hardy and her grand-daughter Penny, who I guessed must have then been around 13. It had been taken two summers back, Mrs Hardy had explained to me; a rare afternoon out at the local park.

'Mummy was happy that day,' Flip had remembered. 'She didn't need her medicine.'

'That's right, sweetheart,' Mrs Hardy said, a tear glistening in her eyes. 'It was a day when she didn't need her medicine, wasn't it?'

She'd glanced at me, and it was enough. There was little more to be said. 'Anyway,' she said, clearing her throat, 'I popped it in a frame and I thought you might like to have it.'

And Flip had thanked her politely and hugged it to her chest, and, as we were already in there, seeing the world she'd created for Pink Barbie, had popped it straight on her bedside table so she could 'look at it in bed'.

I righted it now. 'There,' I said.

'No,' she answered. 'Turn it back over.'

'Why?'

'Because I've decided I don't like it.'

'Don't like it, poppet? Why? It's such a lovely smiley photo.'

'Because I want to forget now. I don't want to see my old mummy's face any more.'

She looked up at me, dry-eyed, and clear-eyed as well. 'I really want a forever mummy. I really, really want one, so I hope they keep searching. But not that one. She's too pretty for someone like me.'

I hugged her tightly and kissed her head, at a loss to know quite what to say to her. To find something that wasn't just a meaningless platitude. 'You are the most beautiful fairy I have ever seen,' I told her, my voice catching in my throat. 'And I'm positive that when we find your new family, that mummy will have been searching and searching as well. To find someone *exactly* like you.'

Chapter 20

Mrs Hardy's visit had changed the mood of the house almost as much as the wall-to-wall fairy lights and tinsel. Perhaps more. The offending photo had disappeared into Flip's bottom bedside drawer and it was almost as if she'd drawn her own line in the sand; a whole week had passed and, though she chatted about Mrs Hardy often, it was as if she'd completely airbrushed her mother out of her conscious. I didn't hear her mention her once.

It was a relief to see Flip back on a more even keel, but that didn't mean I felt all was rosy. It was one thing to move on and accept a new reality, but quite another to simply squirrel the pain away in her head – experience had told me that such a course of action never really worked.

With Tyler due to break up in another week, I decided I'd spend the time we had left together on our own trying to establish which was happening in Flip's case. Perhaps we'd all been wrong about her seeming inability to feel as much as most people. Perhaps her apparent ability to compartmentalise her life was just *her* way of burying things that hurt her.

Yes, the evidence on various FAS websites did point to it being the former (a lack of empathy in children with FAS came up again and again) but I knew I wouldn't feel happy if I didn't at least give her the opportunity to open up, to give me a glimpse of what else might be underneath; to address the vital matter of the state of her emotional health.

I also had another plan in play by the Wednesday: to take Flip to see Father Christmas. It was another of those things that I'd managed to tease out via gentle probing; I'd been right. She had no strong memory of having ever been taken to Santa's grotto. The only Santa she'd ever seen had been the one who had turned up at school the previous year during their end-of-term assembly. 'But he wasn't Santa,' she confided to me. 'He was the school caretaker.'

I had a strong urge to do better, so once we'd had break-fast that morning I told her we were off to do some Christmas shopping and that, if she was good, there might also be a special treat in store.

'And put something warm on,' I called up the stairs. 'It's freezing out there and we might be in town for ages. We have lots to do.'

'Okayyyy!' she called back, in the excited sing-song tone that I'd become so used to. Then, 'Actually, could you help me, Mummy? You only have me to sort out, an' I've got three flipping kids to get ready!'

I smiled to myself. Though there hadn't been the exact horse Flip had wanted in the sacks Mrs Hardy had brought, there were, among all the usual Barbie paraphernalia, two brand new dolls, both still in their boxes, which Flip had fallen upon in raptures of delight. 'Sisters! I always wanted sisters!' she'd squealed, before ripping the packaging off and making their proper acquaintance. She'd asked Mrs Hardy for names for them – which I'd thought was rather touching – and now, as well as Pink Barbie, we had two further family members called Holly and Ivy.

Needless to say, all three now went everywhere with Flip, and as she had so many Barbie clothes to choose from, getting all three dressed every morning was quite the production. As she dithered over boots, bags and hair adornments, each morning felt more and more like a Gok Wan style makeover.

'Oh my!' I said as I walked into her bedroom. Though it wasn't the three naked Barbies that shocked me, lined up as they were alongside three choices of outfit apiece. It was Flip herself. She was sitting at the dressing table, all dressed and ready, and leaning forward towards the mirror, concentrating hard. And in her hand was a lipstick that looked vaguely familiar – a stub of one I'd long since slung in the dressing-up box. An in-your-face, traffic-stopping scarlet.

She'd just finished applying it. Well, in the sense that it was all over her lower face, anyway, as if daubed on in the dark by a four-year-old boy; one trying to channel Ronald McDonald. It looked grotesque.

I crossed the room and inspected her reflection along with her. 'Sweetie,' I said gently, 'I think you've put just a little too much on.' In response, she puckered her lips as if blowing herself a kiss. 'And, you know what,' I went on. 'I think you're still just a little too young to be going out wearing make-up, don't you? Riley wasn't allowed it until she was much older.'

She turned to pout at me then, which only exaggerated her grossly painted lips. 'But I like it,' she said. 'I think it makes me look pretty.' She turned and pointed to the row of dolls on the floor. 'An' all my Barbies have lipstick on, don't they?'

I glanced at the dolls, with their regulation neat, pink painted smiles, and then back at Flip, aware from her expression of a potential flash point possibly being imminent. 'Okay,' I said. 'How about we make a deal? You can use make-up all you like when we're home and you're playing dressing up or mummies, but when we go out you stay just as you are, like all the other pretty little girls. How about that? Is that a deal?'

She grabbed a tissue from the tissue box and started scrubbing violently at her mouth. 'I knowed it,' she said, her chin wobbling. 'It was their fault! They made me do it!'

'What, the dolls?' I asked, following the direction of her jabbing finger.

'*Yes*!' she said. '*They* did! They told me I *had* to. Turn them over and spank their bottoms for being naughty, Mummy! And take their lippy off too. They're much too young for it as well!'

She was scrubbing at her face so hard that it was becoming even redder – red raw, in fact. 'Whoah, there,' I told her, grabbing the hand wielding the tissue. 'Let's take you in the bathroom and use a bit of my special cream, eh? Otherwise you'll make that beautiful skin of yours sore.'

She jerked her hand away at first, but then let me pick her up and carry her into the bathroom, snapping at the trio of dolls over my shoulder. 'See!' she said. 'See what happens when you tart yourself up! You can't make a purse out of a pig's ear! Now you're in *big* trouble, girls.'

I popped Flip onto the laundry basket and ran the hot tap till the water flowed warm. 'What's all this about pig's ears, poppet?' I asked her as I added a little liquid cleanser to a flannel. 'Where d'you get that nonsense from?'

'I *am* a pig's ear,' she said. 'Everyone knows I am. I look like a monkey.'

I smiled at her as I gently wiped the last of the lipstick from under her nose, smoothing the flannel over the equally smooth plane between her lips and nostrils. How could anyone ever convince her that she was fine just as she was when the evidence of her difference was right there in the mirror; the total absence of fashionable, Barbie-style plump rosebud lips?

'Now that really *is* nonsense,' I said, rinsing the flannel off. 'How on earth can you look like a pig's ear *and* a monkey? Or, hang on, have you decided you look more like a – let me see now – a pigski? A pinky? A punky?'

She giggled. She couldn't help it. And, as ever, her smile transformed her little face. But her issues with herself – with the little girl she saw in the mirror – would only become more entrenched the older she got, bombarded as she would be by images that only served to highlight how very different she looked from what the media deemed the 'ideal'.

In reality, those images affected everyone. They affected me. I had my moments; if I put on a few unwanted pounds, say. And when I was a teenager myself I wasn't immune from the odd pang of dissatisfaction. Of wishing I was blonde (such a mug's game), of wishing I was taller; of that corrosive but nevertheless pernicious way of thinking – that if I could only add three of four inches to my five-foot-nothing, all the ills of my world would miraculously disappear.

I'd outgrown such nonsense, mostly, and now, pushing 50, was more or less happy in my skin. But we now lived in a world that distorted reality and then fed it back to us through all the different forms of media now available, enabling us to loathe bits of ourselves every minute of every day.

Ask any girl – or indeed, any boy, increasingly – and they could tell you in an instant which parts of themselves they were desperate to change. And these were kids who most people would immediately classify as 'normal', whereas Flip – well, she had facial features readily identifiable to an experienced medic, but which for most people would cruelly mark her out as just looking 'a bit odd'. And those dolls on the bedroom floor were all a part of it; their exaggerated features – the tiny waists, the massive eyes, the endless legs – only serving to make that 'oddness' even more pronounced.

At that moment I could cheerfully have binned and burned the lot of them, not to mention their teeny dresses and ridiculously vertiginous heels. How about a robust, chunky Barbie, wearing flats and a comfy sweater, daring to face the world without that trademark set of seductive inky lashes? With a much more obvious sense of sleeves up and can-do? And can-do without messing up her flipping hair.

But this was not the moment. 'I tell you a game I sometimes used to play when I worked in a school,' I told Flip, as I scooped her up again and we returned to the bedroom. 'Sometimes we played "What animal would you most like to be?" You had to think of an animal and why you'd most like to be it. I always said a lion, so I could be the queen of the jungle. So I could roar really loud and run really fast, and then sleep all day in the sun if I wanted.'

'You'd make a good lion,' she said as I let her slide back down me, to attend to the dolls and their toilette before we left. Sad to say, she was not about to let them go that easily.

'And how about you,' I said, as I picked up Ivy and dressed her in jeans and a woolly jacket. 'What animal do you think you'd most like to be?'

Flip thought for a long time. 'I *would* like to be a monkey,' she said finally. 'A baby one. I sawed about them on the telly. Their mummys take them *everywhere* with them and everybody cuddles them. I think being a baby monkey would be *epic*.'

The town centre was heaving. Just as I'd expected. It seemed highly unlikely that the day would ever dawn when the shops in December were temples of peace. Not that I minded, and Flip, too, seemed caught up in the atmosphere, engaging with the business of present buying with gusto and showing astonishing insight into which recipient might like what, and reminding me just how far she had come in the few short months she'd been part of our family.

I enjoyed her company too. Enjoyed what was quite a change for me. I'd been so used to boy grandchildren for such a long time now that having a little girl to shop with was a forgotten joy. Yes, there'd been Riley to dress up and shop with when she was growing up, but Riley had never really been a 'girly' sort of girl. More an 'in and out and get the job done' sort of person when it came to shopping; even as a teenager she'd march into town with a list, and would want to come home and do something more interesting and exciting just as soon as she'd completed it.

Flip, however, loved to browse, just to take everything in. From the lights in the street to the trees in each store, everything was magical, everything elicited oohs and ahhs, every new corner revealed vistas that filled her with delight. It's true what they say about looking through the eyes of a child; by the time we were heading back to the car with our booty I was almost as excited about our visit to Santa's grotto as I knew she would be the minute I told her.

'Guess where we're off to now,' I said as we climbed back into the car and belted up.

'Barbie-world!' she cried, jiggling the trio of dolls in her lap. I had no idea what or where this Barbie-world was. In fact, I wasn't even sure it existed – a figment of her imagination? Something Megan had promised?

'No,' I said. 'We're going somewhere better than that. Somewhere cold, somewhere snowy, somewhere way up at the North Pole ...' I watched her eyes begin to widen through the rear-view mirror. 'A place where there are elves ...'

'Santa?' she squeaked. 'Are we going to see Santa?'

I smiled as I fired the ignition. 'Indeed we are. Well, assuming you'd like to?'

'OMG, Mummy! That's –'

'Let me guess. Epic? So you'd better start thinking what you want him to send you on Christmas Day. Think hard, okay? We'll be there in 20 minutes.'

With the lunchtime traffic it was closer to 30 minutes, but when we got to the big out-of-town garden centre there were a good number of empty spaces in the car park, so I knew we wouldn't have to wait too long. And that was just as well because Flip was almost beside herself with excitement and kept up a stream of typical Flip questions from what do reindeers have for dinner to what do elves get for Christmas to why anyone would want to set fire to their pudding.

'Lunch first, though,' I told Flip, herding her to the café, where I bought us turkey and stuffing sandwiches and pulled out a pen, so she could commit her list to a napkin as well as memory.

She began writing almost immediately, curling her arm around her writing hand. 'Aren't you going to tell me?' I asked her.

'Of course not!' she said. 'Don't you know?' she said, angling the pen in my direction. 'If you tell anyone what you wish for it won't come true, will it?'

'But you've got to tell Santa,' I reasoned.

'Course I have. But I'm going to whisper it in his ear so no one can hear.'

At which point, keen to commit her wishes to my own memory, the better to commit it to my 'still to buy' list, I came up with what seemed like a really good idea. 'Ah,' I said. 'I'm not sure that'll be the best plan of action, as I know Santa's getting very deaf. It's all that soot in his ears from going down so many chimneys,' I embellished, feeling rather pleased with myself.

Needless to say, Flip being Flip, she took this information very seriously. So much so that when we were ushered in for our audience with the great man, her 'Hello, Santa!' could have broken several icicles, had they been made of ice rather than glitter-dusted resin.

We all smiled – me and Santa, the two elves in waiting, the huddle of parents and little ones who were all clustered on the other side of the roped-off area, patiently waiting in line.

But I was soon to regret my directive rather more. Yes, it was comical to see her cupping her hands round her mouth, not to protect her secrets but to use them as a megaphone. Yes, it was comical to hear her yell, 'My name's Flip and I'm eight!' as if on stage at a packed Albert Hall.

Yes, it was comical to hear Santa ask her if she'd been a good girl all year, and hear her tell him, 'Almost always, yes, I have! Honest, Santa, I swear down!'

But what was not comical, not at all, was when he asked her what she'd like, and she told him, in the same booming tones thus far deployed, that she'd like 'a boob job, a nose job and a facelift, please, Santa!' because her mummy had promised her she could when she was older and now she was eight she was 'prob'ly' old enough.

Paradoxically, I felt the colour rise up in my cheeks even as the blood drained from my face. There was the odd titter, but soon I felt every eye trained upon me; felt the powerful beams of disapproval all aimed straight at me. Heard the words that weren't exactly on everyone's lips – *yet* – but which I knew were forming in everyone's minds. Did they really hear that right? What sort of a mother *was* I? What a disgrace to put such ideas in an innocent girl's head! I knew they were thinking that because I would have been thinking exactly the same thoughts. But what could I do? Make some announcement that, actually, I wasn't Flip's mummy but her foster mummy? That the mummy in question most definitely wasn't me?

Santa got it. Got it right away, or at least, a version of it. Because he quickly directed Flip to the sack of presents parked beside him and as she bent down to choose one I slipped past the resident photographer – not today, thank you! – and scooped her, the three Barbies and the parcel into my arms. Then, as quickly as I could, I fled the scene.

It was only when we got outside that it really properly hit me, and, to my consternation, I felt tears begin to sting in my eyes. And Flip noticed. At least noticed our hasty retreat.

'What's wrong, Mummy?' she asked me anxiously. 'Did I choose the wrong present? Are you cross? Did I be a good girl? Did Santa not like me?'

It was that last comment that really cut me up. 'Oh, sweetheart,' I reassured her, 'of course Santa liked you. There were just lots of other children waiting, so we couldn't stay and chat. So, how about this present of yours? Shall we see what it is?'

'What?' she asked, the moment over with. 'I can open it *now*?'

It was raining hard now. No longer feeling Christmassy at all. 'Course you can, poppet,' I told her, quickly bundling her into the car. 'It's a special pre-Christmas present, so you're allowed to have it now. Just to keep you going till Santa brings you what, well … what you're getting for Christmas,' I finished lamely.

She ripped off the cheap paper and whooped in delight. 'It's a furry pencil case! Look, Mummy! Aww – the fur's so soft! And some felt pens! I have every colour in the whole *world* now, don't I?' Then she looked at me anxiously through the rear-view mirror, her mouth suddenly forming a frown. 'I forgotted something!' she said. 'I just remembered I forgotted something I wanted for Christmas too! We have to go back! He won't know now!'

I shook my head. 'Don't worry,' I said. 'We'll do him a note when we get home and post it. What was it?' I asked, because I couldn't seem to stop myself.

'All right, I'll tell you,' she said. 'Long as you promise not to tell. I want a water blaster just like Ty has so I can blast him to Balamory and back. That would be epic, wouldn't it?'

I pulled out of the car park and joined the crawling traffic, conscious that there was still so much to do, so much still to be repaired. But not today. It felt ironic, but today I decided I couldn't face it. 'Yes, that would be epic,' I agreed.

Chapter 21

Flip didn't get what she'd asked Santa Claus for, of course. Well, apart from the blaster. But I was determined that she receive everything I could possibly think of to make her happy; not to mention to gently try and steer her towards pastimes and preoccupations more suited to an eight-year-old than cosmetic surgery.

Not that I intended a wholesale move away from all things girly. Flip was very much a girly girl and there was nothing wrong with that; she loved playing Mum to her dollies, loved to nurture and look after them, which, given her background, was wonderful to see. It's often remarked that girls with absent or less than present mothers sometimes fail to acquire mothering skills themselves, so I was glad this didn't seem to be the case with her.

'You're going a bit overboard, aren't you?' Mike had asked as he stared at the ever-growing load threatening to spill out of my shopping trolley.

We were in the local toy superstore; a place I'd haunted for so long now that I could probably find my way around it blindfold. 'Not really,' I said, grunting as I tried to manoeuvre it round a corner without knocking over a display of the latest interactive monster toys.

Mission accomplished, I grabbed a pack of doll's furniture from the shelf and tucked it in between the larger boxes; necessary to accessorise the doll's house I couldn't resist getting, knowing it would come in handy for Marley-Mae when the time came, so it wasn't even an extravagance, not really.

'Except she'll take it with her when she goes,' Mike pointed out, when I outlined what I'd thought was my unassailable logic.

'Well, whatever,' I said. 'It's not like we've really bought her anything yet, is it?'

'No, but there's a perfectly good charity shop just down the road, as you well know.'

But I was already distracted. I knew I was trying to get away from Barbie, but the one thing I really had to get her was the horse. How could I not? Her little face would be a picture. 'Oh, she'll love this so much!' I cooed at Mike.

'I'm quite sure she will. But look, love. Look at the trolley. If you carry on much longer, poor Tyler's going to start feeling hard done by.'

'Oh, don't be silly, love. Tyler's old enough to know the value of things! He knows exactly how expensive a new Xbox is, don't you worry. Not to mention the price of the games. I really don't think he'll give a hoot what Flip has once he sees his own presents. And besides,' I added for good measure, 'there is a purpose to all this. We need to take her mind off what she *really* asked Santa for. Reclaim her childhood.'

It was the deal-breaker I'd known it would be, and, satisfied, I led the way to the tills. 'You win,' Mike said, but couldn't resist making a final point. 'And just this once I suppose it won't harm to go a bit mad. But, Casey, we can't make a habit of this or I'll have to start working nights as well as days!'

I had a houseful for Christmas, as was invariably the case. Kieron and Lauren – plus the bump of course – and it was my turn to have my mum and dad, which was lovely. And, as with every year previously, we also had our first foster child, Justin, who was now a young man and towered over everyone but Mike. He'd even stolen a march on my Kieron. We chatted mostly via Facebook these days, in both good times and bad; with his terrible start in life, Justin was always going to have some bad times. But good times too, and very gradually I felt that things were shifting; that the good might just start outweighing the bad.

I couldn't wait to see him. Though there was only one person a certain person hoped to be seeing. Well, not so much seeing – as I'd explained to Flip, to *see* him was bad luck. But certainly to see evidence of his passing. So it was with some surprise that I was woken by my bedside alarm, at 6.30, because I'd half expected a deputation to come and shake us awake at around four, just as our own kids had done when they were little. That Flip hadn't done that gave me a momentary pang. Had she ever done anything like that? Woken, bursting with excitement in the wee hours? My guess was, if she had, she'd have been either given short shrift or been ignored. Either way, it was a sad thing to consider.

But that was then and this was now, and I needed to be on top of things. With Riley, David and the children all due to arrive at 11.30, it was important I did everything on schedule.

I shook Mike awake. 'Come on,' I whispered. 'Let's go and wake the kids up.'

'Christ, Case,' he groaned, ever Mr Christmas Spirit personified. 'You're *worse* than the flipping kids!'

He was right, of course. 'Tired of Christmas, tired of life' could have been my motto. I was so excited I almost bounced out of bed. I changed my nightie into the Christmas pudding onesie I had been saving especially for the occasion, and pushed my feet into the matching slippers – and, yes, they did have bells on. 'Come on, Mr Grumpy,' I coaxed, punching Mike through the duvet till he submitted and rolled blearily out of bed. He'd drawn the line at wearing a onesie himself (I think his exact words were 'Yes, when hell freezes over') but had at least agreed to a racy, ruby-red satin dressing gown that had been on special offer ('I wonder why?' he'd said to that) and once he'd donned it he was rewarded with a proper Christmas kiss under the mistletoe I'd brought up and hung over the bed the previous night. 'Merry Christmas, sweetie,' I whispered, planting a second kiss on his lips. 'Now, come on, let's create some magic and mayhem for these kids.'

Which we did; at least I hope we did. You never really know, do you? Everyone's memories of life's important days are no one's business but their own. As for me, I could hardly keep the smile off my face. We'd had lots of happy Christmases down the years; we were blessed. But we'd also had several since we'd been fostering that had tugged at our heartstrings, and as I watched Justin and Tyler, deep in conversation about whatever Xbox game they were setting up to play, I was transported back to when Justin had been 11 and Christmas had been oh so incredibly painful for him. And it had been for several other of the children since; some whom I was still in touch with, and some not. Some for whom it had all worked out okay, and others who had totally disappeared from my life.

I raised a glass of sherry to them all as I watched the children playing, Flip in particular, who'd so far passed the day in something of a dream, unable to quite take in the sheer volume of toys strewn around her, muted by wonderment – which was a change – and wholly in a good way.

I looked at Lauren too, who had the same 'pinch-me' dreamy look about her, and I realised exactly what she'd been thinking about all day. I went and sat with her and we watched Marley-Mae and Flip playing together.

'This time next year,' I whispered to her. 'Just think of that. We'll have another little one to buy for. I bet you can't wait.'

She smiled the sort of smile that only a contented pregnant woman can; well, when she's not anywhere near a barbecue, that is. 'We can't, Casey, honestly. But I still can't quite believe it. I can't take it in – that in a few months me and Kieron will actually be *parents*. It's mad!'

Mad indeed, I thought. Even madder that, at my tender age, I was going to be nanna to four grandchildren! Now that really *didn't* bear thinking about.

* * *

If Christmas Day resolved itself into one big happy 'flumpa-thon', as Tyler termed it, Boxing Day saw us up and about early and ready for action. Of which there was plenty to be had, the local council having recently decided that we would henceforth be having a big annual Boxing Day market. It had promised to be a huge affair, with stalls selling hot chestnuts, mulled wine and waffles, street entertainers, old-fashioned fairground rides and amusements, and various craft stalls where I could spend money I no longer had. Or perhaps not, but it was certainly the perfect antidote to stay-ing in, lying on the sofa and scoffing more chocolates, and a chance to grab some much-needed fresh air. It was quite a big production, too – going on all day and then into the evening, where the various vendors would be joined by some of the local bars and restaurants, offering street food and drinks, and a couple of local bands would then play.

My grown-up lot were going to head down there in the evening for a couple of hours, while we – sainted grandpar-ents – looked after the grandkids, but we planned to take Flip and Tyler along during the day; they'd been banging on about the stalls and rides since the moment the leaflet had dropped through the door, so there was no danger of us wheedling our way out of it, however much the sofa beckoned again after our full-on Christmas Day.

And once we got there we got into the spirit of things, and it seemed the money we didn't have was soon going to be spent anyway, as both the men – Mike and Tyler – did that thing males do at fairs. They became obsessed with showing their prowess at some nonsense skill or other, in order to win a cheap, tacky prize.

Tyler was currently engaged on a mission with a set of darts, trying hard to win Flip a teddy bear. He's already spent three pounds – probably more than the toy was worth – but he was enjoying trying so much that, against my better judgement, I'd slipped him a fourth so he could have another try.

Mike, meanwhile, was over at another amusement across the way, and we were both alerted to the fact that he might have been successful when there was a sudden eruption of unmistakable Flip-style shrieks of delight.

I turned around to see her skipping across to me, squealing with joy, Mike carrying something behind her. 'Oh thank you, Daddy, thank you!' she sang. 'Mummy, look what he's won for me!' It was then that I noticed that what Mike was carrying was a water-filled and tightly knotted plastic bag.

'A goldfish?' I asked Mike, arching my eyebrows. '*Really*?'

'She begged me to win them, so I did,' Mike said proudly. 'It took a fair bit of skill as well, didn't it, Flip?'

My husband managed to look proud and apologetic all at once, which was certainly no mean feat. And well might he apologise. *A goldfish*? I mentally rolled my eyes. I had no idea you could still win a goldfish at a fair and, as if in answer to my unspoken question about political correctness and modern ways of thinking, Mike pushed a tiny packet of fish food and a piece of paper into my hand. 'Care instructions,' he said sheepishly. 'It needs decanting into a tank. Or a bowl of suitable dimensions, i.e. a *big* one.'

'I'll bet it does,' I said sternly. Though I was really only teasing. Adopting a goldfish was hardly going to be a major responsibility, after all. And I decided it would be good for Flip to *have* that responsibility. She'd never had a pet, as far as I knew.

Tyler, who'd failed to win the bear, looked on slightly disconsolately. 'How d'you win them, then?' he wanted to know. 'On that hook a duck thing over there?'

'I did indeed, mate,' Mike confirmed, puffing his chest out very slightly. Tyler looked across and adopted a distinctly unimpressed expression. 'Hook a duck! Hook a duck, Mike? A baby could win on that thing!'

'Oh, could they now, young man?' Mike said. 'I'm not so sure. It's a great deal more difficult than you might expect.'

'Not for me,' Tyler replied. 'Bet I could hook one in no time.'

'You want a bet?' asked Mike, fishing in his pocket for some change.

'Hang on,' I began. 'Haven't we already spent eno—'

But there was no stopping a brace of males when they were bent on being competitive.

Which was why we ended up with a brace of goldfish.

'What's that on the side of yours, Flip?' Tyler wanted to know as we all clambered carefully into the car an hour later with the newest family members.

'It's a blob,' she replied, quick as you like. 'A big ugly black blob. That's why I choosed her. She's called Molly and I choosed her because none of the other fish liked her. Because she's got a great ugly black blob growing on her side.'

'I think that's what some of them grow like,' Tyler said, having studied the metallic sliver of fish currently wriggling in Flip's bag. 'A few of them, anyway. I think the blobby ones are, like, a special breed.'

Tyler's own fish was the bog-standard orange, him being less concerned about the design features of his pet than the kudos of having hooked it, as he'd predicted, in an instant. 'Exactly. Molly's special. So she doesn't mind being ugly. And I hope your fish is going to be nice to her and won't call her any nasty names. Or I'll have to smack her bottom,' she finished, waggling a finger towards Tyler's bag.

'I told you, Flip. She's *not* ugly! You're obsessed with that, you are. And you know what?' he said, his eyes meeting mine. 'I think your fish is *may* cool. I think I like her even better than I do mine.'

I could have kissed him.

Sadly, however, in the fostering life, the yin and yang were ever balanced, so perhaps I should have expected that something would soon bugger up what had so far been a perfect day.

Bowing to pressure, Tyler had named his fish Dory ('They have a ten-second memory, Flip – do you think you can remember that? Boom boom!') and once home, and bearing pizza, which I popped into the oven, Mike had dug out the largest of my glass mixing bowls for the fish to live in – well, at least for one night.

'And then, tomorrow,' I told the kids, 'we'll go back to the garden centre and get them a proper tank.'

'And some gravel?' Flip wanted to know. 'Fish always need gravel. And seaweed.'

'You mean pondweed,' Ty corrected.

'All right, *pond*weed!'

'And one of those bits of wreck that they can swim through,' said Tyler, warming to the project.

'And a shark!' Flip enthused.

'Don't be such a madhead,' Tyler told her. 'How can you put a shark in with them? A shark would eat them!'

'Not if it was plastic,' Flip retorted.

'Enough already!' chipped in Mike. 'Are we eating or not?'

So we ate the pizza, plus fries, out of the cardboard, on the sofa, while watching telly, Flip returning to the kitchen on numerous occasions, just to check the fish were okay and still getting along.

'I'll eat the rest of your pizza if you don't hurry back,' Tyler shouted when she disappeared off for the umpteenth time.

'You can have it!' she called back, then a long silence followed. Then she ran back, looking mortified. 'Tyler, Dory is *dead*!'

'What? You're kidding,' he said, putting a half-eaten slice of pizza down and rising from the sofa. 'You sure? Bloody hell – oops, sorry 'bout that – *really*?'

We trooped back into the kitchen and gathered round the mixing bowl. Flip had been right. The orange fish was floating on its side, clearly dead. 'Blimey, that was quick,' Tyler observed. 'I mean, I know they don't often live long, but blimey.'

'Must have been sick,' Mike said. 'Or just shocked. Change of environment, change of water … Difficult to tell.' He placed a hand on Tyler's shoulder. 'Sorry, lad.'

Tyler shrugged. Then he smiled. 'Well, it wasn't like we'd got to know each other or anything,' he said stoically. 'And I'm glad it's mine that's kicked the bucket, and not yours, Flip.'

Flip was staring into the bowl, watching her fish turning circles. 'I'm sorry too,' she said to Tyler. 'Still, at least it was the pretty one who died.'

Her voice was strangely emotionless and I wondered what was going though that damaged mind of hers. She sniffed. 'It was only to be expected,' she went on, sounding as if she'd heard the expression somewhere. 'The reason Mollie's still alive is because she's the strong one. That's how it works. If you're ugly you learn to be strong.'

Again, I got the sense that she'd heard all or part of what she'd said somewhere. And wondered how much of what she'd said reflected what was in her head. Had she actually thought about it before saying it? Did she see herself as strong? As having the tools to cope with a world in which she didn't perfectly fit the mould? I didn't think so – it seemed fanciful – but, still, it made me wonder. I put an arm around her, even though she didn't seem remotely distressed.

'I tell you what,' I said to both of them. 'Tomorrow we'll buy another goldfish. That way Mollie won't have to be on her own.' I turned to Tyler. 'Would you like that?'

'Yeah, why not? If Flip wants to. I'm cool either way,' he admitted.

'And you would, wouldn't you, poppet?' I said to Flip automatically.

But she shook her head. 'No thank you, Mummy,' she said politely. 'Not if Tyler's not fussed. I think Mollie probably likes being on her own, don't you? Like me. I think that's what she's used to.' She paused again, and I fancied I could hear the gears of her brain shifting. 'Actually,' she said at last, 'I think Dory might have died because she knew that. She couldn't take herself out of the bowl, could she?'

The vision of a fishy self-sacrifice taking place while we ate pizza was amusing, but the words, once I thought about them, were both profound and slightly shocking. Was that what Flip thought? Were her words evidence of great insight? I wasn't sure. Wasn't sure if you could really read anything into it, but it was certainly food for thought as all four of us crammed into the downstairs loo for Dory's funeral and official flushing-away ceremony.

'Just like a poo!' Flip observed delicately.

Chapter 22

The remaining holiday period went by as smoothly as I could have hoped, and soon it was that time of year when children usually go back to school, adults go back to work, houses get stripped of their festive glitz and glamour, and everything goes back to normal. For most people I knew, this was a time of new beginnings. They let the New Year in, made resolutions or changes to their lives and looked forward to the future.

Not so me. For me the month of January was evil; the most miserable time of year. I hated taking down my tree and I hated that sudden shift on TV from all those Christmas ads, from the jolly to the bring-a-tear-to-the-eye sentimental, which had formed such a part of the bright December soundtrack; from feeling merry and bright to feeling down in the dumps. And if you weren't, all the new ads took pains to remind you, by relentlessly plugging holiday escapism.

And who wouldn't want to escape, with so much of winter still ahead? Oh, the freezing temperatures, dark mornings and grey days might be fine during the run-up to

Christmas (and yes, I prayed for snow, regularly, because it made everything that bit more magical) but *after* the holiday – well, it just became oppressive, and I counted the days until March. Spring was the time for new beginnings, as far as I was concerned.

'I've got SAD, I think,' I told Mike as I peered miserably out of the kitchen window, waving Tyler off for his first day back at school.

He scoffed. He was clearly having none of it.

'You say that every year,' he pointed out, 'and let me tell you something, Mrs doom-and-gloom Watson. Seasonal affective disorder tends not to be treatable by trips to the January sales, however much you think your next utterance should be "I know! Shall we spend the day shopping?"'

'But –' I began.

'But nothing. As in there's nothing left in the pot for the purchase of any bargains to fill the Christmas-tree-shaped hole in the living room.'

'Or in my heart,' I said, lowering my arm as Tyler disappeared round the corner. 'Oh, just ignore me. I'm fine,' I conceded. 'I guess I'm just a bit fed up that they haven't organised any sort of education for Flip yet. It's been ages and she's missing out on so much education. She should be skipping off to school today, same as Tyler.'

Mike had worked right up to Christmas and gone in over New Year as well, so he was enjoying the last of his belated Christmas holiday, and the last thing he wanted to look at was a long gloomy face. 'Sorry,' I said again, plastering a smile on. 'I'll reboot now. So, what exciting thing shall we do today?'

'Funny you should ask that,' he said. 'Because actually, I did have a sort of plan. I thought I'd take Flip out and buy her a pair of new wellies.'

'But you just said –'

He held a hand up. 'I said I'm going to take her. You're not invited. You have too much to do.'

'I do?' I said, wondering what on earth he was going on about.

'Yes you do. You know when I couldn't sleep last night?' I nodded, further confused now. Mike often found it hard to sleep when he wasn't at work – his job was pretty physical, and when he wasn't properly tired out he tended to be wakeful. But I had no ideas what any of that had to do with buying Flip new wellington boots.

But it seemed he was about to tell me. 'Well, I came downstairs and, for want of anything else to do, I sat down with your laptop and read through all your notes.'

'Really?' I'd been oblivious. I had my manic housework to thank for that. But *really*? It seemed an odd thing to do.

Mike nodded. 'And once I started reading, I started thinking, and you know what occurred to me? That we've done precious little so far to really address Flip's past, have we? We've been so focused on the future, and so locked into her FAS – you know, this whole idea that, because of the way she's wired, the past's best forgotten? And, well, I'm not sure that's the right way to go.'

I agreed. I was no psychiatrist, and I only had a layman's knowledge of the myriad ways FAS could affect a child's development, but Mike was right; we had been working pretty much on the basis that the past was the proverbial 'another country', in my case not least because Flip herself seemed so keen to blot out of her mind all that had gone before. Yes, she loved Mrs Hardy, but as a part of her present, not her past. The photo of the day in the park, however happy her memories of it, still remained where she'd stashed it, in her drawer.

I said as much to Mike. But he shook his head. 'I think we should ignore that. I think we should work with her just as we would any other child on the programme. I think we should do so as a priority.'

It wasn't often that Mike had the time to have a proper talk with me about the kids we fostered. Yes, there were times in bed, invariably following some crisis or other, when we'd lie there and talk long into the night, but that was reactive; me talking things through, Mike responding – he rarely instigated any discussions about the kids out of the blue, preferring to leave that side of things – writing up my log, talking things through with John and the child's social worker – very much to me. He had a full-time job, after all.

Which meant I was keen to make the most of his wee hours analysis, and to hear what ideas it had thrown up. After all, we *were* rather drifting, and perhaps not in a good way, as in the midst of all the Christmas preps she'd settled into a routine, pottering around with me, going out with Ellie twice a week, playing with her dolls, and generally just bumbling along. The truth was that her shrunken world seemed to suit her all too well. It didn't bother her in the slightest that she wasn't going to school. It didn't bother her that, bar Tyler and the grandkids, who had little say in the matter, she didn't have a friend to call her own. It didn't seem to bother her that there were no immediate plans for her future. It didn't seem to bother her that she didn't see her mother any more.

It was almost as if, if we rolled along exactly as we were doing, she was content to live her life that way for ever more, almost as if she was fading into the wallpaper. Which shouldn't, and definitely couldn't, be the case. She had potential, and right now we were heading nowhere towards reaching it, and though I couldn't do much about the lack of schooling, there was plenty I – *we* – could do about the rest.

Which seemed to be Mike's way of thinking. 'I just think we need to go right back to basics,' he said. 'Give her something to focus on. Some sort of structure to her days. Take some steps towards preparing her for life with a new family; all of which, one way or another, has gone out of the window these past weeks – not least because you could barely see her points chart for flipping tinsel!'

Mike was right about that. Chiefly because despite Flip's prodigious amounts of energy, in the past few weeks, a few spats and flounces excepted, she'd become something of a model child. I pointed that out. 'So I'm not quite sure what else we'd put on her chart,' I told him.

He shook his head. 'I wasn't talking about the usual kind of chart,' he said. 'I was just thinking that we should set ourselves some goals. I know there's lots we can't change. Stuff to do with the FAS; the brain damage – that's obviously best left to the professionals. And I think everyone realises anyway that there's nothing we can do about that. But there's lots we can work on in relation to how she functions emotionally, which will help with the transition when she does go.'

I nodded, impressed at this burst of sagacity. But still none the wiser about the proposed shopping trip. To which I was not invited. What was all that about?

'But what exactly does this have to do with buying Flip new welly boots?'

Mike raised a hand. 'One – you need a project. Because it's January,' he added. 'Two – if I take Flip out for a few hours you'll have some time to get it under way. And three, you've been so damned efficient at chucking out every single bit of Christmas rubbish that I can't find a sodding shoebox anywhere!'

It didn't take more than a second or two for me to get what Mike was on about. He wanted to get a shoebox (in fact a boot box; since Flip had grown out of her wellies it made sense for him to get her a pair of them) so that we could help make Flip a memory box – the first practical step on the road to her properly putting her past to bed.

Such activities were a central part of fostering. Children in care often brought very little in the way of possessions, but they often had baggage that belied their tender years. The ones that came to us, particularly, almost always had a great deal of it; a surfeit of memories in which they were victims; in which they felt afraid, felt insecure, felt threatened and confused and, more often than not, guilty for even existing, entirely lacking a sense of self-worth.

Since being with us, Flip had had a chance to make lots of new memories. Happy ones, exciting ones, ones she could return to with joy, and triggers to these, in the form of ticket stubs, photographs, notes and pictures, would form part of the box she created. But making a memory box wasn't just about the immediate, happier past. Along with a timeline, which would also form part of our project, the box would hopefully contain remnants of her earlier childhood – not to distress her, but to give her a sense of identity, to help her understand, as she grew, where she'd come from, and the experiences that had helped shape who she was.

To this end, while she and Mike were out buying wellies (and having lunch at the burger bar and then going to the park to splash about) I used the hours I now had to make a start on the process of filling her box, and, in doing so, banish the usual January blues.

I phoned everyone I could think of for photographs or mementoes. I called Ellie (who it turned out was sale-shopping with Will Fisher). I called John, and asked him to call Megan's social worker, Hayley. I called Debbie Scott and I called Mrs Hardy, keen to see if she could suggest any other contacts, and who proved to be unexpectedly helpful.

'Well, everything in the house got destroyed in the fire, of course,' she explained. 'But I do have a baby photo of Flip tucked up in the loft. I hunted high and low for it before I came round to see her. But my daughter reminded me that when I had my last clear-out it was part of a collection of boxes that went up there. There are a couple of school photographs of her up there too, I'm sure. I hung onto them in case her gran and grandad ever came back.'

There had been little will to trace the grandparents. In fact, Ellie had told me that it was already established that there was nothing to be gained there. That the parting of the ways had been long since and complete; that they'd effectively disowned their daughter. Sadly, it happened more often that you'd expect. But that didn't mean I couldn't ask Mrs Hardy what she knew. Nothing ventured and all that.

'I don't suppose you have any idea where they might be these days?' I asked Mrs Hardy. 'Or know someone else that might? I'm just thinking they might at least have something – a book, or a toy – perhaps some bootees; anything really.'

'I might be able to do better than that,' Mrs Hardy said. 'There's no grandad in the picture now – I believe they divorced, acrimoniously, not long after Flip was born. Between us, I'm not sure if Megan's drinking wasn't a factor. But that's by the by. I certainly know someone who I could ask, if you like. A woman I used to see at our Monday Club in the community hall; she knew Megan's mother quite well. And she still lives on the estate. Shall I try her?'

Just like that. I did a little Tyler-style fist pump.

Of course, getting a contact to contact another contact, who might lead me to the holy grail of a living grandparent, wasn't the whole story by any means. It might lead to nothing, and, equally, it might lead to *something*; but what form that something took was as yet unknown, as was the will of the child to create something out of it. Not all kids were as keen to re-establish connections, however well-meaning such an intervention might be.

I was happy with the prospect of some small tokens from the past; had there been any will for the woman to have anything further to do with her grand-daughter, I was quite sure something would have happened by now.

Which worked both ways. Though Flip knew nothing of Mrs Hardy's mission – and obviously wouldn't, unless anything came of it – she didn't even want to make a memory box in the first place.

'I don't *want* no memories,' Flip said, pulling a face when, the following day, I took her into the conservatory and explained what all the craft materials were out for. 'They just make me upset and all I want's to be happy.'

'Be that as it may,' I said briskly, knowing I sounded just like my mother. 'You need to have some evidence that you existed before coming to us, poppet. After all, you didn't just drop down into our back garden out of the sky, like James Bond.' A possibly inaccurate analogy, but this at least made her smile. I patted the top of her head. 'You know what? Inside there, there are also lots of good memories. They just get buried sometimes, under all the sad ones. And good memories are precious, Flip. They're like little twinkling jewels inside your mind. Memories you can pull out and recall, for when times aren't so good. They're *precious*,' I said again. 'They help everyone, every-where. They help us understand who we are, and they help us feel good. About life, about things that happen, but mostly about ourselves. Go on,' I said. 'Close your eyes. See if you can find one for me. Close your eyes and have a rummage in your head.' She duly closed them, screwing them tight shut and tipping her head back as she did so. 'There,' I said. 'Think back. What can you see that looks hopeful? Perhaps a birthday. Some other party. Perhaps a time when you were out playing. With a friend, or a neighbour. Maybe with a special toy. Or an animal. Perhaps a pet ...'

Her face softened as she thought, the lines around her eyes smoothing out. It seemed a long time – perhaps a minute – before she opened them again.

'Mummy, I think I've found one,' she said. She seemed surprised.

'Right,' I said. 'Let me grab my pen and notebook so I can jot it all down.'

'It was a *long* time ago,' she said, sitting up straight again. 'When we used to have another next-door person – on the other side to Nanny Hardy, this was. They had a boy called Olly and he had a brown face. His mummy used to lift me up high – right over the fence – so I could play in their garden. An' on this day – it was a sunny day; I 'member his mummy put cream on us – we had a picnic in his garden, with tiny cut-up sandwiches. And blackcurrant squash, which I'd never ever had before. And then we played so late that it got dark – really, *really* dark, like night-time. And Olly's mum said that because my mummy had got sick I could stay the whole night and sleep on the blow-up Lilo by Olly's bed. We all took turns and blowed it up together.' She paused, watching me catch up scribbling the bones of it on my pad. 'It was the best day of my *whole* life,' she said. 'Put that as well.'

'Well, there you go,' I said. 'That's a brilliant start, isn't it? So what we need to do next is write it properly – I'll help you turn it into a little story. And then you can draw a picture to go with it. Perhaps of you and Olly enjoying your picnic. And when it's done, we'll fold it up, sort of make it into a little booklet, and pop it in your box so it's there for ever more. Well, that is, when you actually have a box to put it *in*.'

This cheered Flip up no end, and, having got the idea, she set about the task at hand with gusto. The wellington-boot box, now divested of its shocking pink wellies, was transformed by a covering of equally pink paper, and jazzed up with felt love hearts and birds and flowers, and with her name picked out in stick-on diamantés. It was typical Flip and she was rightly proud when she held it up for me to inspect.

'I'm going to write my name on the bottom as well,' she said. 'Like on *Crimewatch*. So even if they pick off the top name so they can steal it, it will still be there, hidden, so they can sling them in jail and throw away the key.'

I was just opening my mouth to laugh when I heard my mobile ringing in the kitchen. 'Excellent idea,' I said instead. 'Now, why don't you crack on with your story while I go and get my phone?'

I ran back into the kitchen and picked my phone up. It was Ellie.

'We've found a school!' were her first words, her first excited words. 'Only nine miles away, and we can organise transport and, best of all – ta-da! – they can take her right away!' She paused to take in air, and I could hear someone laughing in the background. Someone with a deep voice. Hmm. 'Oh, shurrup!' she said. 'Shush! Anyway, I've just come from there, literally, Casey, and I know it's going to be perfect for Flip. Only six students to a class, and they really are brilliant. I've been there before; it's really well-regarded. And if you like, Mr … hang on a tick … yes, Mr Ward – that's the headmaster – says you're welcome to take Flip down any time for a visit. Tomorrow, if you like. Or if not, whenever you want next week. Or I can. But I thought you'd probably want to, wouldn't you? You know, so you're happy in your own mind you know where she is.'

'And they can take her right away?' I asked, conscious that the previous urgency in my head suddenly didn't seem so urgent.

'Pretty much. Usual formalities. Though no uniform to worry about. And the space is available now so, well, as soon as suits you, I imagine.'

I grabbed a pen and scribbled down the number Ellie read out to me, and had just clicked the end call button when the phone piped up again. Yet more encouraging news, this time from Mrs Hardy.

'That was quick!' I said, when she told me she'd tracked down Flip's maternal grandmother, whose name, it turned out, was Jacqueline.

'We have our ways and means, us in the granny network,' she said, laughing. And causing me to wish she really was Flip's nanny. 'Anyway, the news is that she's going to dig out a couple of baby photos and get them copied. Oh, and she's got a matinée jacket of Flip's. D'you think she'd like that? She's not nearby, but she's going to pop them in the post to my friend, and once she's got them she'll pass them on to me. Shall I pop over with them at some point?'

'Oh, I don't want to put you to any trouble. Why don't I drive over and get them from you? Besides, we're early in the process of Flip making peace with her past. I'll have to choose my moment before sharing them with her.'

'Oh, of course,' she said. 'And one thing you might like to know is that my friend says she seemed genuinely keen to be helpful. Keen to know how Flip was. Which could mean something, couldn't it?'

I agreed that it could. And though I didn't know what form the something might take, I felt my happy-ever-after gene go into overdrive. And, in my line of work, that was a rare and precious thing.

Chapter 23

Slowly but surely, things started to fall into place. I took the opportunity to visit the potential new school and, just as Ellie had said, it was perfect.

I didn't take Flip. It felt important not to alert her to anything yet – what if I went there and something about it just didn't feel right? I knew it was hardly up to me to make such assertions – what did I know? But Ellie had impressed upon me, as had John, that I was central to the decision. That I must also be candid about the learning challenges Flip was dealing with; that the school knew in detail exactly what they were taking on.

Because what must not happen, under any circumstances, was a repeat of what had happened in October. If the school took her and she settled, then it was imperative she stay there. There must be no more chopping and changing, no more instability in her life.

Debbie had taken her off to the local farm that day; a day that was bitter but bright. It certainly showed the school – Renshaw House – to its best advantage as I drove up, the lingering frost picking out all the elegant Victorian buildings and carefully tended shrubberies in outlines of silver and glittering white.

Mr Ward, the headmaster, was also everything Ellie had promised, showing me round with the sort of pride in his school that every parent desperately wants to see. And though the exterior was of another age, the interior was purpose-built and modern, and I knew immediately that Flip would absolutely love it.

There were only four classrooms, each decorated in the same cheery fashion as had mine been back when I'd been running the behaviour unit in our local comprehensive. There were colourful plastic chairs, as well as bean-bags and cushions, and, best of all, a well-equipped dedicated arts and crafts room, totally devoted to all things messy. Yes, Flip would definitely love the place, and she would thrive there. Two teachers per class, only six pupils per room. It was exactly the sort of ratio a child like Flip needed, if she was to do that all-important thing – reach her potential.

And there was more. 'I believe Flip only has a mild statement of special needs,' Mr Ward said, as we settled down to chat in his office after my tour. 'I hope you don't mind,' he went on, looking slightly apologetic, 'but we aim to have an educational psychologist come in once she starts, to reassess that. From what I understand from the information I already have, her current statement is quite old.' I nodded. 'And it's already been identified that she will require quite a bit more in terms of support than it entitles her to. Are you happy for us to go ahead and do that?'

Happy? Was the man insane? I could have bitten his hand off. Both hands, in fact. It was exactly what I wanted to hear. I knew some parents were uncomfortable about labelling kids too aggressively, for fear of labels travelling through life with them, but not me. I wanted Flip to get every single shred of help she could. 'No, no,' I said, shaking my head like a wet collie. 'That's fantastic! It's *just* what we hoped for. Will that need to be done before she can be admitted?'

'Not at all, Mrs Watson,' he said, opening a huge leather diary. 'In fact I'm hoping Philippa – no, she answers to Flip, doesn't she?'

'Yes. Well, most of the time,' I quipped.

The warmth in his smile told me all I needed to know. That this was best. That here Flip wouldn't prove a burden in an already stressed system. Here all the focus would be on *her* needs. 'Next Monday, then?' he suggested. 'And we'll start working on her statementing straight away, that week. Nothing too intrusive,' he clarified. 'Just observation and some gentle chats with the psychologist. But all of it very effective. All being well, we should have the revised statement by the end of term, if not sooner.'

I nodded appreciatively. For such words to come out of a teacher's mouth was the best news imaginable. Less than a week and I would have normal life restored again *chez* the Watsons, and Flip would at least be in a place where she could learn, taught by people who knew all about children like her, and would relish the opportunity to enable her.

* * *

I drove home with a huge smile on my face. And when I got home and was able to tell Flip all about her new school she was as excited as I was. Yes, she was a little miffed that she no longer had to wear a school uniform, but by the time Monday came around she was able to see the benefits; within reason she got to choose how to present herself, and looked proud as punch standing in the hall with her little Barbie lunch bag, waiting for the taxi to arrive for her first day.

'You won't forget to check on Molly and the girls for me, will you?' she asked as she stepped anxiously from one foot to the other, beset by last-minute collywobbles when the taxi pulled up.

'I won't,' I said. 'I'll give Molly a pinch of fish food at noon sharp, and I'll look in on your girls every time I go upstairs. I'm sure they won't get up to any mischief. More to the point, a final run-though – what did we talk about last night?'

'If I need the toilet, I just have to ask, if I feel upset or scared I have to tell a teacher, an' if I don't understand anything I always have to say so.' She let out a sigh. 'Honestly, I'm not a *baby*, Mummy. I've growed up a lot since I got my own girls to take care of.'

I reassured her that I knew that was true, which it was. I gave her yet another 'final' hug. 'I just want to be sure you're okay. But I know you'll be *fine*. And you'll probably make some friends today. Won't that be nice?'

The shadow of the driver darkened the glass in the front door. I pulled it open. 'I will, Mummy,' Flip said. 'I'll make a best friend, I promise.'

'No need to promise,' I said. 'That's not an instruction. You just go off and have a supercalifragilistic day, okay?'

She grinned. 'Perhaps I'll even learn how to spell it!'

Flip didn't just have a supercalifragilistic first day, she had a similarly good week, and by the end of her first fortnight Mr Ward himself called to say how incredibly well she'd settled in. And there was more news that same day when I got a call from Mrs Hardy to let me know she, too, had positive news.

She'd already been kind enough to come round the previous week and give me some baby photos, passed on by Flip's grandmother – she'd been passing by, and had stayed for a chat and a cup of tea. She'd also brought a matinée jacket that the grandmother had knitted and which she'd carefully stashed away when relations had broken down.

'She's not anxious to keep it?' I'd asked Mrs Hardy.

She'd shaken her head. 'It belongs to Flip, after all,' she'd said. She leaned closer. 'And d'you know what I think? I think this is something of a peace offering, don't you?'

If so, it had worked, because though Flip had cried when she saw what her grandmother had sent her she assured me they were 'happy tears, like mummies do at weddings'. I didn't ask her to explain how the one was like the other. I was just overjoyed to see the positive effect they had, as all were carefully catalogued and stashed in her memory box.

Today, though, Mrs Hardy had even better news to impart. There had now been some discussion with Ellie about the possibility of contact, but, knowing the background, and in particular the antagonism with Megan, I was the last person inclined to get my hopes up.

But it seemed I'd been wrong in my prognosis. It seemed Flip's gran did want to see her. 'I've chatted to her myself now,' Mrs Hardy explained, 'and I know what the sticking point has been. If it was a case of all or nothing, there was no way it was going to happen. But now it's been explained to Jacqueline that she can see Flip but doesn't have to have anything to do with Megan, she's actually quite driven to make it happen.'

It was wonderful news, though, as ever, I couldn't quite get my head round how anyone could be so entrenched as to disown their own flesh and blood. But it wasn't for me to judge. I hadn't walked a mile in her shoes, had I? So I was just grateful that Flip would have a blood relative taking an interest in her. Even if contact wasn't often, its potential value to her would be enormous.

'That's great news,' I said. Then another thought came to me. 'You might not be able to answer this, but why? Why did she cut herself off?'

'She thought she was doing it for the best,' Mrs Hardy told me. 'Something she regrets now very much. The way she saw it, her daughter would never change and become a proper mother to Flip if she were always there, picking up the pieces. Tough love, if you like. Then it became too much for her to bear; to see her daughter going downhill the way she did. Then after the fire, and Flip being taken, well, Jacqueline just felt that she deserved a fresh start. A chance to forget about her early life and build a new one; a life uncluttered by memories – or people – from the past. I know. Seems odd, doesn't it? Does to me, anyway. But I genuinely believe her heart was – is – in the right place.'

I did too. And I was over the moon. So much so that, with Flip settled in school and the first contact visit imminent, I had a heart to heart with Mike at the beginning of February. Because, now we thought about it, what was the rush to move Flip on, really? Yes, she was still a mile-a-minute Flip, which kept us on our toes. But she was no longer a challenge to us; she was too busy rising to her own challenges, which the new school were so amply enabling her to do.

'So shall I phone Ellie and John?' I said, once we'd both realised we were singing from the same hymn sheet. 'Just let them know that she can stay with us for as long as it takes? That they don't need to prioritise her; you know, don't need to accept something less than perfect?'

'Definitely,' Mike said, and we both knew what we meant. We'd not said as much, but if 'as long as it takes' ended up being another year, perhaps two years … well, we'd just let it ride, and, well, see how it went. Because we'd all grown to love her, and she really was flourishing now. It just no longer seemed to make sense to rock the boat.

But it seemed John had other ideas. It was part of fostering, this yin and yang lark, so you kind of got used to it; it was the job where the words 'emotional rollercoaster' really were well defined. And my personal plunge down the steep bit was 29 February – I remember because when the phone went I was in the middle of explaining to Flip about February being the only month that sometimes had an extra day – something she just couldn't quite get her head around. It was just after half-term, and she'd just got in from school, and was playing with her doll's house, when it rang.

I'd called John and Ellie and had only managed to get hold of the latter, who was unable to speak for long as she was just going into the cinema with another child she was looking after. 'So I'll call you back over the weekend?' she'd said. But she hadn't. Not as yet. Though I supposed I *had* told her it wasn't anything urgent.

'How's it hanging?' John said, as soon as I'd answered, and taken myself off out of earshot

'It's hanging fine,' I answered. 'So did you get my email?' I'd sent a long, rather rambling one, just explaining how Mike and I were thinking. But there was to be no similarly long rambling chat with him today.

'Ah,' he said. 'Here's the thing, and I'm *so* sorry, Casey. But I was already planning to call you today anyway. To see if I could come over. Because, well, because we've found a family. A perfect family. Which – argh – is not what you want to hear, is it?'

I looked through to where Flip was busy rearranging doll's house furniture and trying to shoehorn one of her Barbies into the front bedroom, sideways, a Barbie and a regular doll's house not being quite compatible, size-wise.

I didn't trust myself to speak.

John coughed, presumably to fill the silence, while I gathered myself together. Then he continued. 'I'm so, so sorry,' he said again. 'And it isn't like we purposely kept you and Mike out of the loop,' he hurried on. 'We just wanted to be 100 per cent sure that this couple were right for Flip before saying anything. And of course, with you and Mike, it was only ever meant to be short term, wasn't it? That's what you do. Well, what *you* did do' – he coughed again – 'well, till Tyler, which … God, sorry, I'll shut up, shall I? I just didn't think, Casey. I should have. I know I should. I'm such an idiot. I know how you are with the kids. Oh, I could kick myself. Casey, are you all right?'

I wasn't all right. I was standing there feeling quietly devastated. I think I only realised right then just how much I loved Flip. How much I didn't want to let her go. This was a job, though. I knew what it meant, what I'd been trained for, and it was hardly John's fault that I never got used to it, was it?

'I'll be fine,' I said quietly. 'Honestly, I'm just a bit shocked, you know? I mean, here's me making silly plans, and not even thinking about all the things that are going on behind the scenes. I'm sorry,' I sniffed. 'Take no notice. It's just me being me. I'm really happy that you might have found the right people for Flip. *Really* I am.'

I'd also reached a place of acceptance. That's what I told my brain, anyway. I was getting quite good at lying to myself.

Chapter 24

I got over myself. There was nothing else to do. And just as I'd carefully avoided long run-ups to events when dealing with Flip, lest she get over-excited, so John wasted no time in putting wheels in motion, presumably lest I throw my toys out of the pram.

And, much as it pained me to hear it, the family did sound perfect. A couple in their late forties, they were called Ann and Frank Rawson, and they lived an idyllic-sounding life on the edge of open country and just a couple of minutes' drive from Flip's new school. Honestly, I told Riley as I ran disconsolately through the details, it was almost too perfect to be true.

But theirs was no kind of rural paradise; far from it. For the Rawsons had seen tragedy of the most terrible kind. They had lost their only daughter.

'Eight years ago,' John explained. 'She was19 years old. An only child. She died of an overdose. She'd gone to university, and become a drinker, and they were terribly worried about her, obviously. And then she dropped out –

unbeknown to them because she covered her tracks so carefully – having met and become besotted by an older boyfriend. The usual story. Got into drugs, got into the wrong set, couldn't handle it. One particularly heavy hit of some particularly strong gear, and that was it – she was gone. To a place where they could no longer help her.' He sighed. 'I'm sure you get the picture, but the main thing is that in subsequent years they've worked tirelessly with a charity helping young people with drug and alcohol addiction. And it's through *that* – well, they began to see the wider picture too, including the fall-out from addiction, how badly it affects children – we know all about that, don't we? Anyway, they decided they'd like to make the whole thing more personal. Take in children whose lives have been blighted by it into their lives. Which has led to this. They're now in it for the long haul.'

'Oh that's so tragic,' I said, trying to imagine the depth of their pain. Did you ever get over something like that? 'So how long have they been fostering?'

'Three years as respite carers, usually with older children,' John said. 'But they've now made the decision to switch to fostering long term. They don't want to have another child of their own; never have, even before they lost Katie, their daughter. But they're certain that they have a whole lot to give. And they have, Casey. Just wait till you meet them. Trust me, they're right up your street.'

I allowed myself a smile. That meant they were working class, down to earth and easy to get along with. The sort of people who would call a spade a spade. I smiled again, even as my heart broke just a little. That was definitely another good 'spression'.

I had absolutely no idea how Flip was going to take it. She might shrug and smile and ask when she could meet her new mummy, or she might throw a tantrum and say that she wasn't going 'nowhere no how no way!' as was *her* way.

I felt a bit like throwing something of a tantrum myself. It seemed just plain weird that two weeks previously we'd been talking about keeping Flip long term – with all the soul-searching, heart-string tugging and emotion that implied – and here we were having to tell her she was leaving us. And very soon. It might have been childish but my principal reaction was to stick out my lower lip and shout 'Unfair!'

But it was happening anyway – and Mike and I knew in our hearts now that it should – and on a Friday night in March we simply sat down and told her.

I'd ordered Chinese in for a treat, and had already briefed Tyler what was going to happen once we'd finished our meal. It mattered to us that he was there with us; that this was a proper family gathering, and, though he was disorientated, even though we'd begun preparing the ground a little, he stepped up to the plate.

I chose my moment, which was just after we'd all been having a chuckle about something Levi had said to Tyler the previous day. I waited until the laughter had subsided and then glanced at Mike.

'Flip,' I said brightly, 'do you remember ages ago when we told you that everyone was looking for a forever family for you?'

She stopped laughing and looked at me. Then nodded. 'Yes, I think so.'

'Well, I had a phone call from Ellie and my friend John the other day, and guess what? It looks like they've found you the perfect new mummy and daddy. Well, they will be your new foster parents, just like me and Mike are. A brand new forever foster mummy and daddy.'

The silence swelled, as Flip's face fell and her bottom lip quivered. 'But I don't need a new foster mummy and daddy,' she said quietly. 'I have you.'

I was aware of Tyler's expression even out of the corner of my eye. I saw Mike place a reassuring hand on his arm. These were the tough conversations, and for a moment I regretted my decision to involve him – in this bit at least. After all, we had had these conversations with him. What must be going through his mind right now?

'But why?' he suddenly blurted out. 'Why does she have to go? Why can't she just stay with us, Casey? Why does she have to go just because John says so? He's not *God*.'

Flip began to wail then. 'I have to *go*?' she squealed. 'What does he mean, I *have* to go? Go *where*?'

This wasn't going at all well. I looked to Mike for support. He cleared his throat and reached across to hold Flip's hand as well. 'Sweetheart,' he said, 'you've always known that you were only here with us for a while. They've always been looking for the best family to care for you and love you …'

'No!' Flip screamed, snatching her hand away. 'I didn't know that! I thought that when you made me all pretty *you'd* love me. You *do* love me, I know you do, so why are you sending me away?'

Tyler scraped his chair back and stood up. I could see he was crying. I reached out to try and stop him, but he shrugged me off and ran upstairs. I couldn't remember a time when I'd felt quite so awful.

'Flip, darling, we *do* love you,' I said. 'We'll *always* love you, always. And you'll always be part of our lives. That's a promise. Remember Justin, who you met at Christmas? Like that. For always. But sweetie, I'm not your mummy. I was just your mummy for a *while*. And now, if you like, I can be like your auntie, and you can come and visit us ... But look, we're going to go and see this new mummy tomorrow. Your new mummy and daddy – and they're dying to meet you. They have a lovely house, with fields all round – I think there might even be a stream, so you'll definitely need your wellies – and best of all they love little girls.' I was gabbling on, I knew, but then a thought wandered in. I grabbed it. 'And guess what? They've seen photographs of you. They think you're just the prettiest little girl they've seen in a long, long time.'

Flip looked at me with something other than desolation in her huge, wide-apart eyes. 'They think I'm pretty?' she asked quietly through her sobs. She sniffed. 'Honestly, Mummy? Honest to God and swear down?'

'Honest to God and swear down,' I said, making a cross sign across my chest, just as I'd seen her and Tyler do together when swearing one of their solemn oaths. I pushed my chair back a little and patted my lap, this information seeming to calm her sufficiently to let Mike's hand go and to come and sit on my knee for a cuddle.

Mike tilted his head to indicate that he'd go up and deal with poor Tyler. Job done. Just the fall-out now to live through.

Things moved very quickly after that, as is so often the way of things. Within a couple of days Mike and I were off to the countryside to pay a visit, and, as with the school, I had a sense of rightness that just wouldn't seem to go away, despite a part of me (an unconscious part; I wasn't that mean) half-wishing I'd find the Rawsons horrible.

They'd also done their homework, and seemed to know almost as much about Flip as I did. And, best of all, waiting to greet her there was a neatly wrapped welcome present. It was a Barbie, dressed in posh riding gear; one of the few outfits she didn't have. 'I've got the horseeeee!' she shrieked. 'OMG! This is *epic*!'

She wasted no time after that in making herself perfectly at home. Displaying the same confidence that I remembered the first time she'd stepped over my own threshold, she breezed both in and onto the sofa and then onto Ann Rawson's lap. 'Can I call you Mummy?' she asked her. 'And can you help me choose a name for my new daughter? "I need a new name", she crooned in her dolly voice, "and it needs to match my three sisters who are all pretty just like me!" Oh, and can I bring my fish? She's got a blob and she's called Molly.'

It was a match seemingly made in heaven. So much so that when Mike pulled Flip's coat off the banister rail so she could put it on for the journey home, she looked dumb-founded. 'But I thought I was staying here,' she announced as Mike wrestled her into it. 'Casey, you said I could *live* here!'

Little monkey! Abandoning me at the drop of a Barbie doll.

I didn't even have time to be too dejected, however. On the Monday John phoned me to say that the date was set. Two weeks' time – 27 March, to be exact – would be Flip's official moving day.

'I have other news too,' he said, 'and this is something I'm afraid you won't play a part in. Actually you will, but only to tell Flip about it. The grandmother has been screened and assessed and it's a go. She will be having supervised contact with Flip on a weekly basis just as soon as she's properly settled into the Rawsons'. Don't want to bombard her with everything at once. After that it's hoped to build up to unsupervised and then possibly sleep-overs. We're all hoping that it will be a normal grandchild–grandparent relationship. Something for her to keep of her past.'

'That's brilliant news,' I said, feeling genuinely happy. 'I'm sure Flip will be absolutely thrilled about that.'

'And what about you, Casey?' he asked. 'I know this must be less than thrilling for you. It never gets any easier, does it?'

'No, it bloody doesn't!' I said, with some feeling. We'd been a long way together, had John and I, and I knew he wouldn't mind the odd expletive. 'Oh, I'll be fine,' I said. 'So don't worry. I'm not going to hang my hat up just yet.

I don't suppose I'll ever get used to saying goodbye, but that's not the same as saying I can't cope with having to live with it.'

'And how's our Tyler doing?' he asked then. 'Unsettling for him too. I was just saying to Ellie and Will yesterday, it's incredible to think how time has flown since he became part of the family, isn't it?'

Amazing how a simple question can take your mind off your own worries. 'Oh, he'll be okay,' I said. 'As you say, he's a Watson now, isn't he? In spirit if not in name. And we're not ruling that out either, because he seems pretty keen. Don't worry, John. We're gathered around him. Holding him close. Calming the waves. But, erm, Ellie and Will?'

'What?'

You say you were chatting to them?'

'Yes, in my office, like I said. Why?'

'As in together?'

'Yes, as in together. Will had to pop in with some paperwork and Ellie came with him. What's the ... Oh, hang on. I get it. You don't even know, do you? You're losing your touch, Casey. They've been together now since, oh, at least the New Year, I think.'

Typical, I thought. Do all the spadework and you're the last one to know!

I'd been telling the truth to John. Tyler was struggling a little, but he was so emotionally intelligent that he was at least able to articulate why he felt so strange. And not just to me. He'd also had a couple of little chats with Kieron, who'd been able not just to sympathise but also to empathise with his predicament, which went a very long way.

'This is kind of how it's going to be, kiddo,' I explained to him when we had a few quiet moments that Sunday evening. 'You're going to see lots of kids come and go. They always stay for a while, but they come with a plan usually, and that plan is for them to move on.'

I could almost hear John clapping his approval inside my head. 'I know,' Tyler said. 'Kieron said he still gets upset sometimes. And d'you know what he told me? He told me that if you'd told him *I'd* had to go to a forever family somewhere else, he was going to make you change your mind. He said he just *knew*.'

This was news to me, but such incredibly lovely news. 'I think we all did,' I told him. 'God, look at me. I'm welling up now.'

'But why d'you do it, Casey?' he asked me. 'Why d'you keep doing it if it always hurts so much? Why don't you just keep all of us? I mean, I know that's not realistic. But, you know, why didn't you just keep Justin and, you know, just stop?'

How precisely did you explain that to a 13-year-old? Especially when you weren't sure how to explain it yourself. How did you explain the myriad factors that drove you to follow your instincts? Explain why it had been different for him. 'We do it,' I said eventually, 'because it makes our life richer for doing it. And hey, if we didn't, we would never have met you, would we? Seriously, I'm not sure I can answer you any better. Will that do, sweetie? For now?'

I tried to rugby tackle him for a tickle then but he leapt out of my way. 'I s'pose so,' he said. 'And you did get lucky when you got me, I guess.' And his grin told me he was going to be okay.

It was a first for me the day she left us. A watershed. A moment to cherish and remember. An illustration, right there, of just how emotionally complex a business it was – and still is – being a foster carer. Because there was a new family member there to see Flip off two weeks later, not just Mike and I, or some combination of children and grandchildren. And not the newest youngest Watson; that one was still to be born.

No, it was Tyler. Our Tyler. The boy we'd taken in, just like we had Flip, and who was now there to say goodbye alongside us. Could I have predicted this day happening? Probably not.

In any event, though I felt the usual tug on my heart-strings, I also felt a sense of rightness. A confidence that we'd ultimately made the right choice. Even though it was a choice we'd more or less had made for us by John, I'd come to realise that Flip was going to the very best place for *her*. A home where the focus would be entirely *on* her, and where, basking in such love and, yes, *ambition* for her, she would almost certainly flourish.

It was going to be a journey for Tyler too. Mike and I both understood that. And I didn't doubt that, down the line, he might have a little wobble. That he would miss her. Miss having a sibling. But that was okay. That was life. He was secure in our love and understood why things were the way they were. That there weren't enough hours in the day to take care of everyone for all time. And, no doubt, there would soon be another …

Flip, on the other hand, was in a fizz of excitement. So excited that when Ellie strapped her into the back seat of her car I thought she'd barely glance back, she was so keen to be away.

But just as I'd thought that, she unbuckled her seat belt and hopped back out onto the pavement.

'What now, love?' Ellie asked, having just got into the car herself. 'Flip, where are you off to now?'

'You have to hang on a minute, Ellie,' she called. 'I almost forgotted something!'

She'd clambered out clutching all four of her Barbie dolls, which she now fanned out in front of her. 'We love you,' she sang, in her squeaky doll's voice. 'We love all of you and we've loved living in this house. We …' She stopped then, her chin wobbling and her voice being swallowed up, then dropped the dolls onto the pavement and ran to me. 'I love you, Mummy!' she cried, launching herself at me. 'I love you all. I love you, Daddy. I love you, Tyler. I don't think I'm going to be able to cope very well without you!'

'Silly thing,' I said, tears springing in my own eyes as well now. 'What a funny thing to say. Of course you'll cope okay.' I tilted my head back to look at her properly. 'Sweetheart, do you even know what the word "cope" means?'

She nodded. 'I do, Mummy,' she said. 'I do, really. It's like when you say, "Oh, Mike, I *really* can't cope with these

kids today!'" She smiled through her tears then. 'Me and
Tyler *definitely* know what that means, don't we, Ty?'

Ellie was out of the car and waiting patiently, looking on,
hands on hips, and she and Mike both burst out laughing
as my face turned to beetroot.

'Yep, we definitely do,' Tyler agreed, obviously enjoying
my squirming. 'It's when we're being pains in the bum, and
Casey doesn't want us to be.' He ruffled her hair. 'And, to
be fair, I don't think *I'd* be able to cope with us, either. Not
when I'm being Dennis the Menace and you're in full-on
Minnie the Minx mode.'

Flip giggled, but also managed to bat him playfully
about the head. 'Come on,' I said, while Mike picked up the
abandoned quartet of Barbies. 'Time to fly,' I added, placing her back into her seat. We all took turns to kiss her
again and I finally settled the dolls back in her lap. 'You
won't have a chance to not cope without us,' I whispered,
'because I'll make sure we all see each other often, okay?'

Then they did finally drive off, leaving me with that
familiar hollow feeling, my spirit all at odds with the warm,
sunny day. We all waved until the car went out of sight,
then I put an arm around Tyler. 'Sad day, this, eh, kiddo?'
I said as we walked back inside. 'I think we need a hug,
don't you?'

'Yeah,' Tyler replied, submitting graciously as I squeezed
half the life out of him. 'But don't you worry, Casey,' he
said, patting my head. 'You'll be okay. I'm sure you'll cope
much better with only one of us around to drive you
bonkers.'

Then he ducked and scampered off down the hall.

Epilogue

It's a way down the line now, and Flip continues to flourish. She's absolutely besotted with her new 'mummy and daddy', just as they are with her. It truly *is* a match made in heaven, just as I'd suspected, and believe me, it's not often I'm able to say that without caveats in this line of work. She also spends lots of time with her maternal grandmother, whom I've since met, and actually she's a lovely woman. Straight talking and no-nonsense, she is just what Flip needs, and they get along like a house on fire – no pun intended.

Megan has not been allowed to see Flip again and, though in the early months there were sporadic requests to try and re-establish something (particularly when it reached her that her own mother had re-established relations with her grand-daughter), she has apparently long since stopped asking about her. Tragically, it seems that alcohol is the only family she requires. It's with great sadness that I have to report that Megan has since had another baby; a boy, who was also born with foetal alcohol syndrome and who she immediately agreed to give up for adoption. Flip obviously didn't need to know this, so she hasn't been told. As far as she is concerned, Ann Rawson is her mummy now.

As for our Tyler, well, he's growing into a lovely young man now, and we couldn't be prouder of him. We'd be proud of him anyway, of course, but when you think of all he's been through it's an even greater joy to see him doing so well. As I write, we've not long returned from his most recent parents' evening with him; can you believe how fast time goes? He's already studying for his upcoming GCSEs!

Oh and two more things. Remember Will and Ellie? Well, with Will being Tyler's social worker, we still see lots of him, of course … and also Ellie. Yup, they stayed an item, and, as of a month back, they are also engaged. And I'm reliably informed by Riley that I need to start looking for something called a fascinator.

And, yes, I'm a gran again; the latest Watson is already running around and causing mayhem. So it's business as usual. But perhaps I'll save that for the next story …

TOPICS FOR READING-GROUP DISCUSSION

1. Do you believe the media is doing enough to promote the idea to girls that real beauty comes from within?

2. In recent years dolls such as Barbie have been blamed for giving girls and boys a false impression of how women should look. What effect do you think such dolls have on young people? Should we, as parents, be making choices that are more gender-neutral?

3. Lots of little girls dream of being a princess, then a prom queen and then a beautiful bride. As parents, do we have a right to encourage this? Or are we sending out the wrong message and encouraging our daughters to become superficial?

4. Flip is affected by many of the problems associated with foetal alcohol syndrome (FAS). With the guidelines changing all the time, is it understandable that some pregnant women are confused about safe drinking levels? Should the Government impose a simple 'no drinking' directive, or is it more important to educate and maintain freedom of choice?

5. At what age should we start to teach children the dangers of alcohol abuse? Should this include showing young people graphic images of babies born to alcohol- or drug-addicted mothers? At what age and under what circumstances would you consider giving your child alcohol, and why?

6. During her time with the Watsons, Flip has to leave the local primary school, as lack of funding means they can't meet her needs there. Should more money be allocated to teach children with special needs in mainstream education, or is it better to use the money to fund specialist schools?

CASEY WATSON

*One woman determined to
make a difference.*

*Read Casey's poignant
memoirs and be inspired.*

Five-year-old Justin was desperate and helpless

Six years after being taken into care, Justin has had 20 failed placements. Casey and her family are his last hope.

THE BOY NO ONE LOVED

A damaged girl haunted by her past

Sophia pushes Casey to the limits, threatening the safety of the whole family. Can Casey make a difference in time?

CRYING FOR HELP

Abused siblings who do not know what it means to be loved

With new-found security and trust, Casey helps Ashton and Olivia to rebuild their lives.

LITTLE PRISONERS

Branded 'vicious and evil', eight-year-old Spencer asks to be taken into care

Casey and her family are disgusted: kids aren't born evil. Despite the challenges Spencer brings, they are determined to help him find a loving home.

TOO HURT TO STAY

A young girl secretly caring for her mother

Abigail has been dealing with pressures no child should face. Casey has the difficult challenge of helping her to learn to let go.

A heartrending story of a child secretly caring for her severely disabled mother

Mummy's Little Helper

CASEY WATSON

SUNDAY TIMES BESTSELLING AUTHOR

MUMMY'S LITTLE HELPER

SUNDAY TIMES BESTSELLING AUTHOR

CASEY WATSON

Breaking the Silence

Two little boys, lost and unloved. One woman determined to make a difference

Two boys with an unlikely bond

With Georgie and Jenson, Casey is facing her toughest test yet.

BREAKING THE SILENCE

CASEY WATSON

SUNDAY TIMES BESTSELLING AUTHOR

The Girl Without a Voice

The true story
of a terrified child
whose silence
spoke volumes

Book 1
of Casey's
teaching
memoirs

What is the secret behind Imogen's silence?

Discover the shocking and devastating past of a child
with severe behavioural problems.

THE GIRL WITHOUT A VOICE

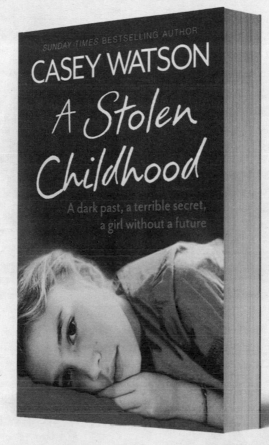

Kiara appears tired and distressed, and the school
wants Casey to take her under her wing for a while.

On the surface, everything points to a child who is upset
that her parents have separated. The horrific truth, however,
shocks Casey to the core.

A STOLEN CHILDHOOD

AVAILABLE AS E-BOOK ONLY

Cameron is a sweet boy with a great sense of humour; he seems happy in his skin – making him rather different from most of the other children Casey has cared for.

But what happens when Cameron disappears? Will Casey's worst fears be realised?

JUST A BOY

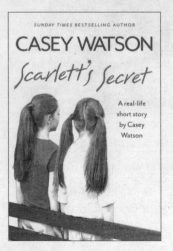

Jade and Scarlett, seventeen-year-old twins, share a terrible secret.

Can Casey help them to come to terms with the truth and rediscover their sibling connection?

SCARLETT'S SECRET

FEEL HEART.
FEEL HOPE.
READ CASEY.

Harper
True.
Time to be inspired

Write for us

Do you have a true life story of your own?

Whether you think it will inspire us, move us, make us laugh or make us cry, we want to hear from you.

To find out more, visit

www.harpertrue.com or send your ideas to harpertrue@harpercollins.co.uk and soon you could be a published author.